PICK ONE

A USER-FRIENDLY GUIDE TO RELIGION

John W. Friesen

Detselig Enterprises Ltd.
Calgary, Alberta, Canada

Pick One: A User-Friendly Guide to Religion

© John W. Friesen, 1995

Canadian Cataloguing in Publication Data

Friesen, John W.
  Pick one

  Including bibliographical references.
  ISBN 1-55059-112-6

  1. Religions--Handbooks, manuals, etc. I. Title.
BL82.F74 1995   291   C95-910580-8

Publisher's Data

Detselig Enterprises
210, 1220 Kensington Road, N.W.
Calgary, AB T2N 3P5
Canada

Detselig Enterprises Ltd. appreciates the financial support for our 1995 publishing program, provided by the Department of Canadian Heritage, Canada Council and the Alberta Foundation for the Arts, a beneficiary of the Lottery Fund of the Government of Alberta.

Cover design by Bill Matheson

COMMITTED TO THE DEVELOPMENT OF CULTURE AND THE ARTS

ALBERTA Lotteries

The Alberta Foundation for the Arts

Alberta

Printed in Canada
      ISBN   1-55059-112-6   SAN 115-0324

To my grandchildren:
Adrian, Anthea,
Brennan, Brittany,
Daniel, Justin and Rachel

Contents

Preface 7

Part One: Pre-Briefing   11

1   Why Check Out Religion? 13
     The Urge to Write, A Theoretical Note,
     Defining Religion and Being Religious,
     The Force of History

2   You May Discover This 23
     Cultural Universals, Religious Universals

3   You May Not Want to Discover This 30
     Religion as Hype, Religion as Help,
     Religion as Hope

Part Two: Assessing The Global Market   41

4   The Aboriginal Way 42

5   Baha'i 56

6   Buddhism 65

7   Confucianism 76

8   Hinduism 87

9   Islam 99

10   Judaism 109

11   Sikhs 120

Part Three: The Christian Cafeteria   137

12   Christianity 138

13   Roman Catholic Church 152

14   Greek Orthodox Church 157

15   Mainline Protestant Churches 163
     Anglicans, Baptists, Lutherans, Pentecostals,
     Presbyterians, United Church of Canada

16   Fervent Protestants: The Evangelicals 183

To Differentiate, Baptists (Some), Christian &
Missionary Alliance, Church of Christ
(Disciples), Church of God (Anderson, Indiana),
Evangelical Covenant, Evangelical Free,
Evangelical Missionary, Free Methodist Church,
Mennonite Brethren, Nazarenes, Plymouth
Brethren, Salvation Army

17   Conservative Protestants 205

Amish, Brethren in Christ, Christian
Reformed, Congregationalists, Doukhobors,
Hutterites, Mennonites, Moravians, Quakers

18   Commonly-Known Sects 223

Christian Science, Jehovah's Witnesses,
Mormons, Old Believers, Seventh Day
Adventists, Unitarian-Universalists

19   Off the Religious Map: The Cults 236

New Age, Scientology, Unification Church

20   Even Less Religious: Atheists & Agnostics 240

Part Four: The Challenge   247

21   Now That You Know 249

The Starting Point, Available Options, The
Search is Personal, Culture and Faith, Fruits
of the Search, Some Comparisons, Points of
Consensus for World Religions, Comparative
Chart on Major Christian Denominations

Preface

Belief systems make people do strange things, at least this is how many religious practices appear to those "outside the faith." Several years ago, in a little northern Alberta village, the congregation was split over the choice of colors to repaint the interior of their church. One staunch group opted for a green-and-white combination, while the other side wanted blue-and-white. One Saturday night the green-and-white group secretly went to work and stayed up all night painting the church. When the congregation arrived for the worship on Sunday morning they walked into a freshly painted sanctuary. It was green and white. Right is right!

In Jerusalem a man remained in prison for 32 years because he refused to say three words, "I am willing." Yihya Avraham and his wife had been separated for 41 years and she had applied to a rabbinical court to end the marriage. The decree was granted, but by rabbinical law it was necessary that both parties state verbally that they were in agreement with the ruling. Avraham had strong convictions about marriage and he refused to verbalize the required triology of admission. By Jewish law he could be imprisoned until he complied with the rabbinical order. He died in 1994, in prison, but still married (*Calgary Sun,* 6 Dec. 1994).

In Manilla, Philippines, an unusual religious cult recently became convinced that deflating the tires of passenger cars was the way to salvation. Terrified motorists abandoned their vehicles and fled for cover through stalled traffic as police chased the culprits. Thirty-two people were arrested, and when police questioned their leader, Alelio Bernaldez Pen, he told them that God had ordered them to let out air out of tires. "Air is from God," he said, "It is the solution to the crisis in our country" (*Cleveland Plain Dealer,* 29 Dec. 1993).

In India brides are being killed because grooms perceive their dowries to be inadequate. In 1994, "dowry deaths" rose to 5 582 from 4 836 in 1990, the government said in a written reply to a parliamentary question. Dowry deaths were outlawed in 1961 but the practice is still widespread among Hindus who form 80 percent of the country's 900 million inhabitants. Young brides whose families cannot meet post-marriage dowry demands are often doused in kerosene which is widely used in India for cooking and burned to death. The husband reports the death claiming it was a kitchen accident (*Calgary Herald,* 25 Aug. 1994).

When the daughter of a fundamentalist Christian family left her husband, divorced him and remarried, her parents were aghast. Though she informed her parents that her husband had been very cruel to her during the marriage, they refused to accept her explanation, siding instead with her husband. Since she was the one who initiated the divorce and she had remarried, they simply assumed that she was the guilty one. In fact, when it came time for the couple to retire from farming, they offered the farm to the "innocent" party, their previous son-in-law. Right is right!

These incidents may be extreme, but to label them so is simply to reflect one's own value system. These actions were probably viewed as entirely in keeping with the oracles of their faith by the people engaging in them. Small wonder that it is very difficult to understand, much less appreciate, religious diversity. Small wonder that so many disputes are initiated on religious grounds.

The Approach

If you accept the adage that "it takes one to know one," this book offers a unique dimension in the sense that it was written by someone who "knows the system" but who has no axe to grind in trying to sell any particular form of it to anyone else. It will be up to the reader to judge how well that mission is accomplished. This admission is in no way intended to belittle any pattern of religion nor downplay the need for each of us to believe in "something spiritual that works" for us. Hopefully, the end result of one's spiritual search will produce a little more, by way of a creed, than that.

Readers will discover at the outset that this book has a distinct bias, perhaps several of them. I was raised in western Canada in a Christian Protestant milieu (in several denominations, by the way), and I still adhere to the Christian faith. This makes it more difficult to be objective about other expressions of faith, but I have tried to compensate for that possibility by examining a variety of sourcebooks for each perspective. For background on the various religions I consulted at least one book written by a member of each faith community, at least one book that tended to be more valuative of each particular religious expression, and at least one that purported to be academic (objective?) rather than either apologetic or polemic in nature. I hope that I have succeeded in this task and if I have failed in any respect, I beg the forgiveness of anyone who is offended by my analysis.

This book has a distinctly Canadian focus, probably a *western* Canadian focus at that. I admit to that. For population data I relied on information published annually by Statistics Canada in the *Canada Yearbook*. It is therefore possible that a few world religions may be omitted from this discussion. It was also difficult to obtain information about many of the smaller and newer evangelical and fundamentalist groups and sects in the country, but I believe that those which are described will serve adequately to represent that particular focus. Some of these groups have probably also been omitted, albeit inadvertently.

The Agenda

There is something very familiar about people when we are faced with similar situations. Anthropologists would probably suggest that we are all more alike than different. To illustrate this, try this experiment. Arrange to attend a variety of basic religious celebrations like weddings, baptisms or funerals, in as many different religious and/or cultural settings as possible. You will witness a great deal of joy at weddings, solemn faces at a christening or baptisms, and tears at a funeral – regardless of the cultural or religious setting. One of the aims of this book is to illustrate the truth of the statement, "We are *all* children of God."

The main focus in preparing this sourcebook was to discover and explain why each particular religious community functions and holds together as it does. What are the fundamentals of each faith, and what kind of behavior is mandated for adherents? What do the various faiths expect of believers and what do they promise them? In plain words, "what makes them tick?" In examining these perspectives there was never any thought of condemning them, and I tried hard not to let my personal experiences with any of these groups affect my analysis negatively or positively. I hope I have achieved this goal. The point is, if this volume is to help someone in selecting a faith group, they will need to know something about them. This book will help in that search.

In preparing a work of this magnitude one always builds a list of obligations to people. In the first instance I would like to thank my publisher, Dr. Ted Giles, President of Detselig Enterprises Ltd., for bringing to my attention the need for this work. I have appreciated his constant guidance and encouragement over the years. I have also benefited from the input of my son, Bruce, a sociologist at Kent State University and I want to acknowledge this. He has been a keen sparring partner in our many discussions of the issues raised in this volume. I would like also to thank the leaders or representatives of many of the religious groups included in this book who were helpful in sharing information about their particular faith. I owe my wife, Virginia Agnes, a heartfelt expression of thanks, first of all for sharing my interest in religious thought and, second, for being so very patient as she listened to my daily rantings about my various discoveries as I conducted my research. Finally, I will admit that the impressions and interpretations in the book are mine, and I am responsible for responding to criticisms. I simply hope there are not too many of them.

J.W.F.

February, 1995

PART ONE

Pre-briefing

I have known anthropologists who accorded a benevolent understanding to the Hopi but denied it to Catholics, Mormons, Buddhists, or Mohammedans. This dichotomy of viewpoint strikes me as ridiculous and completely unscientific. In short, I will study as many religions as I can, but I will judge none of them. I doubt if any other attitude is scientifically defensible.

— Robert H. Lowie, anthropologist.

It is just about impossible to have a calm and rational discussion about religion with anyone. While this is a most unfortunate fact for those who appreciate rational discourse, this reality also supports the contention that religion must matter a great deal to most people.

Recently I had a conversation with an acquaintance about my research in comparing world religions and during the discussion my inquirer remarked, "But aren't you finding that some religions are better than others?"

I replied somewhat evasively that every religion probably appears superior to those who adhere to it, but my response did not seem to satisfy my confrere. Somewhat emphatically I was informed, "Well *I* think some religions are better than others – in fact, a *lot* better!" I could not help wondering how many religions my acquaintance had investigated in enough depth to be able to make such a statement. My guess would be not that many, but apparently this factor would make little difference. Virtually every religious individual believes that they are connected to the *right* creed – theocentric or atheistic; otherwise, logically, why would *they* hold to it? Naturally this statement does not imply that any in depth research has been undertaken. Nor do the adherents believe that any is necessary.

Discussions about religious belief systems have a way of striking at the very core of human existence. In this context everyone has religious concerns, that is, we all have a set of core values that matter very much to us, and we are all prepared to defend them when questioned – with some emotion, if we have to. Few of us can remain objective when someone belittles or attacks things we prize highly. Intensive discussions about religion tend to make us uneasy, perhaps because of an innate fear that we may not personally have all the answers to cosmic questions or worse, we may even be wrong on some point.

This section will elaborate a series of presuppositions about the workings of religion with a view to understanding its importance in human culture. No culture is without a religious value system even though its base may be said to be non-theistic. One does not need to believe in God to be religious if we define a religious person as one who is devout, reverent, or pious about what he or she believes. Another way of putting it is to define a religious person as one who adheres conscientiously (with some attached emotion) to a belief system. Although this truth is not readily appreciated by those who confess to being non-religious, the evidence suggests that in discussions of the topic these folk are quite capable of manifesting emotions and convictions similar to those of individuals who admit to being religious.

1

Why Check Out Religion?

To be ignorant of religion is to be only semi-educated about the workings of the human race. Sociologists suggest that religion is the strongest means by which the lives of individuals fuse to form a cohesive society (Macionis, 1989). Anthropologists tell us that there are three things that distinguish humanity from other animals – religion, the use of abstract language and the making of tools. Religion is the primary target of this study, and much of it consists of specialized (abstract) language. The "tools of the trade" appear to include some very distinctive dialectical techniques which are quite unique to humankind. Some observers think that they have detected among certain birds, mammals and even other organisms the analogues of ritual (Kluckhohn, 1965). To date no one has suggested the existence of myth or theology among these creatures.

To understand the underlying rationale for any national or societal *modus operandi* requires a close look at its underlying religious value system. This cluster of beliefs offers an explanation of origins and purpose, the place of society in the scheme of things and its ultimate destiny. Canada as a nation is no exception. Our national institutions have religious roots, and our history is checkered with religious events described in religious language. To "check out religion," therefore, is to study the rudiments of human society.

People tend to be religious beings. The universality of religion (in the broadest sense) suggests that it corresponds to some deep and probably inescapable human need. People instinctively sense a need for a moral order. Human life is necessarily a moral life precisely because it is a social life, and in the case of the human animal the minimum requirements for the predictability of social behavior that will ensure some stability and continuity are not taken care of automatically by biologically inherited instincts, as is the case with birds and the bees. When standard rules about conduct are put into place they are often invested with "Divine" authority and continually symbolized in rites that appeal to the senses.

Generally speaking, every individual has very sincere beliefs (or opinions) about such matters as the meaning of life, how people ought to regard one another and what, in the end, *really* matters. Religion in this sense represents a response to the wonder and the terror of the ineluctable processes of nature. Religions supply some answers to the profound uncertainties of experience, most especially to the inevitability of death – even though some religions make a pure acknowl-edgement of death and directly, carelessly or undauntedly admit nothingness (Kluckhohn, 1965).

Once convictions about "end things" have been formulated, there are few people who would hesitate to share information about such matters, particularly in times of national or personal crisis. We tend to be creatures who share information that we value – even half-baked information. To illustrate: what "man-on-the-street," regardless of status or occupation, holds back on offering free advice to anyone who will listen about how nationally-elected leaders should run the econ-omy or direct the workings of the nation into the next century? There is a tendency in such discussions for the spiritual nature of basic humanity to emerge. To "check out religion," then, is to study the day-to-day behavior of ordinary people.

There is a third explicit spur to investigating the phenomenon of religion, and that is to fulfill the personal need to know. One of the greatest human tragedies is to stifle this natural drive. As educators know, every individual is naturally curious, particularly about unfa-miliar subjects. One can hardly make an informed choice about anything without undertaking a great deal of study, so why should the spiritual realm be any different? We live in a knowledge-laden age, and most of it is readily accessible. It is therefore a tragedy to deny the young the privilege of heeding the inner call to know, and the tragedy is no less whether it is stifled by external forces or by self-propelled limitations. Still, for some reason some people deliber-ately avoid gaining knowledge about certain aspects of life strictly because this may raise questions about their own convictions. Logi-cally, if one is in possession of "the truth," one should have nothing to fear from studying "false" doctrines. Strangely, it just doesn't seem to work that way!

The Urge to Write

The intrigue of studying world religions has been an itch in my mind for several decades. It began when I was a boy in Saskatchewan, and although reading materials on the subject were extremely limited in our home because of poverty, we *did* have access to two farm publica-tions, *The Western Producer* and *The Country Guide*. Also, I *did* manage to find several advertised correspondence courses in religion which were made available by different religious denominations. After graduating from several such study programs – Anglican, Bap-tist and Seventh Day Adventist, my conviction grew that there was a purpose in these courses beyond that stated in the initial advertise-ment. In the final analysis, each religious organization wanted a kind of personal commitment from me. I was a bit disappointed by this turn of events, and managed to stay clear of any written commitments. After all, all I wanted to do was to satisfy my curiosity.

My boyhood interest in religious diversity was greatly enhanced during the decade my family spent in British Columbia where my parents migrated in search of work and used up their spare time checking out different churches. Having a strong Mennonite background, and with no such church in town, they roamed the area in search of a suitable replacement. The list of "proving grounds" was long, and included Anglican, Christian & Missionary Alliance, Church of God (Anderson, Indiana), Full Gospel, Pentecostal, Plymouth Brethren, Presbyterian, Salvation Army and the United Church of Canada. By the time I was a teenager I was convinced that a meaningful faith cannot be attained solely through the auspices of any one human-invented organization.

As a university student I read a book on the psychology of religion in which the authors contended that people have an innate need to believe in something, minimally, in some *purpose* beyond themselves. Belief in a religious system, most likely a theistic-centred system, comprises a much-adhered to recipe culminating such a search (Ostow and Scharfstein, 1954). Religion has a greater appeal to the individual in times of stress, of course, but an effective religion is also able to offer hope and extract submissive behavior from the adherent at the same time. When the whole of society is in desperate straits, the appeal of religion grows particularly strong, for it encourages optimism instead of the pessimism that reason dictates, and it also acts to prevent the disorganization that panic breeds. Religion tends to make life meaningful by fitting it into the context of an existence beyond the present.

"There are no atheists in the foxholes," is an old saying which implies that every soldier under the duress of battle is a man of faith. Suddenly it makes a great deal of sense to believe in God, and the soldier desperately hopes there is a God. An 18th century writer, Edward Young, put it this way, "By night an atheist half believes in God." Perhaps, when nightfall comes (meaning the "shadows of life's heavier moments"), even an avowed atheist *wishes* for God.

Against this background of diffuse experiences and influences I felt motivated to pursue a study of the phenomenon of religion. This book is the result.

A Theoretical Note

There is no dearth of theoretical speculation about the role of religion in society, and the writings of sociologists of religion are substantive. This does not mean that they are agreed on a definition of religion; quite the contrary, in fact. It is therefore useful to elucidate the ideas of some of the more well-known theorists. A brief elucidation of the ideas of some of the more popular writers may also prove useful here.

Religion as Social Function

One thinker who seriously examined the workings and implications of religion was the French sociologist, Emile Durkheim (1858-1917). Durkheim postulated that religion in its simplest form divides phenomena into two spheres, sacred and profane; the sacred is that which is largely unknown, set apart and forbidden, and the profane refers to the ongoings of daily reality. The sacred comes across as something extraordinary, inspiring a sense of awe, worthy of reverence and even fear. The profane (or secular) includes all of the elements of everyday life. The phenomena of religion (the sacred), are further divided into two fundamental categories, beliefs and rites. The first are states of opinions, and consist in representation; the second are determined modes of action. Durkheim distinguished religious rites, or moral practices, from other practices by the special nature of their object. A moral rule prescribes certain ways of acting just as a rite does. However, a rite can only be described after the belief has been elaborated.

Durkheim claimed that religious beings always suppose a bipartite division of the universe, the known and the knowable. He also suggested that the two categories typically remain separated in the minds of adherents. Religious beliefs are representations which express the nature of sacred things and the relations which they sustain, either with each other or with profane things. Rites are the rules of conduct, which prescribe how people should comport themselves in the presence of sacred objects.

The simplicity of Durkheim's model probably contributed to its rejection by later analysts. In the first place, even allowing for the vagueness of the categories of the sacred and the profane, it seems essential that their existence be recognized not merely by the observing sociologist or interpreter, but by the members of the particular group under scrutiny (O'Toole, 1984). In the case of the Aboriginal peoples of North America, Durkheim's schematic is simply inapplicable. Many Plains tribes, for example, do not delineate between known and knowable, but consider all phenomena to be connected in some way. To some extent this is also true of Buddhism and Taoism. If the Creator deems it essential for people to gain additional insights about these connections, in due course they will become recipients of relevant new knowledge. Other than that it is "life as usual" in the never-ending pursuit of "being with meaning."

Religion and Society

Berger (1967) suggested that religion is a social construction that involves the special quality of the sacred. In fact, it represents the highest order of legitimation in society. Members of society learn the meaning of the sacred through ritual, including religious services, saying grace before meals, and taking sacred oaths as part of various legal proceedings. The primary reason societies construct the sacred is to legitimize and stabilize patterns of social interaction. Because society itself is a precarious human creation it is inherently subject to disruption. Therefore, if certain segments of society are placed safely beyond examination and awarded a kind of "cosmic frame of reference" there is less chance of disruption. Naturally this policy can be abused and its two primary dysfunctions are war and religious persecution. Still, the approach persists and capably keeps many people "down on the farm." Who, without official authority, would dare to raise questions about the sacred world of the "scarcely known?"

Religion as Facade

Karl Marx (1818-1883) suggested that religion was historically a form of ideology used by the social classes in power to legitimize the status quo and divert peoples' attention from social problems and inequities. Marx called religion the "opium of the masses" and claimed that its principal benefit lay in its ability to obscure the true nature of class dominance and conflict, and thus pacify the propertyless. This is usually as far as Marx is quoted, but as O'Toole (1984) points out, there is another side to the story. There is some evidence that Marx acknowledged the active role played by religion in bringing about social change, particularly in the early years of this century when Marxists unashamedly traced the origins of modern socialism and communism to the revolutionary religious movements of classical, medieval and pre-industrial times. These movements were regarded as the offspring of the yearnings and aspirations of the oppressed, struggling for liberation (O'Toole, 1984). In this context, although not much advertised, Marxists may be credited with developing their own tradition of analyzing sectarianism.

During Marx's lifetime the Christian nations of western Europe justified their objective of colonial exploitation by insisting that they were only trying to convert the heathen nations of the world. Major church denominations in the United States justified their domination of Black peoples as somehow consistent with God's will. Support for racial segregation in schools and churches was similarly defended (Macionis, 1989). On this basis it would be hard to accuse Marx of fabricating his theory out of fantasy.

There is a side to religion that Marx seems to have conveniently ignored; there *is* proof that some religious groups have also tried very hard to promote social equality. These efforts have targeted schooling, enhanced medical care and other social programs, and even the abolition of slavery. Religious leaders, like Martin Luther King, were at the forefront of the civil rights movement in the 1960s, and many clergymen participated in the 1970s movement to end USA involvement in the Vietnam War. More recently the injustices committed against the helpless in many countries around the world have been targeted by concerned religious leaders. In Canada, health care was pretty well originated by church-affiliated individuals, as was public schooling and other forms of human care programs.

Psychoanalyst Sigmund Freud (1856-1939), though most often quoted for his writings on human sexuality, also made some severe pronouncements on religion. He suggested that religion is an illusion, a temporary consolation for "immature man." He lamented that the teachings of religion are offered in ways that demand belief in their contents but without producing grounds for their claim. Those being taught are told that the teachings deserve to be believed because they were believed by our primal ancestors. A second claim is that religions possess proofs which have been handed down from those same primeval times, and third, religious neonates are forbidden to raise questions about the authentication of those proofs. Anything so presumptuous as raising questions about revered truth is usually accompanied by severe penalties. It was Freud's hope that eventually people would regard religion like the fairy tale it is and view it with a look of disdain (Freud, 1964).

The Future of Religion

One of the reasons why religion continues to thrive is because it tends to provide individual meaning. This too has been recognized by theorists. For example, although Max Weber pointed out that religion can be a motivating force for individual action in political, economic and other spheres, he did not explicitly fabricate a theory of social change (Hewit, 1993). Weber's investigations of religion in historical and cultural contexts of extreme diversity were crucial to his attempt to account theoretically for those historic processes that led to the emergence of modern society. Weber did not believe that religion is generally and necessarily the source of historical change, but admitted that it did comprise a valuable key to understanding how change comes about (O'Toole, 1984). It is a good bet that the study of religion from the perspective of subjective experiences *does* prove interesting, especially when so many groups have laid claim to having originated on the basis of a unique subjective experience. It is a fact that when an individual experiences something of the Divine by vision or dreams or any other such means, the value of that experience cannot easily be taken away from them. Many individuals claim to have been healed, inspired or given guidance by spiritual means. In fact, most world religions and denominations have been started by individuals who laid claim to a unique spiritual experience. Evidently their witness to events was sufficiently convincing to amass followers – in some cases *millions* of followers. There are very few exceptions to this phenomenon in the origin of religions; most of them appear to have been started by someone claiming to have experienced a direct link with the Divine.

It must be pointed out that the negative speculations about the imminent demise of religion, prognosticated by Freud and Marx and others of that persuasion, were premature. Even more recent predictions, like those promulgated by the "God is dead" movement of the 1960s, have been proven wrong. Established denominations have not rolled over and died; indeed many of them have increased in numbers – Roman Catholics, Mormons, Pentecostals and Jehovah's Witnesses to name a few. In the Western world at least, religion is far from diminishing.

Religionists in this century have shown a remarkable propensity to retreat, retrench, revamp and resurface. Though they remain basically secularized in format and objective, interest in supernatural and spiritual matters has increased (Bibby, 1993). In addition, identification with religious traditions remains high, perhaps because people like to celebrate holidays, even if these festivities have religious origins or overtones. This includes Christmas, Easter or even All-Saints Day. Who cares? As long as it means a holiday.

Defining Religion and Being Religious

Religious influence is everywhere, and, depending on how you define the activity of *being religious,* so are religious people. The *Dictionary of Philosophy* (Runes, 1967) suggests that religion fulfills a separate, innate category of the human consciousness that issues certain insights and indisputable certainties, about a Superhuman Presence. This definition incorporates virtually every system of thought that acknowledges the existence of a greater being with powers beyond those of humankind. In a formal sense, religion has three fundamental characteristics: (i) beliefs which inspire fear, awe or reverence; (ii) a prescribed list of expected behaviors; and, (iii) a long-term promise of eventual respite (hope). Taboos are derived from the first criterion, and are usually translated into a series of "do-nots" for an individual's behavior. Most religions offer a form of relief from the human struggle only as an eventual happening, although not in this life. Adherents are expected to live out their lives with only a minimal experience of happiness or enjoyment.

Being "religious" means that some individuals will be so sincere about things that they will devote their utmost energies towards fulfilling their cosmic calling – with or without any theistic acknowledgement. Their energies may be directed towards the fulfillment of psychological, emotional or spiritual requirements, and their sincerity and devotion can easily parallel that of the loyal followers of any "organized" religious body.

Being Religious

Typically, people think of a religious individual as one who believes in some kind of God, but this is not necessarily the case. To be religious is to be committed to, and act in accordance with, a code of ethics derived from sources outside and considered "greater" than oneself. The code may not necessarily incorporate a personalized theism, that is, belief in Almighty God per se. Melford Spiro (Banton, 1966) defined religion as consisting of some form of organized or patterned social behavior, wherein religious adherents respond, both in daily activities and specific rituals, to the perceived will of some entity that is seen as having greater power than themselves. Durkheim suggested that the *gods* of religion may be nothing more than collective forces, incarnated, hypostatized under a material form. Thus religion becomes a series of beliefs by means of which individuals represent the society in which they are members and the relationships, obscure but intimate, which they have with it (O'Toole, 1984).

Still another way to analyze the phenomenon of religion is to examine its content which generally consists of cultural beliefs to be inculcated and actions to be taken up (Hewitt, 1993). Having been raised in any particular religious milieu, or being converted to it, believers will contend that the attending *code* holds implicit mandatory expectations for the individual, even for society as a whole. This rule applies to "religious" adherence with or without theistic reference. An example of the latter position would be the environmentalist who holds that the cosmos is a given; its origins are not questioned but its maintenance is absolute. There is an obligation on the part of the human race to care for the earth, keep its air and waters pure, and reprimand anyone who violates this code. Some behaviors of members of the "earth-love" movement have at times been quite bizarre, for example, spraying paint on people who wear fur coats made of animal skin. The kind of act suggests that the universe is superior to people, a value that runs counter to most traditional religious creeds. The incongruity of this kind of behavior is most evident when the person with the spray can also happens to be wearing leather shoes!

Everyone is "religious" in the sense of having very firm convictions or "special values" that relate to, or affect, the very ground of their being. The criterion which explicates these convictions as religious is the fact that they are held as universals having cosmic implications. The implied creed ought to be followed by every individual, society and nation. Most people make it easy for themselves to live out their cosmic convictions by adhering to the creed of an established, recognized religious body, but this is not necessarily the only way to go.

Most people have lots of misinformation about religion – religion generally or even their own faith. Naturally they have even less information about other religions. Partly this happens because few of us have been trained to investigate religion without bias. It is usually believed that "either you are religious or you aren't." If you *are* religious, you will be expected to defend the particular religious system to which you are connected. If you are *not* religious, you will probably be quite biased towards *any* form of it. *Anti*-theism in this form is a fairly fervent contemporary societal force.

The above attempt at clarification may not be too helpful in assisting the search for a middle ground on the continuum of religious addiction versus religious hate – if there is one. Naturally, like any other "pursuit of truth" the process is not uncomplicated, nor is it a simple process. However, with a little objective research into the matter most searchers may discover that religion may not be as good (nor as bad) as it seems, and a synthesized personal version of its offerings may be quite attainable and appealing.

The bottom line is that we live in a very religious world. One simply *has* to carve a personally-satisfying path through the maze.

The Force of History

Even a cursory glance at the Canadian past will quickly yield the conclusion that the essence of religion (Christianity, to be specific) was woven into the very foundations of nation-building. Constitution-making, and the formulation of social reforms in the areas of schooling and health care reflect religious values, many of them grounded in biblical language. One of the issues that arose in early Canada in connection with the development of the various provincial school systems, for example, had to do with the religious question. Egerton Ryerson, the first school superintendent of English-speaking Canada, developed an educational system for Upper Canada (later Ontario) that was Christian but not sectarian; it was cost-free, compulsory, practical and universal. His perspective collided directly with that of an Anglican Bishop named John Strachan who fought for a church-operated school system paid for by public taxation. The Common Schools Acts of 1846 and 1850, influenced by Ryerson, made free schooling a reality and a system of local taxation enabled financial backing (Patterson, et al., 1974). Other provinces followed a similar model, and gave the nation the rudiments of a public school system based on very specific Christian values. Although the religious component was eventually eradicated from most Canadian public schools, till very recently the Province of Newfoundland continued to sponsor a church-run, tax-based school system.

The situation in western Canada was similar to that in the East. Many of the first schools in the West were begun by missionaries, although their hopes for a permanent religious system were short-lived. In 1853 Alexandre Tache was appointed the second bishop of the Northwest by the Roman Catholic Church. He worked steadily to formulate an educational system that would be truly Christian (Catholic), untouched by liberality or compromise. He, like many others of his day, wanted to assure that Westerners would be schooled in the rigors of an ecclesiastical structure. Tache turned out to be the wrong man for his times, however, because the rapidly growing secularity of prairie culture motivated a switch to public schooling with only minimal religious overtones.

Clearly the history of Canada comprises a rich and generous admixture of religious institutional influence. Besides the origins of public schooling, most Canadian universities and colleges were begun under religious auspices. The procedures of governance, based on British common law, often find their origins in the rudiments of religious convictions. In the first century of Canadian history most human welfare institutions – hospitals, orphanages, homes for senior citizens, etc. were begun by, and operated by, religious institutions. Most legislation affecting this arena of life was initiated by, or influenced by, people with strong religious (Christian) convictions.

To suggest that this has not been the case is to be unfamiliar with (or to deny) the facts of our nation's history – another reason to be versed in the workings of faith.

References

Banton, Michael. (Ed.). (1966). *Anthropological approaches to the study of religion.* London: Tavistock.

Berger, Peter L. (1967). *The sacred canopy: Elements of a sociological theory.* Garden City, NY: Doubleday & Co.

Bibby, Reginald W. (1993). Secularization and change. In W.E. Hewitt (Ed.), *The sociology of religion: A Canadian focus* (pp. 65-81). Toronto: Butterworths.

Freud, Sigmund. (1964). *The future of an illusion* (W.D Robson, Trans.). Garden City, NY: Doubleday and Company, Inc.

Hewitt, W.E. (Ed.). (1993). *The sociology of religion: A Canadian focus.* Toronto: Butterworths.

Kluckhohn, Clyde. (1965). Preface. In William A. Lessa & Evon Z. Vogt (Eds.), *Reader in comparative religion: An anthropological approach* (2nd ed., pp. xi-xii). New York: Harper & Row.

Macionis, John I. (1989). *Sociology* (2nd ed.). Englewood Cliffs, NJ: Prentice Hall.

Ostow, Morimer & Scharfstein, Ben-Ami. (1954). *The need to believe: The psychology of religion.* New York: International Universities Press, Inc.

O'Toole, Roger. (1984). *Religion: Classic sociological approaches.* Toronto: McGraw-Hill Ryerson Ltd.

Patterson, Robert S., Chalmers John W. & Friesen, John W. (Eds.). (1974). *Profiles of Canadian educators.* Toronto: D.C. Heath.

Runes, Dagobert D. (1967). *Dictionary of philosophy.* Totowa, NJ: Littlefield, Adams & Co.

2

You May Discover This

Social scientists inform us that members of the human race have more things in common that they do differences. This implies that it is also possible that two members of the same cultural group may have greater differences in personality, individual make-up, perception or other characteristics than two individuals who belong to different cultural groups. Individuality knows no cultural bounds.

Did you ever notice that when an event of catastrophic proportions strikes a community and an approach to handle it is formulated, the contrived solution will appear quite conventional? It is often possible to identify a common thread in the way people react to catastrophic phenomena – regardless of race, culture, creed, socio-economic status, racial origins, etc. Perhaps a few examples may be helpful in substantiating this point.

Cultural Universals

Sometimes the statement is made, perhaps too glibly, that the human race has socially developed from the basic unities of family, tribe, village, city-state and nation. Anthropologists also suggest that human societies exhibit characteristics that underscore the universality of human approach to similar challenges.

The cultural pattern in which people grow up is held together by the glue of beliefs which are usually religious in basis. This proposition has been acknowledged by social scientists for more than half a century. Included in each cultural pattern are such common elements or universals as social organization, governance arrangements, cosmic beliefs, artifacts, arts and music, rules about property, forms of caring for the aged and the sick, educational formats and language and stock (Wissler, 1923). A more up-to-date list includes: symbols, language, values, norms, mores and folkways and materials culture, while acknowledging the existence of subcultures and countercultures (Macionis, 1989). If we allow the possibility that there are universal institutional structures among the various cultures, it is possible to apply this perspective to real life situations.

The Common Base

Several decades ago an extensive study of five cultural groups at Gallup, New Mexico was undertaken which demonstrated that persons of basically similar biology, and having different cultures, may settle in the same general geographical area but develop markedly different modes of life (Vogt and Roberts, 1960). Further, the study revealed that when faced with the same crisis (ie., a climactic dry-spell) the five groups responded in kind.

The five cultural communities included Zuni and Navaho Indians, a Mormon group, some Catholic Spanish Americans, and a group of transplanted Baptist Texans. Basically involved in agricultural pursuits to some extent, each of the communities worked out its own solution to the problem of physical survival in a harsh environment. The Zunis, who were the longest-established residents of the area, had worked out an irrigation system to water their crops. The Navahos, originally hunters and gatherers, came into the region a little later and settled in to become sheepherders and dry-land farmers. Livestock raising and wage work were the mainstay of the Catholic Spanish Americans who migrated to the Gallup region at the turn of the century. The Mormons arrived at about the same time and became heavily involved in raising livestock and irrigation farming. Finally, the Texans staked out the last Homestead Act lands and took up mechanized dry-land farming with pinto beans as their principal crop. Then the drought struck, and a variety of cultural value configurations were thrown into gear.

The mechanisms of the five separate communities dictated their varying attitudes towards the dry-spell; the underlying reality was that they all had to deal with it. This was still a fundamental human reality. The Zuni people, for example, regard the universe as a place in which they are privileged to live. They neither feel that they are masters of the universe nor its victims. The universe is to be respected, and it is the job of mankind to cooperate with the underlying forces of nature. The Zunis live in the present although they also appreciate their rich cultural legacy. When the drought came, these various factors came together in their ceremonial celebrations – planting prayer feathers, fasting and rain priests offering prayers.

The Navaho tribe has a value orientation similar to that of the Zunis. They view humans as having an integral part to play in the general cosmic scheme. However, they are more inclined to "do obeisance" to the universe, perceiving natural powers as superior and profoundly threatening to members of the human race. They are not complete fatalists, but recognize that there are limited ways in which the universe may be affected. Thus they engage in rituals and ceremonies intended to beg the universe for favors, like granting rain for dried-out crops.

The Spanish Americans probably come closest in perception to being fatalists, for they regard the workings of the universe as entirely outside their domain. When the drought struck they did little more than gather in small groups on the local plaza and talk about it. They garnered little information about the mysteries of the world, and found concrete expression in traditional fiestas which combined a religious and recreational flare. If the Creator wanted His children to experience drought He must have some reason for it.

On the other end of the scale of the relation between the cosmos and its occupants we have the "immigrant" Texans. They share in common with the Mormons the world-view that nature can be subdued, or at least we ought to do our best to accomplish this objective when possible. The Texans manifest a drive to master nature and the Mormons have a little more subdued concept believing that at least it would *be desirable* to conquer nature. The Texas homesteaders have little respect for the Spanish Americans whom they consider to be lazy and "not getting any place" (Vogt and Roberts, 1960).

When the drought settled in the Texas homesteaders held a quick prayer meeting for rain and then sent airplanes into the skies loaded with silver iodide to sprinkle on any cloud in sight. The Mormons joined in these activities but more regularly said prayers for rain. A few of the more conservative members of the homesteader community objected to the use of dry-ice on clouds suggesting that this kind of activity was "interfering with the work of the Lord." The more aggressive community spokespersons defended their actions by saying: "The Lord will look down and say, 'Look at those poor ignorant people. I gave them clouds, the airplanes and the silver iodide, and they didn't have the sense to put them together' " (Vogt and Roberts, 1960, 117).

Variation in cultural values notwithstanding, the geographic conditions surrounding all five communities were identical. All five groups, therefore, had to work out an approach to dealing with this reality. All five manifested some kind of religious perspective in reacting to the drought and all engaged in some kind of religious ritual. Two of the groups went further, and tried directly to "influence nature." The underlying truth of the case study, however, is that a world/cosmos is common to us all and we must work out a way to deal with it. And we do – almost always on religious grounds.

The Common Reaction

An example that illustrates a more universal approach to dealing with the elements of nature originates from the western Canadian prairies during the immigration period of 1890-1914. During that time literally thousands of immigrants from Britain, Europe and the USA took up residence in the West spurred on by the offer of free land. Initiated by Clifford Sifton, Minister of the Interior, by the time the First World War began thousands of immigrants had been welcomed to Canada. During the peak years of immigration as many as 2 500 settlers left the Winnipeg train depot each week, and helped prompt the development of the railroad to further points.

Life in the West for many would-be Canadians initially meant living in over-populated immigration sheds with minimal supplies. Those who subsequently made their homes in the cities suffered crowded conditions, because Canadian urban living at that time did not meet European standards. Those who opted for a farming career often developed a lifestyle similar to their neighbors', even if the neighbors represented an entirely different heritage culture. The sod huts of the immigrants all looked very much the same, and all farmers struggled with exactly the same kinds of challenges: making a living, establishing a home life and getting along with others.

All newcomers had to select a geographic location for their permanent dwelling, in the city or in the country, and they all worried equally about how their children would be educated, who they would marry and how their culture, language and belief system would be retained (Friesen, 1989). Historian G.F.C. Stanley once observed that there were five basic seasons with which all newcomers had to contend: mosquito, blackfly, horsefly, housefly and winter (Gagnon, 1970). On a parallel note a Saskatchewan pioneer defined the natural challenges of that territory in terms of four seasons: dreading winter, preparing for winter, enduring winter, and recovering from winter. In such conditions, we are all kin.

Religious Universals

Once a year a group of religious thinkers from nearly every world religion assembles for the purpose of determining how much they have in common with one another. The gathering is called the Parliament of the World's Religions and includes Buddhist, Christian, Hindu, Jewish and Moslem representatives, et al., right down through the alphabet to Zoroastrians. In 1971 the conference decided that the following themes were respected by all of their communities:

1. unity of the human family; the dignity of all human beings

2. value of the human community

3. might is not right; human power is not self-sufficient and absolute

4. love, selflessness and truth have ultimately greater power than hate and self-interest

5. stand on the side of the poor and the oppressed against the rich and oppressors

6. hope that good will finally prevail.

In 1993 the Parliament met in Chicago for their 100th anniversary with ample representation from the various faiths. The following statement of "a global ethic" reflects the nature of consensus endorsed by the participants:

> We must strive for a just and economic order,
> in which everyone has an equal chance to

reach full potential as a human being.
We must speak and act truthfully, and with
compassion, dealing fairly with all, and
avoid prejudice and hatred . . .
We must move beyond the dominance of
greed for power, prestige, money and
consumption to make a just and peaceful world.

Statements about acceptance of others and goodwill abound in religious circles. In 1992 the Federal Ministry of Multiculturalism & Citizenship funded a project of the Pacific Interfaith Citizenship Association of British Columbia. The project's editor compiled a series of religious expressions from scriptures and writings on human dignity and respect from a multiplicity of sources (Khaki, 1992). The following are exemplary of the prepared statements – all of which most Canadians could readily endorse.

(Anglican) "At the centre of both the Hebrew scriptures and the New Testament is the double commandment to love God and to love the neighbor. Jesus saw this double commandment as summary of the law of God. . . . both the Hebrew scriptures and the New Testament point to the fulfillment of God's promise when those of every race and language will be included in the kingdom of God" (Anglican Diocese of New Westminster, 1992).

(Baptist) "We call upon all Baptists to teach their children respect for all people; and to build bridges of common concerns and interests with the people of other nations, races, cultures, language and religion" (Tingley, 1992).

(Hindu) "What good is it if we acknowledge in our prayers that God is the father of us all and in our daily lives do not treat every man as our brother? Together we are better" (Prameya, 1992).

(Islam) "Islam has proclaimed the unity among human beings, based on the fundamental doctrine of oneness: 'Verily this, the Brotherhood of Yours is a single Brotherhood' " (Khaki, 1992).

(Jew) "God's role in human history cannot, therefore, be presumed to be limited to the affairs of one or the other single nation. Rather, the prophet bids us recall that all human beings are the children of God, all equally, or rather potentially equally sharing in His caring interest and governance" (Cohen, 1992).

(Roman Catholic) "The message which [the Roman Catholic Church] has drawn from biblical revelation strongly affirms the dignity of every person as created in God's image, the unity of humankind in the Creator's plan, and the reconciliation among peoples brought about by Christ the Redeemer" (Roman Catholic Archdiocese of Vancouver, 1992).

(Sikh) "The Sikh Gurus declared that humanity was one and that a person was to be honoured, not only by virtue of belonging to this or that caste or creed, but because he or she was a human being, an emanation of God, having been given the same sense and the same soul as others" (Jheeta, 1992).

(Unitarian) [Our congregations] "covenant together to affirm and promote the inherent worth and dignity of every person; justice, equity and compassion in human relations. . . . the goal of world community with peace, liberty and justice for all" (Unitarian Church of Vancouver, 1992).

(United Church) "The United Church of Canada's faith calls people to value the building of bridges of understanding and common action with those of other faiths so that God may be praised, humankind may be enriched and so that God's creation will know justice and love" (How, 1992).

The above quotations indicate that religious writers of various persuasions can certainly formulate generous, similar-sounding statements about people of other faiths. More than that, when they disperse to their separate congregations they engage in similar kinds of religious enactments – offering up prayers, and participating in (or observing) ceremonies and rituals related to their interpretation of people's relationship to the universe. One can only hope that the underlying thrust of the prepared statements is translated into their interactions with others.

It is most lamentable that sometimes individuals perceive that their way of doing things and of believing things, is unique and therefore superior. To this end a study of at least several variations of religious interpretation may prove useful. If nothing else this procedure should fortify the assumption that human beings are more alike than different. Now *that's* a worthy discovery!

References

Anglican Diocese of Vancouver. (1992). Religious expressions (pp. 25-27). Aziz Khaki (Ed.). Vancouver, BC: The Pacific Interfaith Citizenship Association of B.C.

Cohen, Martin Samuel. (1992). Jewish reflections on religious & Inter-Faith tolerance. In Aziz Khaki (Ed.), *Religious expressions* (pp. 17-20). Vancouver, BC: The Pacific Interfaith Citizenship Association of B.C.

Friesen, John W. (1989). The human side of prairie settlement: 1890-1914. *Multicultural Education Journal, 7*(2), 28-36.

Gagnon, David P. (Ed.). (1970). *Prairie perspectives: Papers of the western Canadian studies conference.* Toronto: Holt, Rinehart and Winston.

How, Gordon. (1992). Tolerance & the Christian. In Aziz Khaki (Ed.), *Religious expressions* (pp. 13-16). Vancouver, BC: The Pacific Interfaith Citizenship Association of B.C.

Jheeta, Mota Singh. (1992). Sikhism and race relations. In Aziz Khaki (Ed.), *Religious expressions* (pp. 11-12). Vancouver, BC: The Pacific Interfaith Citizenship Association of B.C.

Khaki, Aziz (Ed.). (1992). *Religious expressions.* Vancouver, BC: The Pacific Interfaith Citizenship Association of B.C.

Macionis, John J. (1989). *Sociology* (2nd ed.). Englewood Cliffs, NJ: Prentice Hall.

Prameya, Rukmini. (1992). Hinduism: racism & racial discrimination. In Aziz Khaki (Ed.), *Religious expressions* (pp. 7-8). Vancouver, BC: The Pacific Interfaith Citizenship Association of B.C.

Roman Catholic Archdiocese of Vancouver. (1992). Towards a more fraternal society. In Aziz Khaki (Ed.), *Religious expressions* (pp. 9-10). Vancouver, BC: The Pacific Interfaith Citizenship Association of B.C.

Tingley, J.A. Raymond. (1992). Baptists build bridges. In Aziz Khaki (Ed.), *Religious expressions* (pp. 3-6). Vancouver, BC: The Pacific Interfaith Citizenship Association of B.C.

Unitarian Church of Vancouver. (1992). Unitarians & racial justice. In Aziz Khaki (Ed.), *Religious expressions* (pp. 23-24). Vancouver, BC: The Pacific Interfaith Citizenship Association of B.C.

Vogt, Evon Z. & Roberts, John M. (1960). A study of values. In Edgar A. Schuler, et al. (Eds.), *Readings in sociology* (pp. 109-117). New York: Thomas Y. Crowell.

Wissler, Clark. (1923). *Man and culture*. New York: Thomas Y. Corwell.

3

You May Not Want To Discover This

This is probably the most important chapter in this book because it tells the truth about religion. Of course lots of people make this claim, but most of them usually have a hidden agenda. Some of them are pushing a particular brand of religion. I am not. Others have something against religion. I don't. Many critics claim to have at their disposal an abundance of reasons why people should not be religious, but that is not the intent here. Rather, the objective is to explain the workings of religion in order to be better informed. Hopefully my years of involvement in, and study of, institutional religion have yielded some insights which may be beneficial to others as well.

Some of the traditional criticisms of religion are just. There *are* charlatans in the business, *some* churches are overly concerned about money, and *some* religious leaders *are* basically interested in empire-building. One only has to point to the ex-careers of Jimmy Swaggart and Jimmy Bakker to know that "some TV preachers are just big phonies." Persistent begging for money is synonymous with the role of those same television evangelists, plus a few other we could name – like Oral Roberts, who suggested that God was going to strike him dead if he did not come up with several million dollars by a certain time. Luckily he duped enough people with his threat that they awarded him with sufficient funds, and he also managed to "squeeze extra time out of God" as well or local TV stations would have found themselves with plenty of extra air-time to sell.

Criticism notwithstanding, religion still plays a vital part in many individuals' lives. Granted, in some cases it appears to have the same effects as a huge dosage of emotional hype, but those affected will fervently insist that their faith simply cannot be labelled anything other than a valid resource. A few examples may illustrate the extent to which the "hype" aspect is a factor to be considered in studying religion.

Religion as Hype

A good starting point for the discussion about emotional highs is the world of sports which probably thrives on hype more than any other social sector. It is quite amazing to witness the speed with which a crowd can be brought to its feet when a grown male manages to violently kick an inflated pig bladder between two designated poles on a playing field – thereby engaging in a highly cerebrally-developed activity called football. An amazing act of herculean proportions is apparently heightened significantly by the team colors the respective player wears.

It is an interesting fact that the hype of sports is directly related to the city, province or nation of its origin. If one hails from a particular city or province one is thrilled beyond description when one's "home team" scores a point or, better still, wins a game. The irony is that in professional sports, at least, in most cases the heroes do not even originate from the city or province in whose name their team plays. It gets even more unbelievable when one finds anti-American Canadians cheering for their "home" team which is comprised mostly of American players who are citizens of the United States or perhaps from other countries. Apparently, logic does not apply in sports – identifying with a team and watching them win does!

The hype of sports is not excluded from church circles. Just because one is spiritually-inclined does not eliminate one's enthusiasm for sports. Many times devoted church board members have had to struggle with paying attention to local business matters during sessions of the board while trying to keep one ear tuned to the latest sportscast. It is amazing to see the ingenuity of individual board members who manage to keep one ear tuned to a transistor radio and the other to the business at hand. When the 1994 hockey strike began in Canada, one columnist suggested that the lack of televised hockey might produce better board members (*Mennonite Reporter,* 31 Oct. 1994, 14).

There are other sectors of life that utilize hype as a component of operation – politics, media, advertising and propaganda agencies of all sorts. Exemplary promotion slogans might include these gems: "Get people excited and you can sell them anything. Encourage folks to take ownership in your enterprise and you can get them to buy plenty of shares. Present your program in an exciting and stimulating fashion and people will buy anything!" As P.T. Barnum, the circus promoter put it, "A sucker is born every minute." With this kind of environment in which to function, small wonder that religion also embraces an element of hype in its repertoire.

Hype as Essence

Religionists are sometimes accused of operating on emotion when they celebrate their faith in public gatherings. Truthfully, some religious gatherings (including Christian), do take on rather stimulating proportions, particularly those of the charismatic nature, where a lot of hand-clapping, loud singing and shouting "Amen" takes place. This is usually more than your average "high church type" can stomach. Nevertheless, this kind of religion apparently has a great deal of appeal for young people who like noise, former street people who value belonging to something, or folks who simply like a little more "life" in their church services. The debate about the nature and extent of the use of "charismatic gifts" in churchdom has long raged, and it is doubtful that it will be resolved here or in the immediate future.

People often participate in religious activities for what they get out of them, and often this is simply to experience an emotional high. One individual claimed that he stopped attending charismatic religious services in his church because "you can only take so much of that kind of activity and then you have to get back to real life. Emotional highs are a temporary avenue to spiritual satisfaction." Well, that was his view.

Columnist James Beverley recently described a Toronto revival campaign of the California-originated Vineyard movement started by John Wimber. Beverley suggested that some of the charismatic displays might be hard to justify by reference to the Holy Spirit or the Day of Pentecost. According to Beverley:

> Two women near the front were rocking so strongly in their seats that their heads were almost banging into people in the row behind them. Little children were duplicating the frenzy in wild dancing that looked artificial and contrived. One man roared like a lion during Wimber's sermon. A few individuals hit the concrete hard when they were "slain in the spirit" (*Faith Today*, Sept/Oct. 1994, 13).

Beverley's analysis may seem a bit harsh to Vineyard followers, but it does support the point that there are significant differences in religious practice – even among subsections of specific religious camps like fundamentalists, conservatives, pentecostals, charismatics or evangelicals. Naturally, Beverley was severely chastised by a Vineyard leader, Roger Helland, in a subsequent issue of *Faith Today*. Beverley was warned that:

> Those who pretend to pass judgement in spiritual matters must be prepared to show their credentials of personal spiritual experience. Unfortunately, many people condemning manifestations of and experiences birthed by the Holy Spirit have had little personal experience with either" (*Faith Today*, Nov/Dec. 1994, 8).

Of course it is not exactly clear from this quote whether Beverley was now being judged for his stance, but it does show that spiritual unanimity has not yet been achieved. Ah, the joys of brotherly acceptance and understanding!

There is some indication that individuals who regularly participate in religious services with one group or another may have very little knowledge of the underlying belief system of that body. Further, they may also be uninformed about which particular denomination acts as sponsor for their group. Apparently none of this matters. Recently I met an individual who claimed that he attended a non-denominational "community church." When I asked for further information he insisted that it was a Christian interfaith church with no specific prescribed doctrinal creed. Apparently this was a church that accepted the belief systems of *all* Christian denominations. Having a little information about this particular congregation, and knowing that it was a baptism-by-immersion-only affiliated group, I suggested that my acquaintance approach his minister about having a child baptised. After all, *most* Christian faiths endorse this Sacrament. He reported back to me a few weeks later with a, "Whew! I see what you mean! That's no interfaith church!" Evidently his request had met with some sort of reprimand and doctrinal clarification. The "community" label for this particular church was simply a smokescreen to lure unsuspecting people to what was being advertised as an "interfaith" church. This church was not even "inter-Christian."

Some friends told me recently that they were attending a new church with a new name – something about "Christian fellowship" in the title. They enjoyed the services very much, but they did not know what kind of church it was; they thought it might be a Lutheran-affiliated congregation. A few days after our conversation they checked with the pastor and discovered that they were attending a fairly well-established evangelical kind of church. Still, this did not seem to matter to them. They were not after labels, simply enjoyment and good feeling.

Another acquaintance indicated to me that the church of his ethnic heritage no longer appealed to him, so for the past five years he had found a more ideal denominational linkage. When he identified the denomination in question, I mentioned that he was attending a "holiness" type of church. Did that matter to him? He enquired about the meaning of "holiness" and I explained the doctrine of the "second work of grace" to him. It means that once persons are converted to Christianity, they still have to strive for a *second* spiritual experience, namely the "infilling of the Holy Spirit." This person had no knowledge of the concept, and he was sure that he had never heard a sermon preached on it during his sojourn with that group. No matter; he kept right on attending this church. His spiritual needs were being satisfied.

So why do people go to church or attend religious functions? Probably for a variety of reasons, but one of the most pronounced is simply because of what they get out of it. Denominational identities or affiliations often do not seem to matter. Feelings do.

Hype as Exclusivity

Perhaps the saddest thing about religion is the phenomenon of elitism. Every Christian church I have been affiliated with has made this claim, usually not directly, but by inference or innuendo. Once, during a summer vacation in British Columbia, my wife and I stopped at a church to ask for directions to a certain address. The minister of the church graciously helped us out and then asked casually about our own church affiliation. When we indicated it, he quipped, "Oh that denomination; second-best church, eh?" I may be over-sensitive or too analytical, but I really did not think that this "joke" was appropriate. Surely it is not necessary to play church one-upmanship when people are simply asking for directions.

There are many indications that exclusivity is alive and well, at least among more evangelical Christian groups. In testimony meetings new adherents often make reference to their former church connections as being to "dead churches." Usually mainline denominations are identified. Baptism is another intriguing phenomenon. Some denominations require that adherents be baptized by certain means, particularly the baptism-by-immersion-only variety. Others will insist that converts be rebaptized by them even if they *have* been baptized by immersion previously. Apparently that isn't good enough. Then there are those congregations who convince new arrivals that they must be rebaptized as adults even if they have previously been baptized as infants. In at least one evangelical denomination, previously "sprinkled" adult adherents may have *full* membership privileges without being rebaptized – except they cannot be candidates for the ministry. Complicated, isn't it?

A similar phenomenon exists among other world religions as well, and often a great deal of condemnation will be heaped on parallel religious bodies, especially those originating from within the parent group. While visiting a Baha'i retreat centre recently I indicated to my resident hosts that they seemed to be a very tolerant group. Were there no religious groups or individuals that they did not accept or endorse? Their answer was that any religion claiming Divine revelation *before* that of their own leader was acceptable. Any claims made after *his,* were not acceptable. This meant that any religious group originating *after* the midpoint of the 19th century was considered invalid. A further discussion revealed that the Bahai's were also quite opposed to individuals who once have belonged to the Baha'i faith and then left it. Such is an act of unforgivable apostasy. Apparently these individuals are to be ignored, shunned or condemned. So much for unconditional universal brotherly/sisterly love. It has its limits.

The Hype Attack

Canadian journalist Roy Bonisteel recently observed that some of the most vicious attacks made on American president, Bill Clinton, were coming from conservative Christian circles. TV Evangelist, Jerry Falwell, is apparently selling $43 videotapes accusing President Clinton of being involved in murders. In Virginia, supporters of the religious right endorsed Oliver North for the US senate, well aware that he had been found guilty of involvement in selling arms to the

Iran-Contras. Apparently North was now saying the right things – religiously-speaking, and strongly condemning the president. This was good enough for the religious right. Columnist Brian Stiller comments that no critic "can match the hostile and ridiculing commentary of open-line radio and television host Rush Limbaugh" who enjoys belittling the US president though he has never met him *(Faith Today,* Sept/Oct. 1994, 70). Stiller concludes:

> The "Bubba" show is not a glorious saga. It is sad. And cheering on Rush Limbaugh finds no symmetry with the fruits of the Spirit. The role of America in setting the moral agenda is too overpowering for us not to pray that God in His mercy will bring resolution to troubled leadership *(Faith Today,* Sept/Oct., 1994, 70).

Unfortunately an analytic study of religion will quickly bring the investigator to the conclusion that not all is well in the land of faith. As previously cautioned, you may not *want* to discover these things about organized religion, but they are still there – an attribute of being human, no doubt. It is most regrettable that even when proponents of religion reduce their campaigns to denigrating others in an effort to show their moral superiority, the number of people attracted to the membership of their particular organizations still rises dramatically.

Attacks on each other, on "enemy" denominations, or on the "wicked," are not the only arenas in which religious self-righteousness manifests itself. A certain portion is reserved for adherents as a means of generating faithfulness to the creed. This tendency has intriguing dimensions in the Anabaptist world of my upbringing. The case of one Mennonite pioneer, a southern Manitoba businessman named Abram K. Loewen, who was 105 years old on 15 May 1994, is interesting. During his long lifetime Loewen sold a variety of goods – tires, postcards, kerosene and gasoline and suits. He was always ahead of his time with his church who frequently questioned his buying into the "ways of the world." Loewen was first in his church to buy a car for his business, a crystal set (radio receiver), the first pull-type combine, and the first self-propelled combine. Once he bought a shirt with pink stripes on it, and the gossip lines hummed. Even though his church was against the use of musical instruments, he learned to play the accordion and the mouth organ *(Mennonite Reporter,* 2 May 1994, 16). He was never excommunicated from his church, but the elders were almost constantly "breathing down his neck" with warnings.

The Amish community holds an equal kind of intrigue for the observer, and congregational splits are frequent. Although basically a farming people, the Old Order Amish do not use tractors, nor trucks or cars and they do not endorse the use of electricity. Still, there is a wide variety of interpretations of these principles, each manifest in a different form in each congregation. One church, for example, will not allow rubber tires on farm wagons while another will. One will allow cabs on horse-drawn buggies and another will not. Like Hutterites, the Amish forbid their men to wear pockets on their shirts lest they put things of pride into them – like fancy-colored pens or pencils. In one church the men are permitted to wear only *one* suspender to hold their pants up. In other congregations normal suspenders are permitted. Some Amish congregations endorse the growing and use of tobacco, others allow its production but frown on smoking, and still others will have nothing to do with the weed. In each instance these differences emerged because someone broke the rule, others sided with them and a new congregation with its own unique set of rules was born. Religion *does* have its stipulations.

Religion as Help

Despite any and all criticisms of religion, for many people it is their faith that keeps them going in rough times. It gives them comfort, meaning, a sense of belonging, inspiration and spiritual security. Skeptics may denounce the claims of those who have seen visions or experienced personal healing, but the faithful will not be deterred from believing in the value of their personal miracle.

If we accept the axiom that people have a need to believe, we can surely concede that they also have a need to feel good about themselves. If religion helps in this regard, can it be all bad? This happens in different ways, of course, sometimes through the inspirational modelling of respected heroes. If these individuals are (or have been) religious, it may helpful to adopt their particular form of faith and practice, e.g., Saint Francis of Assisi, Mahatma Ghandi, Buddha, Jesus Christ or Confucius. In similar fashion, people are sometimes assisted in "getting through their day" by inspirational readings, poetry or music. Who has not been encouraged or inspired through the poetry of Helen Steiner Rice, Edward Markham, Elizabeth Barrett Browning or John Donne, or the hymns of Fanny Jane Crosby? Sometimes these works emanate from religious experiences, even from individuals attached to particular religious bodies. Those being helped may want to further their inspiration or healing by obtaining more of this kind of medium. A trip to the office of the respective religious body may provide the seeker with obtaining additional materials. Perhaps regular weekly attendance at a synagogue, temple or church may be useful.

Perhaps the most convincing evidence that participation in religious activities is desirous is derived from personal experience. Despite the most intense efforts of the skeptic, it is very difficult to dissuade a firm believer with a profound personal spiritual experience that this attachment has no validity. And why should one undertake to do this? Why is it necessary to rob someone of an inspirational or otherwise useful resource? Some take joy in this kind of deed, and I suppose that is understandable as well. After all, those who are in possession of the truth simply have an obligation to set everyone else straight as well.

In many instances the assistance offered by religious organizations is conditional. There is often a hidden side to their proffered solace, namely that one should really join their organization and toe the behavioral lines which their rulers have drawn up. In this sense these "spiritual" agencies operate much like other societal institutions, and appear to be built on the same model. The secular world says, "For so many purchases you get so many air-miles" which, interpreted in "religious" terms means that if you attend, believe, obey, tithe and pray a lot, God will reward you. Did you ever notice that the "rewards" seem to accrue in greater amounts to the persons doing the advertising? And when the rewards are not forthcoming to the new initiate, they are explained away in terms of one's apparent "unbelief" or lack of spirituality.

There *are* benefits to joining an established religious organization, for example, you get a full explanation for any moral or metaphysical question you might ask. True, at times you may be warned that your queries could be in areas which "we cannot talk about," or you may receive an evasive response to a query, but for the most part religious systems do cater to philosophical closure. They offer a full set of interpretations of absolute truth, the universe, the meaning of life and the destiny of peoplekind. They also set out a fairly full routine to be followed in terms of rituals, sacraments, prayers etc., and spell out the repercussions for deviation. For some people, this is very comforting.

Several years ago some friends joined a very conservative Christian group with its own vocabulary for such standards items as church buildings, budgets, church meetings or ministerial personnel. When I inquired as to the reason for their new faith pursuit they remarked, "Finally we have found the truth. These leaders have a complete answer for *every* question that we have about the Christian faith." According to this interpretation, faith is not "the substance of things hoped for," but a humanly-contrived answer to every possible question. There is very little room for hope in that stance. We should all be so lucky; come to think of it, I forgot to ask these folk if they knew who Adam and Eve's son, Cain, had married when he grew up. Most likely, their leaders would have provided them with an answer.

To a real extent, religious systems are in business to stay in business. After all, if an agency serves a vital purpose, and provides a bit of employment on the side, why not sustain it? For those operating on the more dubious side, if you have a good thing going, why not keep it going? So, if the agency and its message are to be perpetuated, a means of support must be established. Naturally, adherents, or those who benefit, should pay their just dues. Everything costs money or takes effort, so why should the helping function be extended without a little something expected in return? Besides, higher-ups have a lot to lose if the membership is not faithful or, worse, if numbers dwindle. Not the least of these worries is the matter of financial support. The logical conclusion is that a full plethora of techniques must be developed for capturing the imagination of potential members for getting them to join the ranks, *and* means by which their loyalties will be maintained. Lure tactics often duplicate those used in the secular world, including those of the huge marketing giants. Off-beat organizations may even revert to deviant methods such as the "sex evangelism" approach used by the Children of God cult founded by David Berg. Retention devices may range from gentle admonition to threatening to withdraw the guarantee of personal salvation. Deviation, or backsliding, therefore, can be a very excruciating and/or isolating experience for the individual.

Fortunately, not all religious organizations complement their helping function with a hidden agenda of promises and threats. This possibility is mentioned here for caution and information. It may be quite possible to obtain spiritual help and encouragement through an established religious order without having to fulfill a whole series of corollary requirements. So go ahead, pick one, but check out the small print first.

Religion as Hope

There is a good reason why books that offer words of hope and courage to people in need chalk up huge sales every year. The search for solace and inner peace takes many roads. Books with promise are one of them. True, many of these volumes are probably written primarily to make money, but in this instance the end may justify the means. A colleague told me recently about her mother who had joined a very conservative, yet charismatic Christian group – and her mother loved it. My friend said, "I personally wouldn't engage in the kind of irrational and emotional behavior endorsed and encouraged by that particular organization, but it makes my mother happy. Why would I want to spoil her fun or upset her joy with *my* logic?" A wise woman, that!

The base of religion does not need to be rational or true to be useful. For people in need, be it poverty, physical illness or mental depression, the promise of hope is often sufficient to help them face another day. In the Gospel of John there is a story about a man who had been stricken for 38 years and spent his life lying next to the "Pool of Bethsada" which was reported to have magical properties. At certain times the water in the pool would move, and people entering the pool at exactly that time would be healed of their ailments. One day the man met Jesus Christ for the first time and in answer to Jesus' query informed the Lord that he had remained at the site for so long because when the "waters moved" there was no one to help him into the water. This is truly a story of faith and hope. The Gospel does not tell us whether or not the water was indeed magical, but we do read that Jesus healed the man.

I would imagine that no one was able to talk that man out of his opinion that his experience with Jesus was valid.

The Task at Hand

This chapter was intended to be informative about the downside of organized religion in Canadian culture. Perhaps the discussion will also be useful in determining the direction for undertaking one's own individual spiritual quest. In Part Two the gamut of world religions operant in Canada is presented. Hopefully, a perusal of this section will help clarify this cafeteria of metaphysical systems.

PART TWO

Assessing The Global Market

As the content of the forthcoming chapters will attest, it is not particularly useful to distinguish between major world religions on the basis of the number of their adherents in Canada. For example, Confucianism is a world religion and is included here, even though it has limited influence in Canada – statistically speaking. Taoism, on the other hand, is not discussed because *The Canadian Yearbook* reports no adherents in the nation.

Most religions, whether they attract great multitudes of people or only a few individuals, reveal a remarkable similarity in terms of the nature of their origins (usually they start on the basis of someone having had a "Divine" vision), doctrinal principles and methods of operation. Eccentricities, specialties, sanctions and taboos also bear a remarkable human similarity. Each religion in this section is described in terms of its origins (pedigree), its principles, precepts and practices and its unique features (peculiarities).

We begin our assessment where it should begin – with the First Peoples of Canada, the Aboriginal people. Though the Indian Affairs Department of Canada lists only 533 451 Status Indians, there are over a million Canadians who can lay claim to Native descent.

4

The Aboriginal Way

One of the great religious tragedies of modern times occurred during the period of first contact between incoming Europeans and the North American First Nations. The European invaders who landed on this continent about 500 years ago were armed with a religious value system which they perceived to be superior to anyone else's; they believed it had been handed to them by the Creator. From their perspective they were given the mandate to investigate, analyze and make judgments on any religious system they might encounter in the new land for the specific purpose of determining and undermining its inadequacy or shortcomings. Any system they deemed inadequate would most certainly be revamped or stamped out altogether and replaced with various forms of imported Christianity. European contact with the First Peoples of this continent, therefore, resulted in an inevitable theological clash. For the purposes of this discussion we shall refer to the First Peoples by various ascriptions currently in use, i.e. Aboriginals, AmerIndians, First Nations, Indians, Native peoples, Original peoples, etc.

Pedigree

No one knows how the Aboriginal peoples got their religion, how old it is, nor how many practices or rituals have been retained or lost through time. Perhaps this is as it should be, for Native spirituality is a way to live rather than a way to talk about. It is a way of seeking harmony with the universe. It is regrettable that from the time of first contact the Aboriginals were targeted for takeover – physically, socially, economically and spiritually. The invaders had no intention of learning anything in the new land except that which was necessary to complete the task of domination. When they met the First Peoples they did not bother to discover if a religious or social system was in place, and if so, how could they relate to it. Their intention was that even if they *did* discover any identifiable institutional forms, they would quickly destroy them and replace them with their own.

The First Nations met the newcomers at their boats and welcomed them. True to their long-standing approach, they listened intently to the new interpretation of truth imparted by their incoming brothers and tried to incorporate aspects of it into their own system. To this very day there are many Indian tribes who celebrate a religion born of two distinct origins, their own traditional spirituality, and that of imported Christianity (Friesen, 1991).

At first the Indians listened eagerly to their visitors but wrongly perceived that by doing so they were not necessarily committing themselves to major changes in their lifestyle. Besides, the Black Robes (priests) and missionaries who followed the fur-traders declared themselves to be "men of God," so the Indians took them at their word and paid careful attention to them (Snow, 1977). This was the Indian custom – to respect anyone making this kind of claim and heed their words so as to catch any messages they might have from the Creator. Later the Indians discovered that by being good hosts they had apparently committed themselves to abandoning their traditional religion and adopting Christianity. The ownership of their hunting lands was now also in question.

It would be unfair to suggest that regard for the Aboriginal peoples by fur-traders and missionaries was always negative. Indeed, many fur traders married Native women and "lived happily ever after." There were also some missionaries who developed a strong respect for Native cultures and described them as making up an honorable and religious civilization. One Jesuit missionary, Father A.M. Beede, after 25 years of service, described the Sioux as a "true Church of God with a religion of truth and kindness." He suggested that the tribe had no need for a missionary, so he abandoned his assigned role and studied law in order to assist his new friends in that capacity. He was defrocked, of course, but spent his last days in service to his particular tribe (Seton, 1966, 38).

One wonders what might have happened if the North American immigrants of a half century ago would have taken time to learn more about Indian ways. With that possibility gone forever, however, it is reassuring to know that a fairly reliable configuration of the Aboriginal belief system can be outlined in much the same form as it existed before European contact.

Principles & Precepts

A key to sharing in the lament for a once badly battered religious institution requires an appreciation for the difference between the oral tradition and a preference for the written word. Traditionally, the First Nations never developed much by way of written forms; at least we have little proof of that except in the form of petroglyphs and pictograms which some tribes left behind. Like the Psalmist, the Indian people believed; "I have hidden your word in my heart that I might not sin against you" (Ps. 119:11). Naturally, their belief system and rituals changed slightly from generation to generation, partially reflecting an inbuilt design of adjusting to time and place. A good example was the practice of telling stories and legends which comprised a valued form of moral teaching. Stories would vary slightly from storyteller to storyteller and from one occasion to another, but no one worried about this. The tribe was sure that the essence of the particular truth being imparted was still being preserved. Children used to spend hours with their grandparents and with tribal elders and acquired their beliefs in informal settings.

On the other side of the ledger is the written tradition whose proponents believe that nothing can be proven, nor have any epistemological value, unless it can be located in some written form. As it turns out, in retrospect, both forms have a measure of validity, and both stand in need of a degree of healthy skepticism in terms of comprising an absolute form (Friesen, 1994). One wonders if some degree of compromise might have been worked out at the time of first contact, would both systems not have benefitted a great deal as a result? Alternately, if our incoming agents had been raised to show at least a modicum of respect for other spiritual systems, a great deal of unnecessary stress and recapitulation might have been avoided.

The Contrast

When first forced up against the European perspective, with its penchant for philosophical dissection and analysis, Indians were baffled by the white man's being enamored with wanting to explain and control every element of the universe. There was apparently no respite from this assignment. The Europeans even gave the impression that this was the main purpose for which humankind was put on earth. This fixation persistently dogs European descendants to this day and appears to be embedded in every philosophical, scientific, cultural and religious institution.

The Aboriginal perspective towards openness augured well for the European invaders. When their philosophical captors indicated that the traditional Native lifestyle was out of sync with God's commands many Indians believed them and attempted to change their ways. After that it was only an extension of logic to convince the Natives also to give up their lands and transfer their control to their spiritual superiors.

The Indian orientation of respect for the universe logically blossomed into a resignation to work *with* the forces of the universe. The power of these forces was invisible, yet rhythmic, and by respecting these reliable patterns, it was possible to sustain a perpetual form of cultural life on earth. A further extension of this mind-set was an inherent warning not to seek to dominate or exploit nature, but to work in harmony with it.

Interconnectedness

It is difficult for non-Natives to comprehend the implications of a holistic view of the universe, but Indians have always believed that all phenomena, including material and non-material elements, are connected and interconnected. AmerIndian peoples do not adhere to any "scientific" breakdown of how people function or how the universe operates. The modern scientific view further allows and encourages the development of separate "hard-core" academic disciplines which seek to ferret out and explain the basic components of varied phenomena. For example, when such fields as geography, physics and biology are further broken down into even finer distinctions, they comprise elements of interdisciplinary cross-over, i.e., astrophysics, biophysics, etc. The social sciences feature similar distinctions such as anthropology, sociology and psychology with further subdivisions, such as biopsychology, anthro-archaeology or social psychology, with even more subdivisions in the making as these fields continue to develop. Although the proponents of each of these areas of expertise may make sophisticated claims about interdisciplinary parallels and concerns, there is always an element of academic ethnocentrism involved in their professional deliberations.

The delineation of disciplinary specialties is quite foreign to the Indian way of thinking. Indians view the world as an interconnected series of only sometimes distinguishable, or understandable, elements. They experience no uneasiness at the thought of multiple realities simultaneously operant in the universe, and they do not differentiate among the varieties or qualities of entities, i.e., between physical and spiritual elements. Their world-view allows for the possibility that a variety of "structurally-different" elements may simultaneously be active, for example, in the process of holistic healing. This also explains why dreams and visions comprise as welcome a source of knowledge as scientifically-derived truths or personal experience. In short, you never know where you might gain knowledge or where you might learn something.

In the traditional Indian world there was only one universal and absolute truth – the universe exists. Often described in terms such as respect for nature or working in harmony with nature, the underlying truth requires much more pondering – not necessarily more analysis. Coupled with the concept of connectedness, for the Indian the universe remains the object of reverence, albeit its workings are veiled in mystery. There are no satisfying scientific explanations in this approach, and the deeper mysteries are only partially understood and then only through an intensive lifelong spiritual search.

The mystique of the universe suggests at least two limitations. An unknown and hallowed entity cannot and should not be approached with the idea of exploitation or domination. Second, one should not tamper with the elements or workings of the universe, but respect its modus operandi. Actually the term "respect" is not strong enough to portray the Indian attitude towards the universe; in fact, it is better described as a hands-off approach reinforced by awe. The universe is sacred territory. The fact of its eternal perpetuity, affirmed through the oral tradition, requires obeisance.

Pelletier (n.d.), describes the difference between a Native and non-Native approach to the universe in a scene that places him on the top of a mountain in British Columbia. There he imagines he has been assigned the awesome responsibility of improving his natural environment. His first inclination is to stock the sky with a few more birds or perhaps move some clouds around to provide balance. Then his eye falls on an old plank lying on the ground at his feet and he decides to relocate it to a more appropriate place. As he lifts the plank he notices that the underside of it contains a whole colony of insect life. Ants are scrambling to move their eggs to safety, wood-lice are digging to get down into the ground, earthworms are coiled up like snakes, and a spider is staring him straight in the face demanding, "What have you done to my world?" Pelletier immediately puts the board down as close to the original place as possible, and apologizes to the insects for disturbing their society. Then he thanks them for the lesson they have taught him not to interfere with the doings of the universe.

Contrast this perspective with that of the staff of a construction company charged with digging basements to prepare the ground for new homes in an urban development project. Their mandate is to rearrange the earth in a pattern that is virtually unrecognizable when compared with the previous format; nothing in the way will remain untouched, if not completely destroyed – the terrain, trees, and any and all forms of vegetation. *This,* after all, is *progress.*

The Indian hands-off approach to the universe generates several spin-offs which, from the dominant North American perspective, have varying implications. The positive aspect has to do with providing the would-be learner with a more open attitude towards personal growth. By placing oneself at the disposal of the inner workings of the universe, its every component and process become potential teaching-learning situations in the manner that Pelletier's experience demonstrates. There may be some resistance to the nature of these potential teaching opportunities on the part of more scientifically-minded observers, since the essence of the experience will necessarily be intuitive and/or spiritual. Seldom is even the "truest" scientist prepared for, or open to, learn about Nature's inexplicable mysteries (Knudtson and Suzuki, 1992, xxx). In addition, the orientation and pace of everyday human goings on in dominant society virtually dictate a total disregard for this sphere.

The downside of "universe reverence," if it may be so labelled, is that the resultant attitude towards the universe can take many forms. The strong penchant towards "maintenance," so strongly valued by many successors of the European tradition, for example, might be viewed by Aboriginal peoples as comprising a form of tampering with the operations of the universe. Nowhere is there a better illustration of this than when formerly "developed" communities paralyzed by "progress" wither and fall into disuse. Abandoned townsites serve to substantiate the Indian view that non-Native people tend to build and destroy. They dig holes, erect buildings, lay paved roads and develop streets, and then install elaborate underground wiring and pipe systems. When a town dies, however, in many cases the modern trappings of convenience are simply left to rot, often inflicting permanent damage to the earth as well as comprising an eye-sore (even by non-Native standards). Native people find this state of affairs quite intolerable. In their view, in time, the earth will return to find its own form – provided that in the meantime the damage inflicted by "civilization" is not irreparable.

The vision of permanency, particularly the notion of building a bigger, better future for one's successors or, better still, in heaven, is not a vital plank in Aboriginal philosophy, and in light of today's happenings, it does seem somewhat pointless to value such ends. And towards what purpose? Indians continually see non-Natives using up all their energies "building for the future" but they end up dying anyway. Perhaps a better way would be to adjust one's energies towards fulfilling the Creator's wishes in *this* life.

The First Peoples see themselves as part of a great chain of existence that includes all aspects of creation; all elements in this natural chain are interrelated and interdependent. If any single element is subjected to undue attention or pressure, or is tampered with, there will be repercussions in the grand scheme of things. Modern scientists may wish to argue with this non-professional view of things, but when one ponders the tremendous changes that have occurred in society that have affected the workings of the universe only in recent decades, the mind boggles. If the earth has been a working enterprise for "millions of years" as we have been led to believe by those same scientists, even a non-scientist can imagine what the effect of increased chemical use such as pollution will ultimately have on the earth. In the final analysis we may also discover that the irregularity caused by each new scientific "invention" cannot be rectified by still another scientific adjustment.

The Spiritual Mandate

One of the hardest "truths" for a devotee to the work-ethic to accept is for anyone to claim that efforts to fulfill a specified objective (often called "work") may not necessarily have any virtue in itself. Yet, an important underlying presupposition of the traditional Native lifestyle is to shun work for its own sake, and even demean any colleague who buys too strongly into the work-ethic. Virtue emanates from living in the perennial "now." An acquaintance of mine, a young Indian man in his thirties was enrolled in extension university courses in his home community. About half-way through his studies towards completing a degree he abruptly decided to stop. When queried about his reason for doing so he simply remarked, "I am going too fast; there is so much to learn, and I am not getting out of the process what I should. I want to make the most of it." Subsequently he spent several years engaged in a job quite unrelated to his area of study and then, when he felt he was ready, began again – taking only one course at a time.

The Aboriginal attitude towards those who value the exertion of a great deal of effort towards the fulfillment of a specified task as virtue certainly did not originate in the present-oriented, survival-centred society of the Ancients. Game used to be hunted to fulfill immediate needs, and with the exception of being stored as pemmican, meat could not be preserved for long periods of time anyway. When the circumstances of hunting and gathering called for hard work, it was done, but there was no concept of holding a job as a means of validating one's existence. Work was undertaken to fulfill a specific task or to satisfy a pressing need; nothing more.

The Native attitude towards negating the virtue of work for its own sake has spawned the misguided notion of "Indian time." For example, observers often joke about "Indian time" as though to imply that Indians are always late. The truth of the matter is that Indians, like any other people, *are* sometimes late, and sometimes they do not even show up for an appointment when another party may be expecting them to do so. This does not mean that a sense of time is *always* irrelevant, but rather that time per se is not the *only* criterion by which to determine how a particular moment ought to be acted out. It is certainly not a top priority in and of itself. There *are* times when Indian people are actually *early,* depending on circumstances or purpose and the relative importance of an event. Above all, clock-watching simply does not happen. It is a completely irrelevant (and perhaps irreverent) entity in the Indian scheme of things. The important thing is to keep time with the universe, with one's tribe and with one's spirit.

My Brother's Keeper

It is a common stereotype to conceive of Indian society as a sharing society, and this claim is often made by Native spokespersons as well. This is a "true" statement, depending on the context and meaning ascribed to the term. In the dictionary definition, "sharing" simply means that those who possess things or have access to resources may use those resources to assist others who may be in need. Implicit in the definition is the assumption that those who have resources *may* want to help out the needy. In Aboriginal cultures, however, the question of *wanting to* is seldom a relevant factor because of very limited individual choice in the matter.

The Indian twist to the definition of sharing leans quite heavily toward the obligatory component of the process, almost to the point that they who have, *had better share.* This tradition has deep historical roots. When a warrior returned from a successful hunt he was expected to give some of the meat to his immediate family members and relatives and then to other tribal members. In times of famine the meat was stretched out as far as possible. Rare was the warrior who refused to fulfill this obligation because there were strict implicit and explicit rules about sharing. Conversely, there were also taboos about not fulfilling this requirement reinforced by various means of disapproval including gossip, teasing, humor or outright shunning.

At the time of first contact there were many formalized institutional approaches to sharing among North American tribes such as the potlatch, which was practiced by West Coast Indians, and giveaway dances sponsored by several Plains tribes. Joe Dion describes a particular giveaway dance among his people, the Crees, in which a woman experienced such joy and euphoria during a giveaway dance that she virtually gave everything away. Her husband was away from home at the time and he was somewhat chagrined on returning home to discover that even his horse and gun had been "danced away" (Dion, 1979).

A Native student who moved to the city in order to complete her education soon found that her small apartment had 14 occupants. Relatives who moved in with her had either come to town to look for work or simply to visit. The crowded conditions made it difficult for the student to fulfill her assignments, but asking her family to move out was unthinkable. Her solution was simply to ask her landlord about the availability of a larger apartment to accommodate her additional room-mates.

An elderly Indian man in his late seventies, clearly perceived by his tribe as a much-respected Elder, lamented that he found it very difficult at times to keep working as a consultant for his band because of his gradually fading energy. "I have to keep working," he responded to a question. "My children come over and look for meat in the freezer. If there is none I disappoint them, and I simply cannot do that. So I must keep on working." Outsiders would no doubt be astonished that an elderly man would have to assume such a degree of responsibility for his middle-aged "children." The underlying principle was that he had a job; a job means income, and the benefits of income are to be shared. The fact that this man was of advanced age did not diminish nor negate this obligation in any way.

Respect for Individuality

Native people, according to one Native observer, possess a kind of self-reliance which non-Natives often interpret as uncooperative, stubborn, belligerent or even "dumb" (Couture, 1985). Indians also act with an aloofness which is easily perceived as a reluctance to ask for, or receive, help other than in an emergency or crisis. Their live-and-let-live philosophy reflects an attitude of non-interference, for to interfere is to be discourteous, threatening or even insulting (Couture, 1985). Although group goals are paramount and individual identity is primarily awarded through community channels, the Indian community reveals a very strong tendency to avoid direct disagreement with the individual.

The inherent difficulty in trying to understand this aspect of Indian philosophy originates in the European-inspired appreciation for talking things out. The Indian way is more inclined to stifle or repress issues or, if necessary to go beyond this point, find a means by which to handle the matter by avoiding direct confrontation as much as possible. When some measure of confrontation becomes necessary, it is often accomplished by telling a story or by relating a legend. In this context, the purpose of story-telling is simply a means by which to let the second party know that his or her behavior has been inappropriate. The hearer is then supposed to figure out that he or she is the target of the story and is to consider amending his/her ways. If the point of the story is missed, or if the listener perceived its purpose to be other than informing, another means may be sought to amend the situation. Usually this kind of undertaking is not attempted more than once. Parenthetically, when this process *is* attempted on the uninitiated non-Native the scene can have quite humorous side-effects. It is possible that non-Native listeners may become so engrossed in the story that they will make comments that clearly indicate their lack of awareness about what is transpiring. In one instance it did not occur to several individuals that they were the target of a particular story until one of them later related the incident to a third party. At that point the insight sparked and they got the point.

Respect for individual privacy in Native cultures is strong, including respect for personal opinion. This also applies to the area of communication; Aboriginal society is not a talkative society, and people are not usually in the habit of asking nosey questions nor providing extensive responses to questions of a personal nature. Ask a non-Native Canadian why they were absent from an occasion at which they were expected to be present and an endless verbal harangue may result. Ask a Native person the same question and you may be rewarded with a one-word response or none at all. After all, if you respected the person, you would not even *ask* why they did not show up. A curious non-Native was walking down the street with a Indian woman of his acquaintance and he enquired of her if it was acceptable for him to ask about her family background; she replied, "Yes," and kept walking.

Community

Belief in the interconnectedness of all things and a reverential awe for the operations of the universe produced a deep, almost withdrawing sense of patience among the Aboriginal peoples of the past. Add to this the concept of time already described and a perspective of tolerance, and a "wait-and-see" attitude results. This orientation is applicable to virtually all areas of human behavior and the general attitude towards cosmic phenomena. Thus if a problem appears in the community, the people coalesce in an attitude of "let's wait-and see, and maybe it will disappear." Besides, no unauthorized individual would dare to undertake the resolution of a problem and risk community disapproval by appearing too bold, interfering or eager.

Few followers of Robert's "Rules of Order" would retain their sanity at a traditional Indian meeting. Not only are the "rules" different, often prescribed by the person in charge, but individuals may leave intermittently during a meeting for no apparent reason (at least it may appear so to an outsider), except that a mood may take them and they may return sporadically or not at all. Elders, chiefs and respected spokespersons often prescribe the procedures for a meeting simply by their behavior, and no one takes issue with this. Traditionally, every challenge faced by a tribe had to be resolved communally and with community consensus. This practice still continues. Recently, when discussing the lateness of a particular meeting of Indian leaders, one chief observed, "There was one hold-out to the idea and it took us till past midnight to talk him into it. There simply *had* to be consensus." This concept of community reflects the essence of Aboriginal faith in the universe, in cosmic operations and in the power of the Great Creator Spirit who made it all possible.

Practices

The recorded first descriptions of the Aboriginal faith and practice in Canada were furnished by outsiders – missionaries, explorers, fur-traders or Hudson's Bay employees. Most of this literature is negative, premised on a set of ethnocentric concepts culminating in the unfortunate conclusion that the religion of the newcomers was superior to that of the Native peoples. If that outlook was not sufficiently denigrating, most of the newcomers went further and denounced Aboriginal beliefs as heathen. Had the invaders been socialized with a more tolerant or sensitive mind-set they might have discovered that the traditional ways of the First Peoples were premised on some very valid and meaningful concepts – meaningful even within the very context of the faith system of these harsh judges. This kind of investigation, by the way, would still constitute a very healthy learning experience for today's critics of Indian ways.

It is difficult to describe all of the many varied religious practices of Aboriginal peoples because of the tremendous tribal and regional differences within their communities. In fact, there are more significant cultural differences among the various regional Indian groups than among European cultures, for example, Southwest (Pueblo)

Indians, West Coast Indians, Woodland Tribes or Plains Indians, are quite unique, to say nothing of the Metis People. Traditionally, in some tribes, their religious leaders spent the majority of their waking hours in religious activities of some type. Because of the extensiveness of the range of tribal variations, however, this discussion will focus primarily on the culture of the North American Plains Indians, emphasizing especially the Blackfoot, Cree and Stoney (Nakoda Sioux) cultural configurations.

Traditions, Ceremonies and Rituals

Religious people of all persuasions express their faith through uniquely-devised vehicles, and the Aboriginal peoples are no exception. Before contact, their sacred practices highlighted the seasons, the various circles of life, their livelihood and their daily life in general. With some modification these phenomena still persist. Unfortunately, due to space, only very brief descriptions of these practices can be offered here.

To begin with, there is the sundance, an annual event among Plains tribes, staged something like a contemporary church conference. Although explanations regarding the origin and nature of the sundance vary slightly among its descriptors, most agree that it is essentially a four-day event comprising an expression of joy and ecstasy of a religious life, of being thankful for creation, the rain, the sun and the seasons (Snow, 1977, 111). Blood Tribal members of the Blackfoot Confederacy celebrate their sundance as a joyful renewal of acquaintances featuring feasting, playing games and the exchange of properties. At least one day is devoted to spiritual activities. Some viewers also suggest that the sundance is a form of petition with the Almighty to guard the people from possible disaster (Hanks and Hanks, 1950). When the Canadian government at the turn of the century outlawed the sundance at the recommendation of the missionaries, the action struck at the very heart of Indian culture. Thus in many tribes the sundance observers went underground and observed it "behind closed doors." Due to strong government regulation and missionary influence some tribes were more easily influenced. In some quarters the sundance is still observed by substituting the traditional centre pole with a cross and flagpole (Lincoln, 1985, 173).

A special feature of the sundance is the exchange of medicine bundles; these objects are leather pouches containing such articles as feathers or bones, and put together by the originator who saw the special message contained in the bundle in a vision or dream. Medicine bundles are deemed sacred articles and they are not to be handled by just anyone. If they are touched by someone other than a designated guardian, a purification ceremony may be conducted. Medicine bundles are viewed as possessing special powers or insights which accompanied the original vision. Bundles may be bought and sold, and the price may be set by recognized elders. The new owner may then access the power of the bundle. A closely-related artifact is the medicine pouch which may be worn by an individual seeking spiritual mercy and protection, or healing from a certain ailment. A medicine pouch may contain plant material prescribed by an elder.

Many physical items are believed to play a vital part in spiritual ceremonies. Pipes, for example, may be used during private and group ceremonies in connection with fasting or cleansing ceremonies. The pipes are used exclusively by either men or women. Sweetgrass or herbs are used as incense in connection with the pipe ceremony, or as a purification ritual. Sweetgrass is often braided and used in a cleansing ceremony because it symbolizes positive energy, good thoughts and purification. Tobacco is similarly considered, because it is the first plant given by the Creator, thus it is used in ceremonies for prayer requests and in thanksgiving. Rattles are believed to help "shake up the spirit of life," and may be used by elders during healing ceremonies. Drums represent the heartbeat of the nation, the pulse of the universe. Eagle whistles are blown to honor the drums. Eagle feathers are used to adorn costumes and for other purposes. These feathers are special because the eagle is considered a Divine messenger; its feathers represent power, protection and solar majesty.

Many tribes also erect sweatlodges, structures about five feet high, made of willow branches and covered with hides. Functioning much like a sauna, sweatlodges are used mainly for communal cleansing purposes and include a series of songs and prayers.

The religion of the First Nations incorporated many fasts, prayers and dances, often in connection with ceremonies emphasizing the circle of life – birth, adolescence, marriage, old age and death. For instance, a family celebrating a member's formal entry into the dance circle, or wishing to commemorate the death of a loved one, could host a giveaway dance during a pow-wow. Gifts such as blankets, beadwork or crafts may be given to friends or visitors followed by appropriate songs and dances. A pow-wow, by the way, is a frequently-staged social to celebrate a special happening or to honor an individual (Horse Capture, 1989). Pow-wows consist of dancing, feasting and having fun; old ways are remembered, friendships are renewed, and unity is highlighted. They are a time to share the sense of one-ness with one another and Mother Earth, a sense of inter-dependence with all living creatures. Some of the names Indian dances are grass dance, fancy dance, sneakup dance or traditional dance.

Peculiarities

The theological essence and structures of traditional Plains Indians' religion cannot be ascertained with any degree of specificity because of their adherence to the oral tradition. In a deep sense, this is its beauty. The precision of the mechanism of a ritual, or the epistemological exactness of a truth, are never as important as the way these phenomena are lived. We are fortunate that enough of a knowledge base about Indian practices can be formulated so that a fairly accurate configuration can be framed. Fortunately, many respected and knowledgeable elders have also been generous in sharing information about Indian Native ways. Undoubtedly the nature of ceremonies may have changed through time, but consultation with respected elders has always been, and still is, a major avenue for the perpetuation of dominant beliefs (Kirk, 1986). The fact that various rituals and ceremonies are still practiced in many communities today bears testimony to the validity and tenacity of the oral tradition.

Indian rituals of spirituality are presided over by elders – men and women who have demonstrated their appropriateness for that office over time. Consistent with the "vagueness" or elusiveness of the oral tradition, elders are not elected nor appointed, nor do they have special training for their task. They simply "emerge over time" and their wisdom is informally recognized by the tribe, particularly their talent for giving guidance when it is sought. The current resurgence of interest in seeking direction from these spiritual advisors is evident among many North American tribes today and comprises a strong indication of the increasing importance of their role and the vitality of the Aboriginal ways (Lincoln, 1985; Couture, 1991). It might be too much to hope, but this time it would be most encouraging to discover a genuine intrigue on the part of those given the opportunity to share in this revival.

References

Couture, Joseph E. (1985). Traditional Native thinking, feeling, and learning. *Multicultural Education Journal, 3*(2), 4-16.

Couture, Joseph E. (1991). The role of Native elders: emergent issues. In John W. Friesen (Ed.), *The cultural maze: Complex questions on native destiny in western Canada* (pp. 201-218). Calgary, AB: Detselig Enterprises Ltd.

Dion, Joseph F. (1979). *My tribe: The Crees*. Calgary, AB: Glenbow Museum.

Friesen, John W. (1991). *The Cultural maze: Complex questions on native destiny in western Canada*. Calgary, AB: Detselig Enterprises Ltd.

Friesen, John W. (1994). *The Riel (real) story: An interpretive history of the Metis people of Canada*. Ottawa, ON: Borealis Press.

Hanks, Lucien M. Jr. & Richardson Hanks, Jane. (1950). *Tribe under trust: A study of the Blackfoot reserve of Alberta*. Toronto: University of Toronto Press.

Horse Capture, George P. (1989). *Pow wow*. Cody, WY: Buffalo Bill Historical Center.

Kirk, Ruth. (1986). *Wisdom of the elders: Native traditions on the northwest coast*. Vancouver, BC: Douglas and McIntyre.

Knudtson, Peter & Suzuki, David. (1992). *Wisdom of the Elders*. Toronto: Stoddart.

Lincoln, Kenneth. (1985). *Native American renaissance*. Berkeley, CA: University of Berkeley Press.

Pelletier, Wilfred. (n.d.). Two articles. In J. S. Frideres, *Canada's Indians: Contemporary conflicts* (1974, pp. 105-106). Scarborough: Prentice-Hall.

Seton, Julia M. (1966). *The gospel according to the redman.* Santa Fe, NM: Seton Village.

Snow, Chief John. (1977). *These mountains are our sacred places: The story of the Stoney Indians.* Toronto: Samuel Stevens.

5

Baha'i

Although somewhat limited in terms of numbers of adherents, in comparison to other world religions, believers in Baha'i proudly point out that they are the second most "global" religion in the world. There are about five million Baha'is in 232 countries worldwide and about 15 000 in Canada. They have established "significant communities" in more countries and territories than any other independent religion with the exception of Christianity.

It should be mentioned that in Baha'i literature many words are loaded with diacritical markings, most of which are eliminated in this chapter to make reading easier. It is hoped that no one will take offense at this, because it is not our intent to be disrespectful.

Although the Baha'i faith originated in the Middle East and its founders had Islamic ties, Baha'is do not like to be considered a sect of Islam. They point out that each manifestation of God has to have *some* cultural roots, and theirs happens to have begun in that particular part of the world. In fact, the history of religion in Persia is complex. The religion of the ancient Iranians (Aryans), who invaded Iran about 2000 BC was that of their kinsmen, the Vedic Indians. They worshipped gods of nature and gods of human society. They recognized the inflexible nature of the world, developed rituals and devised a mythology of creation.

Parenthetically, in 660 BC a prophet named Zarathustra (or Zoroaster) arrived on the scene and attracted a sizable following. The name of Zarathustra is sometimes associated with the Magian movement, which figured heavily in the story of the coming of the wise men to the site of the birth of Jesus, but there are limitations to this association. The Magians existed already before the time of Zarathustra, and we know they were masters of learning in ancient times. Zoroaster certainly stood for this kind of learning, and although the religion he founded never attained world-wide recognition, it did influence Roman, Hellenic, Jewish, Islamic and Christian thought (Jackson, 1965).

Zoroastrianism was the state religion of Iran until about AD 600 and survives today with about 90 000 followers in Iran and 60 000 on the Indian subcontinent. Those who practice the faith continue many of the beliefs and practices of their common ancestors, particularly those relating to purity and pollution (Choksy, 1989). After the Moslem conquest of AD 637-650, the Persians adopted Islam as their major religion, but after AD 1500 they switched to the Shiite move-ment which regards Ali and his descendants as divinely inspired Imams (prophets).

Pedigree

Baha'i is a relatively recent arrival on the Persian scene and was formalized in 1844 when a 25 year old Persian named Ali-Muhammad declared himself to be the herald of the Divine Will in Persia. As he put it, "I have never aspired after worldly leadership. My sole purpose has been to hand down to men that which I was bidden to deliver by God" *(The Baha'is,* 1994).

Ali-Muhammad assumed the nick-name the "Bab," an Arabic con-cept meaning "gate," and he was martyred on 9 July 1850. For six years he suffered persecutions and was incarcerated in various pris-ons until his martyrdom. The Bab sent his first 18 disciples throughout Persia to spread his version of the teachings of Moham-med, the founder of Islam. Persian religious officials interpreted his ministry as political treason and had him put in prison. It is believed that Bab was a prophet of God whose mission it was to prepare the world for the arrival and ministry of a great teacher in the person of Baha'u'llah (Sabet, 1975).

Interpreted, the name "Baha'u'llah" means "Glory of God," and he began his ministry in 1863 by declaring himself "The Promised One of all ages and religions." For 40 years he confirmed his prophetic claim through countless writings and letters which he addressed to believers, clergy and political leaders. He died in 1892. He believed he was one in a long line of prophets whom God raised up in every generation to bring the truth in a relevant form to every generation. In his words:

> And since there can be no tie of direct intercourse to bind the one true God with His creation, and no resemblance whatever can exist be-tween the transient and the Eternal, the contingent and the Absolute, He hath ordained in every age and dispensation a pure and stainless Soul be made manifest in the kingdoms of earth and heaven *(The Baha'is,* 1994, 17).

Before Baha'u'llah's death he appointed his eldest son Abbas Ef-fendi as "Centre of the Covenant" and interpreter of his writings. Abbas Effendi was also made a prisoner and remained as such until the Turkish Revolution of 1908 when he was released. For the next few years he travelled across Europe and the United States preaching his father's gospel wherever he could gain an audience. By the time of his death in 1921 the Baha'is had gained a foothold in 35 countries. Abbas Effendi appointed his grandson, Shoghi Effendi as "Guardian of the cause of God" and the official interpreter of Baha'u'llah's writings. During Shoghi Effendi's ministry Baha'u'llah's teachings were disseminated in 250 countries and translated into 240 languages and 4 500 Baha'i communities were established. He worked according to a very specific three-point, seven-year plan, beginning in April, 1937. The plan was to (i) establish at least one local spiritual assembly in every state of the United States and Canada; (ii) to make certain that at least one Baha'i teacher was resident in each Latin American country; and, (iii) to complete the exterior design of the first Baha'i house of worship in North America. The cornerstone of this house of worship had been laid in 1912 and the building was finally completed in 1944 *(The Baha'i World,* 1993).

The Seven Year Plan

In 1946 a second seven year plan was formulated with a focus on European developments which at that time had only two spiritual assemblies – in England and in Germany. One of the major goals of this plan was to establish an independent national spiritual assembly in Canada which was achieved in 1948. In 1953 a formal dedication service was held in Wilmette, Illinois, for the North American house of worship. That year also witnessed the opening of 132 additional assemblies in as many different countries and territories.

After Shoghi Effendi's death on 4 November 1957 the question who would be the next leader arose, since Effendi had not designated a successor. Subsequently the leadership was passed into the "Hands of the Cause of God" which was later changed to "Chief Stewards of the Faith." In April 1961, 21 new national spiritual assemblies had been established in Latin America and 11 more in Europe. Two years later, a century after Baha'u'llah's first pronouncements, the nine member Universal House of Justice was elected by the representatives of the Baha'i world. Members of 56 elected national assemblies around the world participated in this election. This institution is the chief authority of the faith and makes all major decisions concerning the community. Its location is in Haifa, Israel (Sabet, 1975).

Appropriate to the philosophy of the Universal House of Justice, the original nine elected members represented four continents, several varied ethnic origins and three major world religions – Jewish, Christian and Muslim.

By 1993 the number of participating countries in the elections of the Universal House of Justice had increased from 56 to 165. The number of local spiritual assemblies rose from 3 555 in 1963 to 20 435 in 205 countries. Officials estimate that there are at least 2 112 different ethnic and cultural backgrounds represented in the makeup of the membership. Literature is currently published in over 800 different languages *(The Baha'i World,* 1993).

Principles & Precepts

The purpose of Baha'u'llah's ministry was to support the work of those prophets who had gone before, and to restate the basic truths of their teachings in a manner that would conform to the spiritual needs of the people of his time.

Basic Teachings

Baha'u'llah's principal teachings are contained in a number of documents known as "Tablets," most of them addressed to individual followers over time. His ethical teachings are included in a small book entitled, *The Hidden Words,* but his foremost writing is *The Most Holy Book,* the contents of which were revealed to him during his imprisonment in Acre. The process of translating Baha'u'llah's works into other languages is still ongoing.

Baha'u'llah believed that there is one God, and people can be united only through His power. If one were to characterize Baha'u'llah's teaching in a single word, that word would be unity. The plan of Divine Revelation incorporates the essence of a whole series of religions, i.e., Buddhism, Christianity, Hinduism, Islam, Judaism and Zoroastrianism. Parallel with the ideal of Islam, Baha'is believe in the never-ending revelation of God, who will establish the unity of mankind and found a Divine world civilization. To live and work for the salvation of all humanity is the highest and noblest task for every Baha'i.

In specific terms, Baha'is claim to believe in the oneness of humanity, equality of the sexes (despite the fact that only men can serve in the Universal House of Justice), religious tolerance, universal education and the harmony of religion and science. They oppose discrimination and racism. Believers are expected to exhibit the following characteristics in daily living: honesty, trustworthiness, chastity, service to others, purity of motive, generosity, deeds over words, unity, and work as a form of worship. The following behaviors are forbidden: killing, stealing, lying, adultery and promiscuity, gambling, substance abuse and gossiping and backbiting *(The Baha'is,* 1994).

Future Hope

Baha'u'llah believed that the ages of infancy and childhood of the human race were over and the age of human adolescence was emerging. Slowly and painfully mankind will learn to attain adulthood. When that state is achieved, there will be peace on earth. Swords will be beaten into plowshares, and the Kingdom of God promised by Jesus Christ will be established. Baha'u'llah did not claim finality for his revelation, but saw his ministry as filling a vital place in a succession of revelations.

Baha'u'llah taught that every believer is endowed with absolute divine authority and innate knowledge. Individual revelations, however, are subject to changing conditions and the needs of the people. Truth, therefore, is perceived as relative and revelation is seen as progressive. This implies that all the great religions of the world are divine in origin, and their basic principles are in harmony. Their aims and purposes are one and the same, their various teachings are but facets of one truth, and in essence their functions are complementary. They differ only in the non-essential aspects of their doctrines, and their missions represent successive stages in the spiritual evolution of human society (*The Baha'i World,* 1993).

Baha'is envisage the eventual formation of a world commonwealth with recognized and secure borders for all nations. Freedom of travel and thought, general disarmament and a world federation of nations are vital parts of the ideal structure. An international military to enforce peace through the principles of collective security would assure the protection of human rights and cultural diversity.

Absence of Clergy

The Baha'i faith does not have clergy, nor officially recognized laity. In fact, anyone can become a teacher because there is only one essential qualification for a teacher – an upright and praiseworthy character. Baha'i emphasizes group decision-making through equal representation, but there are some groups of individuals who play a special role in inspiring and advising the community. They may not have decision-making power, but their ideas and opinions are often sought out by elected officials. In 1968, in fact, the Universal House of Justice began to designate a number of spiritually mature and experienced individuals as "Continent Counsellors." There are 72 counsellors world-wide and they are appointed for five year terms.

Members' Obligations

All members have the obligation to share with others the truths they have discovered. Thus the movement is also missionary-oriented or evangelical. If listeners express interest, they should be told more. If they are not interested, they must be left to go their own way.

Baha'is are expected to give generously to the cause. In fact, donations cannot be accepted by the organization except from members. Giving is encouraged on a regular basis but amounts are not stipulated and giving is confidential.

The source of the believer's zeal for evangelism is the Word of Baha'u'llah. He told his believers that the greatest gift of the believer is to teach others, although he also warned them against aggressive proselytizing (*The Baha'is,* 1994). Baha'is are "merely the instruments through which the divine fragrances are diffused" (Farraby, 1987).

Practices

Every religion has a code of laws, some of them more explicitly spelled out than others. These laws have specific and strict behavior expectations. The Baha'i faith is no different from other world religions in this respect, and since the origins of these laws is quite recent, given the youthfulness of the movement, it is easier to determine the exact nature of these commandments.

Social laws

Baha'is have a unique calendar of their own. It consists of 19 months of 19 days each plus 4 days added to the second last month to make 365 days. The Baha'i calendar was given by the Bab and confirmed by Baha'u'llah. Nineteen-day feasts are normally held on the first day of each month, but may exceptionally be held on some other day. All Baha'is are expected to fast, since fasting is considered a time for meditation and prayer, and for spiritual recuperation. During this time the believer must strive to make the necessary adjustments latent in his or her soul. Fasting is also a reminder of abstinence from selfish and carnal desires. The annual Baha'i fasting period lasts from March 2nd to March 20th and is immediately followed by the Feast of Naw-Ruz. Fasting takes place during the day, from sunrise to sunset, and both eating and drinking are forbidden. These activities may be engaged in after sunset. Certain groups of people, such as the aged or pregnant women, are exempt from fasting.

Anyone can become a member of the Baha'i faith through application to a local spiritual assembly. While adhering Baha'is do not like to label themselves as "members," a specific vow is required for admission. It includes a full recognition of the role of the founder of the faith, a dedication to the Baha'i cause, a total submission to the works of Baha'u'llah and other accepted prophets, and close association with the present-day administration of the Baha'i communities throughout the world (Ferraby, 1987). Membership in the Baha'i community is seen to be incompatible with membership in any other organization whose policies differ with the oracles of the Baha'i faith. Anyone who takes up such associations or membership, and is warned of the consequences, can be excommunicated and subsequently shunned.

Baha'is are not to involve themselves in national politics of any kind since their purpose is to achieve world peace – not to advance the cause of any single nation. Support for the United Nations, however, is another matter. Baha'is are encouraged to work for peace and harmony through this organization and its subsidiaries such as UNICEF and UNEP, and to function as promoters of general human welfare in their own countries.

Family Life

In terms of following their social order, Baha'is are encouraged to marry; and the purpose of marriage is procreation. To promote unity and avoid friction, a central Baha'i tenet, one must first gain the permission of all four parents before a marriage union can be entered into. Parents, however, do not have the right to choose a mate for their children, since the consent of both partners is considered essential to entering a sacred covenant. While Baha'is are expected to marry members of the faith, it is permissable to enter into a marriage union with a non-believer, provided that the believer does not formally commit to another religion through the marriage ceremony. In addition, a Baha'i ceremony must also be conducted on the same day as the wedding. Weddings do not have to be conducted under the auspices of a Baha'i assembly, and the Baha'i ceremony must culminate in the saying, "We will all, verily, abide by the Will of God" (Ferraby, 1987).

Under certain circumstances, couples may divorce, particularly after "mistakes have been made" in choosing a partner. Attempts at reconciliation should be undertaken, however, and Baha'i law tries to be consistent with the civil laws of the various countries in which their membership is represented.

Baha'is must bury their dead within one hour of death. Cremation is forbidden, and Baha'i funeral services are conducted in much the same manner as those of other religions. Baha'u'llah confirmed the existence of a separate, rational soul for every human in this life. He said that the soul is related to the physical body and provides the underlying animation for the body, and is our real self. The soul lives on after death, but the exact nature of the afterlife remains a mystery.

Peculiarities

When one joins the Baha'i community one commits to the rules and regulations of the organization. A nine-pointed star is a symbol of the faith, symbolizing various important events in the history of the movement. For example, nine years after the announcement of the Bab, Baha'u'llah received the initiation of his mission. The number nine is also believed to represent completeness, hence unity. The Administrative Order of the Faith, which is responsible for setting community and individual regulations, tries to blend freedom and authority. This Order also provides opportunity for individuals to express their views, and if they do not like particular requirements placed upon them, they may say so at the annual Nineteen day Feast. Once a decision has been made, however, individuals must abide by them. Anyone who flouts the authority of the Assembly may have voting rights taken away, and thus lose all membership rights in the organization.

Excommunication and Shunning

Baha'is believe that when individuals renege on their commitment to the Baha'i covenant, they invoke the wrath of God and they are considered enemies of God. They are to be expelled from fellowship and shunned, lest they, as an evil cancerous growth, affect the spiritual well-being of the entire community. Further, if dissidents are not expelled they may contribute toward the fragmentation of the faith (Taherzadeh, 1992, 255). When individuals *are* excommunicated, believers are forbidden to have anything to do with them – including interactions or conversations of any kind. It is difficult to understand how a religion that by its own testimony appears so interested in promoting kindness and understanding and unity for all members of the human race, can so cold-heartedly condemn any *sector* of the human community, even if their only crime is that they have changed their minds.

Relation to Islam

Baha'is believe themselves to be a special target of Islamic officialdom, though they originated in that context. This may seem a bit unusual in light of the fact that both organizations appear to value the same objective of global unity. The history of the Baha'i faith is punctuated with outbreaks of fanatical persecution of its followers, especially in Iran, the land of its birth (Farraby, 1987). In 1955 the Baha'i international community appealed to the United Nations for assistance, and that organization sympathetically helped to relieve the pressure against members of the faith. In 1979 the Iran government again initiated a full-scale persecution of the Baha'i community, and by April 1983, well over 100 adherents had been martyred.

The Baha'i interpretation of these events is that Islam sees Baha'i as a threat. It was this way from the beginning. Islam saw the Bab as one claiming to be the *Koran* incarnate, and for this reason he was imprisoned and martyred (Nash, 1982). The followers of his teachings are therefore considered heretics, and according to Islam (as with Baha'i), heretics are to be condemned. To an outsider it might appear that Baha'i, as a new revelation of Islam and other avenues of Divine truth, may well have retained at least one, very harsh doctrine, while offering new illumination on an old faith.

A difficulty central to the Baha'i faith is with regard to the Baha'i assertion that the truth must be reinterpreted afresh for every generation and in every culture. This claim, however, is subject to severe limitations because the words of Baha'u'llah are seen as absolute. For example, despite current pressures towards recognizing the equality of the sexes (a stated Baha'i claim), Baha'u'llah forbad the election of women to the House of Justice and this apparently cannot be changed.

Baha'u'llah claimed that the wisdom of his various stipulations would become clear in the future, so that is the final word on a "flexible" faith.

References

Choksy, Jamsheed K. (1989). *Purity and pollution in Zoroastrianism: Triumph over evil*. Austin, TX: University of Texas Press.

Ferraby, John. (1987). *All things made new: A comprehensive outline of the Baha'i faith* (2nd rev. ed.). London: Baha'i Publishing Trust.

Jackson, A.V. Williams. (1965). *Zoroaster: The prophet of ancient Iran*. New York: AMS Press.

Nash, Gregory. (1982). *Iran's secret pogrom*. Suffolk, UK: Neville Spearman.

Sabet, Huschmand. (1975). *The heavens are cleft asunder*. Oxford: George Ronald.

Taherzadeh, Adib. (1992). *The covenant of Baha'u'llah*. Oxford: George Ronald.

The Baha'i world, 1992-93: An international record. (1993). Haifa, Isr: Baha'i World Centre.

The Baha'is: A profile of the Baha'i faith and its worldwide community. (1994). New York: Baha'i Publishing Trust.

6

Buddhism

The religion of Buddhism originated in India in the 5th century BC with the teachings and philosophy of Siddhartha Gautama who began his life in the splendor of a palace environment. Buddha (meaning "teacher" or "master") is an honorary title attributed to Gautama. There are about 163 000 Buddhists in Canada.

Pedigree

Gautama was the eldest son of the Raja of Kapilavastu who was also Chief of the tribe of the Sakyas, an Aryan clan. The area they occupied is about 80 kilometers south of the Himalayan Mountains. While the young prince was growing up, his every wish and whim were granted by adoring and obedient servants. When he was still a teenager, according to custom, a bride was found for him and he married. For the next decade he bravely bore the burden of lavish living, then experienced four earth-shaking situations that greatly affected his thinking about life. Eventually a new world religion was born following the vision of the Buddha.

The Four Visions

Gautama was known as the enlightened one. The first traumatic experience which influenced his departure from royal living occurred one day when he instructed his favorite charioteer, Channa, to take him to a particular garden. Enroute to his destination he came upon an old man, bent with age, showing all of the afflictions produced by the ravages of time. When Gautama enquired of his servant as to the cause for the man's condition he was informed that the aged one's dilemma was the result of a very normal process. We are born to die from the moment of birth, Gautama was told. We all grow older each day and then get feeble and weak – our senses, our bodies and our minds. It was too much for the prince; he ordered that the trip to the garden be cancelled and he returned at once to the palace.

The second experience was similar in nature, except that Gautama encountered a man suffering from a debilitating disease rendering his body swollen, emaciated and pale. He was leaning on another man for support. The scene was too much for the prince who immediately returned to the palace. The third experience had the same effect on the youthful Gautama. It had to do with death and occurred when the prince's company came upon a funeral entourage. On inquiry Gautama's servant explained that the individual they were viewing was dead. He then explained that this was the end of all humans. They would simply cease to be. The encounter ended in a third quick return trip to the palace.

Finally, a fourth chariot ride ended when Gautama discovered a holy man, a beggar, who had renounced worldly life and lived without a permanent home. Although the various accounts of the four experiences differ somewhat, most agree that they formed the essence of his enlightenment. Some say that all four events occurred on the same day; others say they happened at different times. Some sources suggest that an angel appeared, visible only to Gautama and his charioteer, and delivered a special message to them. In any event, at the age of 29, these experiences motivated Gautama to change the course of his life and take up the pursuit of the path to purity.

The Leaving

When Gautama's father found out about his son's concern with eternal destiny, and his subsequent disillusionment with wealth and station, he immediately tried to divert him to other causes. He sent Gautama to a farm, hoping the young man would become interested in agriculture. Instead, Gautama saw a different picture. Instead of being engaged in a worthwhile occupation, he saw hard-working men and beasts working without relief, tormented by flies and sweat. When Gautama learned that the farmers were his father's slaves he freed them on the spot – including the oxen.

Shortly after Gautama's son was born, the prince left the palace. Though his wife had had a dream about his probable leaving, she begged to go with him. Gautama desisted, saying that he would return to his wife once he had gained enlightenment and become a Buddha. He rejected his wife's entreaties to accompany him arguing that their child was too young for such an undertaking. Then, one night when everyone was asleep, accompanied by his faithful servant, Channa, Gautama stole out of the palace. After only a short time he sent word to his father that he would never return to the lap of luxurious living.

Search for Enlightenment

In due course Gautama learned how to beg for food and how to find a place to sleep. One day he saw a vision in the sky – the Great Tempter appeared and promised the aspiring Buddha a universal kingdom over seven continents if he would only return to his home. Gautama bravely resisted, even to the point of becoming disturbed that such lustful, malicious or angry thoughts could enter his mind. He resolved that he would someday conquer these temptations. He began his life of denial by taking a sword and cutting off his long hair, then divesting himself of his fancy ornaments. He sent these back to the palace. Then he entered a seven day fast and began his spiritual search in earnest.

Eventually the young aspiring Buddha heard about a holy man named Master Arada (sometimes spelled Alara), and joined his company. After being accepted he quickly mastered all of the holy man's teachings including the traditional seven levels of meditation. Soon Arada invited Buddha to become his assistant, but the latter was not satisfied. He did not yet feel that he had attained enlightenment. He then sought out another teacher, Rudraka Ramaputra, and achieved yet another higher level of meditation. Still dissatisfied, he continued his search.

As the years passed Gautama (Buddha) continued the life of an ascetic, often eating only one meal a day. At one time he was so weak from fasting that his five disciples thought he was dead and abandoned him. Still he kept on with his search, and although he now began to eat meals regularly he was basically an ascetic. He determined more than ever to attain enlightenment and then declare his doctrine to the world. His biographers report that his motivation was love and pity for a humanity ruled by desire.

The Enlightenment

Eventually, the day came when Buddha's search was rewarded. It came about by the realization that birth is the cause of old age, sickness and death. It happened while he was sitting under a tree, "the Bodhi tree, literally the "tree of enlightenment." He saw that human beings are born and pass away in accordance with karma, the laws of cause and effect. He sought and found the means of liberation.

Buddha perceived that through the cessation of birth (if one could "do away" with it), old age and death would not exist; through the cessation of becoming, there would be no birth; through the cessation of grasping, no becoming – and so back to the sequence of causation to ignorance. He saw suffering, the cause of suffering, the cessation of suffering, and at last also the path to cessation.

It is useful to keep in mind that the nature of Gautama's pursuit of enlightenment via asceticism represented a fairly common phenomenon in India during this time. The fragmented political situation contributed towards this kind of development. The country was split up into little principalities, each governed by a petty despot whose pursuits were not necessarily in the best interests of the community. Promoting the doctrine of reincarnation satisfied many of the poor since they were told that if they were good, they might have a better chance at success in their next life. Reincarnation also offered a welcome potential release from the miserable situation in which the poor found themselves. Partially, the assurance for a better future was cemented by the way the people treated the priests who had an extraordinary connection to forthcoming spiritual states. Further was the belief that a more preferable status might be envisaged by respecting and soliciting the assistance of holy men.

During Gautama's lifetime the aspiration of youth towards asceticism was fairly commonplace. The ascetics strove to raise themselves to higher spiritual planes so as to offer advice on the basis of achieved self-attainment. Many of these individuals became teachers of the common people who sought their advice because they promised explanations of the mysteries of life. Some of these wandering holy men also represented the antithesis against the established religious orders and no doubt lent an element of revolution to their cause. This was not unusual for the religions of India. Their leaders have hardly ever been concerned with dogmas and dogmatic definition. Even heresies have been no problem to them, for they are only opinions (Fernando, 1985).

Sharing the Vision

Having attained what he set out to conquer, Buddha looked for his past teachers to share his secret discovery. When he found that they were dead he sought out his five former disciples who were less than impressed with his declaration that he had completely conquered all evil passions and was no longer tied down to material existence. From their Hindu point of view they felt he had failed. He had not yet proven the superiority of mind over body while he still served and yielded to his body. Undaunted, Buddha stated that he was dedicating his life to living out and being the prophet of perfect truth.

Time proved to be on Buddha's side, and eventually his followers were "reconverted" to his doctrines. For 45 years Buddha ministered in an area no more than 240 kilometers from his home community and even many of his relatives joined his movement. One cousin named Dewadatta, who was jealous of Buddha, started a rival sect. Influenced by Hindu Brahman opposition, this group made several attempts on the life of Buddha and his followers. Certainly the Brahmans had no use for a philosophy that preached equality for all ranks and castes and the possibility of salvation without sacrifices or the assistance of priests.

Buddha died when he was 80 years old, having appointed 12 disciples to carry on his work. Shortly before his passing he offered his last words to his beloved disciples, "No doubt can be found in the mind of a true disciple. Beloved, that which causes life, causes also decay and death. Never forget this; let your minds be filled with this truth. I called you to make it known to you."

Buddhist Influence

At the time of his death around 483 BC, Buddha's organization was well-established in central India. There were many followers, but the heart of the community were the monastics or Sangha. Two faithful followers, Ananda and Upali, soon called a council to establish the whole of Buddha's law. Still, when a great leader dies, there is usually dissension in the ranks, and Buddhism suffered the same fate. One disciple, in fact, even going so far as to suggest that finally the order was free from control and they would not always be told what to do. Of the factions that evolved, one clung to the old ways, while another tried to encourage more lay participation in the movement. In less than 150 years after his death, the new religion had become most powerful in Northern and Central India and also the state religion of Magadha whose kings claimed superiority over the whole peninsula. By the end of the 3rd century after Buddha about 18 schools with varying shades of opinion in points of doctrine had developed. For the next ten centuries the stronghold for Buddhism remained solely in India, probably because of suppression by Islamic conquerors (Bercholz and Kohn, 1993).

Efforts to establish Buddhism in other countries varied. In China, for example, there were positive results about the 4th century. Several centuries later, around AD 845, there was a major persecution of the Dharma community and the monasteries had to be evacuated. After that Buddhism never recovered its former popularity. Buddhism spread to Korea from China in the 4th century, flourished for a time, and slid into the background starting with the 14th century when Confucianism was made the state religion. Today a kind of syncretic Buddhism is widespread in Korea (Bercholz and Kohn, 1993).

Buddhism moved to Japan from Korea, through the efforts of Prince Shotoku, who made it a state religion around AD 593. It was rivalled by the appearance of Zen towards the end of the 12th century. Zen remained a powerful force in Japan after that. Although this fact may not necessarily be related, Japan boasts the highest number of Buddhist sects today.

Many countries were affected by the spread of Buddhism – Burma, Cambodia, Ceylon, Mongolia, Nepal, Thailand, Tibet, Vietnam, and finally the West. The interest of academic scholars in university departments of religion has aided in attracting attention to the religion and popular English versions of Buddha's writings have become available in the last half century.

There are two kinds of Buddhists in North America today. The first group, located mostly on the West coast, comprise 60 churches of descendants of Japanese immigrants. They meet for worship much in the style of North American Christians. The other group are mostly Caucasians, partly spurred by the hippie movement of the 1960s, and quite representative of a populist movement (Robinson & Johnson, 1982).

It is impossible to deal fairly with the various subdivisions of Buddhism in this short a space, but because of its popularity, a few explanatory notes must be said about Zen Buddhism. Although Zen originated in China in the 6th and 7th centuries, knowledge of it on this continent is almost entirely due to the labors of a single Japanese scholar, Dr. Daisetz Teitaro Suzuki, who worked for seven decades to interpret this brand of Eastern thought to Westerners. Essentially Zen stresses the primary importance of the enlightenment experience and teaches that sitting is the shortest, but also the steepest way to awakening (Bercholz and Kohn, 1993). Zen is a way of life that appreciates facts and despises abstractions. It does not deal with concepts, but with life. Zen is in the here and now, and consists of doing the right thing (Humphreys, 1977). It is an honorable religion.

Principles & Precepts

Buddhism seems like an incredibly complex and dense religion, but everything in Buddhism really does go back to a few simple basic teachings that encapsulate the entire tradition (Gross, 1993). In the first place, everything corporeal is material, and therefore impermanent, for it contains within itself the germs of dissolution. Persons bound up in material living are subject to sorrow, decay and death. The reign of unholy desires in one's heart will contribute towards the perpetuation of unsatisfied longings, useless weariness and cares. Oppressing the body will be of little value since it is the morally degraded condition of one's heart that keeps us chained to materialism and decay. The exercise of virtuous acts will similarly have little benefit because evil can only be temporarily subjugated by virtue. Only the complete eradication of evil can set the individual off from the chains of materialism. This is the philosophy of the Buddha.

Buddhist Teachings

It is not difficult to memorize the basic Buddhist "catechism" since there are only four items (truths) to remember. To understand them, however, is quite another matter. Besides, these are only the beginning.

The *first* truth is that misery always accompanies existence. Life is predominantly characterized by "suffering," translated to mean that all of life is pervaded by an unavoidable sense of inadequacy. Contemporary expressions are that "life is a drag," laden with irritating inconveniences like chores, requirements, dealing with people and facing a never-ending stack of unfulfilled obligations. Fortunately, Buddhism offers a way through this tedium.

The *second* truth is that all modes of existence – people, animals and plants – result from passion or desire. Thus the cause of human inadequacy is craving or desire. The Buddhist believes that there is no real delight in passion; real delight is to be free *from* passion (Stevens, 1990). People want too much, we are never satisfied with what we have; in today's world of the propaganda, epidemic advertising and hot-sell, who can blame us?

The *third* truth is that there is no escape from existence except by destruction of desire. There is good news, however; we *can* get out of the rat-race because the *cause* for our cravings and resultant troubles can be overcome. This is possible by following *the path* or fourth truth, which in turn consists of four stages and is attainable primarily through the process of meditation.

Before discussing the "four stages to happiness," however, the reader might as well know that there are also other Buddhist truths to be comprehended. Most of these are "old truths," pertaining to the three marks of existence – impermanence, suffering and egolessness. It is not necessary to go into these at this point. Buddha and his disciples engaged in the subtlest metaphysical distinctions and memorized the smallest details of belief. To illustrate:

> scattered through space there are innumerable circular worlds in sets of three. All of these are exactly similar to our own, in the centre of which rises an enormous mountain which is surrounded by seven concentric circles of rock of an enormous height, and the circle enclosed by the outermost is divided into four quarters or great continents, part of which is the earth on which we live. On the heights of the mountain and above it and the rock circles, rise the twenty-four heavens, and beneath it and the earth and the eight great hells. The heavens and the hells are part of the material world, subject like the rest of it to the law of cause and effect, and the beings within them are still liable to rebirth, decay, and death (Davids, 1910, 387-388).

One can only leave it to the efforts of the true believer to decipher, and perhaps conquer, other equally intriguing aspects of Buddhist philosophy. A good starting point might be to determine what "karma" means, which is the sum total of one's merits and demerits. Usually demerits are the greater of the two and roughly analogous to sin or error. Demerits usually arise from ignorance; destroy the ignorance and there will be deliverance.

The *fourth* truth (following the path) provides release from the tyranny of materialism and the attachment to this world through four stages. The first stage is the awakening of the heart. This is the "moment" of salvation, the specific time when the scales are removed from the mind. One begins to realize that life is unfulfilling. The second stage occurs when awakened believers rid themselves of all impure desires and revengeful thoughts. The third stage requires additional cleansing, this time from ignorance, doubt, heresy, unkindliness and vexation. When impurity, evil longings and desires for revenge disappear, doubt and heresy will logically be voided. Right actions will naturally follow when evil has been eradicated (Rinpoche, 1986).

By the time believers have reached the fourth and final stage such undesirable entitles as ignorance, passion and sin will have been eliminated. Although most Buddhists would deny the possibility of reaching the fourth stage in this life, they believe that one must practice a lifelong commitment to the paths. The final perseverance of the saints is sure.

Practices

Buddhists reject the notion of a priesthood with magical powers because personal salvation is entirely dependent upon the modification, or growth of, one's inner nature. Growth results from one's own exertions. Contrary to fairly orthodox interpretations of Christian principles which stress the need for human fellowship (sociability) and the importance of outreach or evangelism, Buddhists believe that salvation is attained solely through personal effort. There is an element of faith involved, however, because faith denotes a freedom from self-power and the total trust of the believing heart in the power of the vow they have taken. Buddha alone can elicit faith (Yoshinori, 1983).

This does not mean that evangelism is rejected out of hand, for the message must be told. It is just that the decision to enter the life of believership is personal, and any spiritual progress must also be credited to the individual. Naturally, the life of a personal recluse is held to be the most conducive to achieving serenity which is the ultimate goal for the believer. However, even a believer who cannot completely tear away from the perceived obligations of home or business may "enter the paths" and through a life of kindness and upright living attain a rebirth towards growth in holiness. So there is hope, even for the "lukewarm" believer. Grace is an active force in Buddhism (Pallis, 1980).

Buddha initially commissioned his disciples to embark on their own spiritual journey while spreading the word so that a greater number might hear the gospel. He usually travelled with several of his most devoted disciples, perhaps as a means of assuring that in the event of his death his philosophy would be passed on intact.

Two Stories

Perhaps the best way to delineate the mandated practice for a Buddhist believer is through two incidents alleged to have occurred during Buddha's ministry. The first concerns a merchant convert who stated his intention to preach to his unbelieving relatives. When Buddha warned him that members of this particular tribe were quite violent and would probably not take kindly to the convert's views, the merchant replied that even if his relatives reviled him, struck him or tried to kill him he would not retaliate. After all, death, for the Buddhist, is no evil in itself. Thus Buddhist believers opt for the truth, no matter what the consequences. This is because the material world, even in its most attractive form, is inferior to "the enlightened way."

The second incident illustrates the futility of holding on to elements of the material world – including mourning for deceased loved ones. A woman who lost her young son to death sought out herbal medicines from holy men which might bring her son back to her. When she heard about Buddha's ministry she felt compelled to seek his counsel also. He advised her to bring him mustard seeds from any home in the community. He would receive a mustard seed from any home where no son or husband, parent or slave had ever died. Carrying her dead child she went from house to house in search of the mustard seed. Naturally, she did not obtain any seed and discovered in the process that all members of the human family have been affected by death in some way. Buddha then explained to the woman about the permanency of the spiritual state which is attainable only by devoting oneself to truth, and she became a devoted convert.

The specifics of Buddha's orders for believers were manifold, and only a few examples must suffice to illustrate the intricacy of the system. Though Buddha hoped that all adherents would eventually join the monastic order, he appeared to compromise, by suggesting that they should obey at least five of the "ten (rather negative) precepts," i.e., not to take life, not to steal, not to lie, not to commit adultery or fornication, and not to drink strong drink. Stated positively, and given as an answer to a query about what constitutes the good life, Buddha apparently replied that it consisted of serving wise men, giving honor to whom honor was due, helping loved ones, engaging in pleasant speech, being long-suffering and meek, living righteously, etc. An easy parallel to these teachings could be found in the oracles of most any world religion.

Peculiarities

The Priestly Office

The Buddhist priestly order (Sangha) is unique. Members of the order are not seen to have mystical powers, and at first they were admitted solely on the basis of application. All one had to do was shave one's head, put on yellow robes, and lead an ascetic life. Later a few restrictions were imposed.

Initially Buddhist priests or monks had to live by rules laid down by the Buddha. With regards to nourishment, they were not to eat solid food except between sunrise and noon and to abstain completely from intoxicating beverages. Monks were expected to beg for food and there were strict rules about begging. For example, stricter monks were to abstain from animal food, eating a whole meal without rising, refusing all invitations and all food brought to them, and eating everything in a bowl without leaving or rejecting anything. Much later on, these same ascetics owned rice-fields and let them out to be cultivated on a share crop basis. The allowance to own land and thereby engage in a form of dreaded materialism also contributed to a loss of humility among the priesthood and made them appear little different from their lay peers. According to one source, this order eventually became wealthy, lax and idle (Davids, 1910).

The ascetic lifestyle had rules about virtually every aspect of life. A lonely lifestyle was preferred, away from the jostle of the public so that one's spiritual journey would be free from interruption. They were to dress in clothing of no value and even the length of their robes was stipulated. A monk was allowed to own only eight things: three robes, a girdle, an alms bowl, a razor, a needle and a water-strainer through which he had to strain all the water he drank. To engage in sexual activity meant immediate expulsion from the order.

To the Westerner all of this discipline might imply the submergence of individuality. The Buddhist thinks of it as a mental culture, not mental death. Consciousness, in the language of Williams James, a contemporary psychologist, "is at all times primarily a *seeking agency*" (Kalupahana, 1987). The mind is a dynamic that keeps functioning at all times in an effort to achieve the ultimate state (Johansson, 1985). Five forms of meditation are constantly practiced: (i) love, in which the monk longs for happiness for all human beings; (ii) pity, in which he thinks of all human beings in distress; (iii) gladness, which is the converse of distress; (iv) purity, in which the monk thinks of the vileness of the body and the horrors of disease and corruption, and (v) serenity, in which the monk thinks of all things that men hold good or bad (power and oppression, love and hate, riches and want), and regards them with fixed indifference, with utter calmness and serenity of mind (Davids, 1910).

The office of priest or minister in contemporary North American religious terms virtually applies across the board to Buddhists. Although this was historically not the case, Buddhist priests today are expected to be "seminary" educated, ordained and charged with a pastoral role. There are three levels of ordination: the first is equal to that of a recognized lay person; the second requires seminary training; and the third compares roughly to that of the missionary in Christian terms (Kashima, 1977).

Role of Women

The role of women in Buddhism goes back almost to its beginning when women attempted to join the order. After an initial refusal, they were allowed to join but Buddhist nuns were seen as subordinate to monks. Many women gained *nirvana* (The Blessed State), and gathered their own literature, the Songs of the Women Elders. After the death of Buddha, however, attitudes towards women hardened. Then through the evolution of the centuries women continued to claim equality in the organization. Currently, in the West, women are active and influential in all forms of Buddhism (Gross, 1993).

To state peculiarities without acknowledging similarities is unfair in light of the basic assumption of this work – that we are more alike than different. To illustrate this we can refer to the beliefs of the Northern group of Buddhists known as Lamaism. This system, with its shaven priests, its bells and rosaries, its images and holy water, its popes and bishops, its abbots and monks of many grades, its processions and feast-days, its confessional and purgatory, and its worship of the double Virgin, so resembles Roman Catholicism that the first Catholic missionary thought it must be the imitation by the devil of the religion of Christ (Davids, 1910). We need only decide; was this a coincidence or a remarkable similarity?

References

Bercholz, Samuel & Chodzin Kohn, Sherab (Eds.). (1993). *Entering the stream: An introduction to the Buddha and his teachings.* Boston: Shambahal.

Davids, T. W. Rhys. (1910). Buddhism. *Werner encyclopedia, vol. IV* (pp. 381-392). Akron, OH: The Werner Company.

Fernando, Anthony. (1985). *Buddhism made plain: An introduction for Christians and Jews.* Maryknoll, NY: Orbis Books.

Gross, Rita M. (1993). *Buddhism after patriarchy.* Albany, NY: State University of New York Press.

Humphreys, Christmas. (1977). *Zen comes west: The present and future of Zen Buddhism in western society.* London: Curzon Press.

Johansson, Rune E.A. (1985). *The dynamic psychology of early Buddhism.* London: Curzon Press.

Kalupahana, David J. (1987). *The principles of Buddhist psychology.* Albany, NY: State University of New York Press.

Kashima, Tetsuden. (1977). *Buddhism in America.* London: Greenwood.

Pallis, Marco. (1980). *The Buddhist spectrum.* London: George Allen & Unwin.

Phillips, Bernard. (1962). *The essentials of Zen Buddhism.* New York: E.P. Dutton & Co.

Rinpoche, Kalu. (1986). *The Dharma: That illuminates all beings like the light of the sun and the moon.* Albany, NY: State University of New York Press.

Robinson, Richard H. & Johnson, Willard L. (1982). *The Buddhist religion: A historical introduction* (3rd ed.). Belmont, CA: Wadsworth.

Stevens, John. (1990). *Lust for enlightenment: Buddhism and sex.* Boston: Shambhala.

Yoshinori, Takeuchi. (1983). Notulae on the Buddhist-Christian Encounter (Hans Küng, Trans.). *The heart of Buddhism* (pp. vii-xii). New York: Crossroad.

7

Confucianism

Statistics Canada indicates that there are only 400 adherents to Confucianism in the nation. Basically a contemporary of Buddhism, Confucianism originated in China which is still its stronghold. The religion, if it may be called such, seems to have been spawned as a system to regulate the relations of people, according to certain beliefs concerning the fundamental forces operant in nature and society. From a Christian perspective there is little that appears religious in Confucianism; rather, it is a humanistic, people-centred philosophy of life. Evangelicals who target secular humanism as a modern Christian antithesis would do well to study Confucianism if only to discover just how old the roots of such a perspective really are.

Defining Religion

When contrasting Confucianism to Judaism, Christianity or Islam, where ethics have always been firmly linked to religion, some critics suggest that Confucianism actually divorces ethics from religion. These critics point out that Confucius never discussed such questions as the immortality of the soul or the existence of God, nor did he even question the origin or nature of the universe. His philosophy was purely concerned with humanity and human relationships, and, there is in his teaching no philosophy of nature or the cosmos (D.H. Smith, 1973). Confucius states in the *Analects,* for example, that one is to attend to the duties of man and keep one's spirits at a distance. When he was asked about death he responded that he had as yet to understand life, and he most certainly knew nothing about death. In this context it would appear that Confucius was not a religious man. If the definition of religion does not focus on the practical components of a pre-defined world-view, but rather on religion's soteriological capacity for transformation within the setting of ultimacy, then these particular responses of Confucius become, at best, secondary to the adjudication of a religious point of view (Taylor, 1986). Having said all this, it is still useful to remember that an adherent to Confucianism can be strongly motivated by its precepts, emotionally, motivationally *and* spiritually. On these points Confucianism certainly qualifies as a religion.

Sociologists who study religion point out that a religious tradition has at least three elements, each handed down and developed in the multitude of ways that traditions are passed on. The first element is the formulation of a mythical, or philosophical cosmology to define the

rudimentary structures and limits of the world. This set of postula-
tions will explain the fundamental structures and limits of the cosmos
and calculate the basic ways of explaining how things are and what
they mean. Ancient Confucianism has such a cosmology, and by
inference one can determine within reason what its parameters and
purposes are. The ancient writings even intimate moral obligations
in the realms of heaven and earth. This comes out more expressly in
the writings of Neo-Confucianism, whose authors elaborated such
themes with elegant philosophical arguments and presented the
Confucian tradition as an explicit alternative to Buddhism and Taoism.

The second element of religion is ritual. Rituals are a finite set of
repeatable and symbolizable actions that epitomizes the things a
tradition treats as crucial to defining the normative human place in
the cosmos. Early layers of ritual epitomize the hunt, nurturing of
agricultural fertility, acknowledgement of political authority (worship of gods as lords) and acts of commitment to other individuals.
Clearly the rituals involved in filial piety qualify Confucianism as a
major religion.

The third essential element to defining religion is that a religious
tradition have some conception of and practical procedures for fundamental transformation aimed at relating persons harmoniously with
the universe – a path of spiritual regeneration or perfection. In theistic
religions this usually means salvation – "getting right" with God. In
Confucianism it may well mean the path of the sage towards spiritual
perfection (Neville, 1990).

It has been argued that the beliefs of Confucianism have a history
that long predates the man for whom it was named. Its evolution
comprised a union and subsequent dominance of certain tribes, cultural patterns and what were once divergent elements (W. Smith,
1973). This unusual weave of ideas eventually produced a national
religion.

Pedigree

The Chow Dynasty

The coming of age of Confucianism in China occurred in the 5th and
6th centuries. The dynasty of Chow, the third within historic time,
had ruled the country since 1122 BC, and had passed its zenith, so the
country was ready for change. Chow was a feudal kingdom and the
lords of the different territories belonged to five orders of nobility,
corresponding to the dukes, marquises, earls, counts and barons of
feudal Europe. The theory of the constitution required that princes,
on every succession, should receive vestiture from the king, and

thereafter appear at his court at stated times. The princes paid dues to the king, and his control was directly related to the military strength that he was able to maintain over his subjects.

In 770 BC a northern group plundered the capital, killed the king, and effectively dismantled the Chow dynasty. The king's son escaped and settled himself in a nearby city, but the influence of the dynasty was gone. The new rulers held power for the next four centuries but their influence never reached the success of the previous administration. From the 5th to the 7th century China was fraught with wars, crimes, heroic acts and devoted friendships.

Chinese culture continued to flourish. Literature abounded and many of the arts of civilization were evident. Not only the royal court, but every feudal court, had its musicians and historiographers. Institutions of an educational character multiplied. There were histories and poems and codes of laws and books of ceremonies. In the midst of this, the central organization of government was weak and there was widespread and ever-increasing suffering and degeneracy in the country (Ledge, 1910).

Early Life of Confucius

The man who arrived on the proverbial white horse to "save the country" was born in the winter of 550 BC. His clan name was K'ung and the name by which his beliefs were popularized – Confucius – means "the philosopher or master." Confucius had a grand lineage, traceable through the sovereigns of the previous dynasty of Shang, to Hwang-ti, whose figure looms out through the mists of fable in prehistoric times. By the end of the 8th century the family name of K'ung had been stabilized.

Confucius' personal history is more interesting. He was the son of an elderly man who had already sired nine daughters and one son. Because the son was handicapped, however, Confucius' father, an officer named Heih, wanted another son. He therefore went to a gentleman of the Yen clan who had three daughters. When Heih asked to marry one of the daughters the gentleman agreed, recognizing the value of an alliance with a man of noble birth. The youngest of the three daughters, Ching-tsai, agreed to the union simply because her father thought it was a good idea. A year later she gave birth to the sage.

Confucius' father died when he was three years old. From an early age the child showed a remarkable interest in learning. As was the custom, he was married at 19, his wife being from his ancestral state of Sung. The couple had three children, one son and two daughters. Confucius immediately became employed by a king, motivated by the fact that his father had left very little inheritance to the family.

Confucius as Teacher

By the time he was 22, Confucius had become a teacher. He was not particularly interested in his students' mastery of "the 3 R's" but rather that they reveal themselves to have inquiring minds. His pay for this task was nominal and spasmodic, and he was forced to rely on other means to support his family. When his mother died two years later, he began to become concerned about future states. He mourned for her for the required period of 27 months.

In due course Confucius was able to make a trip to the capital of the kingdom where he examined the treasures of the royal library and studied the music of the court. He also met Lao-tze, the father of Taoism, and was impressed with the man's commitment to transcendentalism. When Confucius returned home he discovered that the state was in political disarray, and he was forced to flee to the neighboring state of Ts'i. By now he had attracted several disciples who also accompanied him to Ts'i.

For the next 15 years Confucius devoted himself to things of the mind. He tried to maintain a polite relationship with the various political leaders in Ts'i. Dissatisfied with the way things were in Ts'i, he returned to Lu. Eventually, in his 52nd year he even took a government position as minister of crime. He managed this position so well that crime was virtually eradicated from the state and he became a hero of the people. Clearly the marquis of Lu was much impressed, and his enemies, patriots of Ts'i, devised a plan to pry away his admiration for Confucius. They feared that Confucius' influence would extend the influence of Lu beyond what it deserved. The plan was to send a company of beautiful women to Lu, trained in music and dancing, together with a troop of attractive horses, and seduce the court. The bait took, and the lure of the harem was powerful enough to upstage the sage. Disillusioned, Confucius left the state. He was 56 years old.

For the next 13 years Confucius visited a number of different states, frequently encountering recluses who had given up on the world. Some of them had misgivings about Confucius whom they saw as a bit of an unrealistic visionary, a man always hoping against hope. Still, Confucius would not give up on the people. Defeated he might be, but he remained true to his belief that humaneness and righteousness would eventually prevail.

Confucius as Sage

Confucius returned to Lu when he was 69. While there he experienced the death of his son, but he mourned little. Unlike his own behavior at the death of his own mother, Confucius had forbidden his son to show emotion when his son's mother died. Some sources say that Confucius had divorced his wife before her death, and his love for her had diminished. When his faithful disciple, Yen Hwni died, however, Confucius was visibly crushed by the loss, and his emotions showed. Confucius' own death occurred in 478 BC, shortly after the death of another faithful follower named Tze-lu. He was buried by his followers amidst a great deal of pomp and splendor, and his elaborate tomb bears this inscription, "The most sagely ancient Teacher; the all-accomplished, all-informed King."

Two centuries after the death of Confucius, the Chow dynasty perished, giving way to the dynasty of Ts'i. The latter eliminated the feudal system and blamed Confucius for trying to justify that form of social and political structure. Books were burned and the name of Confucius was banned from use. The plan did not work and the dynasty of Han which followed restored Confucius' place in the kingdom.

Neo-Confucianism

The term Neo-Confucianism refers to the growth and expansion of the Confucian tradition during and following the Sung dynasty from AD 960-1279. It is closely associated with state orthodoxy in China, Korea and Japan. There are two major schools of Neo-Confucianism, the School of Principle and the School of Mind. The former promotes a step-by-step method of learning in which there is gradual accumulation in the understanding of true desirable nature. The School of Mind emphasizes the *sincerity* of intention. The School of Principle contends that learning must proceed by a process of study from external sources, while the School of Mind sees learning as a process of realization and manifestation of the inherent principle, i.e., one must reveal wisdom by one's actions. The most vivid departure of Neo-Confucianism from the classical interpretation is the notion that sagehood is universally a reachable goal. In the classic tradition, sages were figures of high antiquity (Taylor, 1986).

Principles & Precepts

Confucius perceived his role to be that of a transmitter rather than that of a framer of ideas, and he refused to put his thoughts into writing. He also did not lay claim to having a special or unique Divine revelation, but postulated that righteousness could be attained if men would look inside themselves. On occasion he hinted that he was on a special heavenly mission and would remain free from harm until it was fulfilled. Essentially, he was devoted to a reasoned analysis of existing thought and literature.

Confucian Literature

In one work, *The Analects,* there is reference to four things of which Confucius seldom spoke – extraordinary things, feats of strength, rebellious disorder and spiritual things. He is quoted as saying, "To give oneself earnestly to the duties due to men, and while respecting spiritual things, to keep aloof from them – that may be called wisdom" (Ledge, 1910, 235). This might be translated to say that Confucius would approve of a religion that makes no greater claims than it can feasibly practice.

Adherence to this maxim today would surely put into question the lengthy doctrinal lists of pretty well every Christian denomination.

Lest we become hasty, there are also sources which contend that though Confucius may not have articulated a great deal about spiritual things he certainly implied them. Neo-Confucianism certainly contends that self-cultivation and the attainment of sagehood are aimed at transcending mundane goals. While self-cultivation is morally significant, the stress on the unity of heaven and the human being endows this concept with religious significance (Eber, 1986). The spiritual element of Confucianism comes out in the need of individuals to live beyond themselves, thus overcoming existential loneliness and isolation.

It is estimated that Confucius compiled about 305 pieces of literature. The content of one book, entitled *Yih King* (The Book of Changes), is purported to have especially attracted him (Blofeld, 1970). It is supposed to give a theory of the phenomena of the physical universe, and explicate moral and political principles. Some also hold that he wrote the *Annals of Lu,* but this work tells little of his philosophy. Essentially, he admonished his disciples to live according to what amounts to a negatively-stated version of the Christian Golden Rule, "What you do not like when done to yourself, do not to others." Someone once asked Confucius what he would do if he held political power in the State of Lu and he replied that the state would first have to come to order, a natural order of peace and harmony. Confucius believed that the decay of the state came about because of the unbridled passions of men. He strongly believed in the goodness of human nature; good rulers could and should model correct living for their subjects. Rulers should be exemplary figures, a high ideal for humankind to emulate, regardless of how difficult it might be to attain this goal. The sage was to be an example both of *something,* as an embodiment of the Way of Heaven, and an example to *someone,* as a model for emulation (Taylor, 1990). Live like a model ruler and model subjects will emerge.

The Basic Premise

The central doctrine of Confucius' thinking is *jen,* translated to mean "goodness, benevolence or humanheartedness." It is defined in terms of loving others and having personal integrity – indeed a form of altruism. Confucius was remarkably silent on heavenly things, but he believed that heaven gave him his message and protected him.

In modern terms Confucius could be said to have a very high image of himself. He believed that the wisdom of the sage had made previous dynasties great and it could happen again. "If any ruler will take my direction for twelve months," he said, "I will accomplish something considerable in the state" (Ledge, 1910, 232). Needless to say, his dream was never realized. However he did succeed in attracting about 3 000 disciples, including some 70 scholars of "extraordinary ability."

Practices

Confucius emphasized rituals, arguing that they govern human relationships, especially among aristocrats. He expected model rulers to exhibit proper behavior or propriety. He believed their followers would emulate ideal moral behavior. This dedication can be aided by a constant self-examination: "When you meet someone better than yourself, consider emulating them." There are three criteria for self-examination: (i) in my undertakings with others, have I done my best? (ii) in my dealings with my friends, have I been faithful? and, (iii) have I passed on to others what I have not personally practiced?

Confucius is credited and much quoted for this saying:

> At fifteen I set my heart on learning to be a sage; at thirty I became firm; at forty I had no more doubts; at fifty I understood Heaven's Will; at sixty my ear was attuned to truth; at seventy I could follow my heart's desires, without overstepping the line.

Stressing his version of the Golden Rule, Confucius believed that inner forces could propel an individual to moral living. The following guidelines reveal how this works:

> What the superior man seeks in himself, the small man seeks in others. The superior man is dignified, but does not wrangle; he is social, but not partisan. He does not promote a man simply because of his words, nor does he put good words aside because of the man. A poor man who does not flatter, and a rich man who is not proud are passable characters, but they are not equal to the poor who yet are cheerful, and the rich who yet love the rules of propriety. Learning, undigested by thought, is labor lost; thought, unassisted by learning, is perilous. A man can enlarge his principles; principles do not enlarge the man; that is, man is greater than any system of thought. The cautious seldom err (Ledge, 1910, 234).

Four Practical Steps

Those interested in specifics will be happy to note that Confucius' interpreters have been graciously accommodating. As Howard Smith (1973) has pointed out, there are four distinct dimensions to Confucius' ethical system. The first has to do with the past. Confucius had a profound respect for the past and therefore promoted worship of ancestor-spirits. Sacrifice to a Supreme Deity was linked to reverence for ancestor-spirits. The over-ruling providence of Heaven, its majesty, benevolence and righteousness, are constant themes in the poetry and other literature.

The second practical area designates family relationships as the crucial arena in which to practice *jen* (love) and *i* (righteousness). During his own time, Confucius witnessed the decline of family life and he identified it as a primary target for the practice of virtue. He specifically identified five relationships: ruler and subject, husband and wife, father and son, elder brothers and younger, and friends. There was an implied rule in the one position and submission in the other. The rule should transpire in righteousness and benevolence, and submission should reflect righteousness and sincerity. Between friends the mutual promotion of virtue should be the guiding principle (McNaughton, 1974).

The third area for religious practice is the economy, the arena of making a livelihood. Confucius recognized that warring tribes often fought over hunting areas, places to grow crops or the occupation of settlement lands. He believed that community interests must supercede individual greed. The virtues of sharing, reciprocity, faithfulness, love and justice must be practiced in community.

Fourth and finally, a Confucian code or ethics must apply to the development of a community culture (Wright, 1960). Ritual and music were seen as the essential manifestations of culture. Music, which included mime and dancing, was a powerful stimulus to community spirit.

Post-Confucian Developments

In the centuries that followed Confucius' death, a form of spirituality developed which *did* emphasize both ritual and music, and the religious belief in a Supreme God as Lord on High diminished. Formal music was performed at ancestral sacrifices and other religious ceremonies. Music was seen as a form of joy, and since man cannot help but feel joy, he must find an expression for it. Music fulfills that need. Combined, music and rituals serve to maintain an inner harmony, like that between heaven and earth (Eber, 1986).

After Confucius died the rituals of the state cult began to be practiced in celebration and honor of Confucius himself. It is somewhat ironic that what Confucius had argued for retaining as the proper display of the relations between Heaven and mankind should come to be considered a proper display of respect for Confucius himself. The twice yearly sacrifice initiated after Confucius' death consists of three separate offerings. The first consists of singing and dancing and prostrations, made to Confucius and to other figures in the temple. The second consists of the presentations of offerings of sacrificial animals, the celebrant placing his hand on the animal, accompanied by the sound of drums. The third sacrifice is a ritual address offering adulatory words of worship to Confucius, accompanied by appropriate prostrations (Taylor, 1986).

Peculiarities

How does one practice a religion that at first glance seems void of rituals and rules or a well-spelled out concept of God? Is one's own experience and point of view sufficient enough a base upon which to draw in addressing metaphysical questions or in seeking comfort in the time of need? Westerners used to living out the oracles of a "well-defined" faith would find it frustrating and lonely. Surely the study and practice of the arts would comprise an insufficient base for meeting daily problems. Thus a religion almost totally void of "dos and don'ts" is likely quite unappealing to the occupants of this continent.

Ancestor worship

The Confucian practice of worshipping the spirits of the deceased is an anathema to the Christian. In Chinese culture it makes a great deal of sense, set in the context of the Chinese family complex. Not only do such obvious matters as the laws of inheritance and the holding of land depend on the organization of the family or clan, but the influence extends into trade, where families control certain industries and trade processes are held as family secrets. Politics is honey-combed with nepotism and criminal law is based on family relationships. This is especially true in moral sanctions, and although ancestor worship appears to have no connection with morals, the whole system of Chinese family, past and present, is interconnected and built upon the fundamental virtue of filial piety (Shryock, 1966). Not to respect or render obeisance to the family is to neglect the very roots of one's existence.

Ceremonies connected with the worship of ancestors fall into two classes, those connected with death itself, and those which are part of the regular and continued "cult of the dead." Chinese funerals are elaborate, and pay appropriate homage to the deceased. Cult ceremonies represent several variations, but historically they were usually welded to state religions (Shryock, 1966).

Confucianism as State Religion

Perhaps the most cynical observation about Confucianism is that it is a state religion designed for bureaucrats. It was probably not Confucius' intention that this interpretation would evolve, but his enchantment with the ruler as moral sage clearly produced that perspective.

The cult of Confucius was hero worship deliberately adopted by the state at the instigation of a social group of scholars who acknowledged the leadership of the sage. This hero worship occupied a place in the state religion between the cults of nature deities and the worship of ancestors, from both of which it borrowed. While there have been many cults recognized by Chinese governments, it is doubtful that these existed before Confucius' time (Shryock, 1966). The first indication of a regular cult of Confucius was in AD 37. Sacrifices made to Confucius were instigated by Emperor Chang Ti in AD 85 and Emperor An Ti in AD 124. These two leaders sacrificed to Confucius and their officials sacrificed to Confucius' 72 (some say 70) disciples. Gradually Confucian principles were adopted by the state and schools were set up, led by a privileged scholar class, to teach his ideas (Shryock, 1966). By the 2nd century the cult was fairly well established.

It is easy to criticize the assignment of undue or elevated positions to sages, from a western perspective, unless one takes the parallel view that hero worship is a cultural universal. Consider, for example, the extraordinary status awarded to national sports heroes, Hollywood movie stars or even politicians who manage to excite public adulation to the point of unreasonable frenzy. Ancestor worship may find a ready western parallel in the persons of Marilyn Monroe, Elvis Presley or JFK.

When Neo-Confucianism came to fruition in the 11th century it emerged as a protest against the success of Buddhism with its emphasis on otherworldliness and the illusionariness of all phenomena. Neo-Confucianists wanted China to return to her original religious roots. Buddhism posed a threat to this vision by purporting to have answers to intellectual and metaphysical questions. Proponents of Neo-Confucianism settled on finding Confucius-type answers to questions pertaining to human nature and the cosmic order, the way to achieve human perfection and an ideal human society, the principles of government by example, and the importance of education. The Buddhist challenge therefore set Confucian philosophers to thinking in universal terms (D.H. Smith, 1973). However, although Neo-Confucianism took its rise among intellectuals, and commanded the adherence of other intellectuals, the influence of the state, if it counted at all, counted adversely (de Bary, 1969). The attainment of peace and harmony for the individual was the focus of attention.

One Neo-Confucian thinker, Chu Hsi, postulated that human nature is "principled," and inherently good. The Confucian aim in life is to eliminate everything that stands in the way of uncovering true human nature, which is "Heaven implanted," is perfectly sincere, and contains in itself the virtues of love, righteousness, propriety and wisdom. The aim of education is to allow one's heavenly-bestowed nature to shine forth (D.H. Smith, 1973; de Bary, 1991).

Lest this discussion be extended to the point of making Confucius sound like a 20th century pedagogue urging the universal pursuit of knowledge, we shall cease.

As Confucius said, "To know is inferior to *to love*. To *love* is inferior to *to delight in*" (McNaughton, 1974, 96). Let us therefore delight in the new knowledge we have of Confucius' thoughts.

References

Blofeld, John (Ed.). (1970). *The book of change*. London: George Allen & Unwin.

de Bary, Wm. Theodore. (1969). Some common tendencies in Neo-Confucianism. In David S. Nivison & Arthur F. Wright (Eds.), *Confucianism in action* (pp. 25-49). Stanford, CT: Stanford University Press.

de Bary, Wm. Theodore. (1991). *The trouble with Confucianism*. Cambridge: Harvard University Press.

Eber, Irene (Ed.). (1986). *Confucianism: The dynamics of tradition*. London: Collier Macmillan.

Ledge, James. (1910). Confucius. *Werner encyclopedia, vol. VI* (pp. 229-235). Akron, OH: The Werner Company.

McNaughton, William (Ed.). (1974). *The Confucian vision*. Ann Arbor, MI: The University of Michigan Press.

Neville, Robert Cummings. (1990). Foreword. In Rodney L. Taylor, *The religious dimensions of Confucianism* (pp. ix-x). Albany, NY: State University of New York Press.

Shryock, John K. (1966). *The origin and development of the state cult of Confucius*. New York: Paragon Book Reprint Corp.

Smith, D. Howard. (1973). *Confucius*. London: Maurice Temple Smith Ltd.

Smith, Jr. Warren W. (1973). *Confucianism in modern Japan* (2nd ed.). Tokyo: The Hokuseido Press.

Taylor, Rodney L. (1986). *The way to heaven: An introduction to the Confucian religious life*. Leiden, Neth: E.J. Brill.

Taylor, Rodney L. (1990). *The religious dimensions of Confucianism*. Albany, NY: State University of New York.

Wright, Arthur F. (Ed.). (1960). *The Confucian persuasion*. Stanford, CT: Stanford University Press.

8

Hinduism

A study of the Hindu religion returns us to India, and draws attention to the unusual fact that this religion originated from two radically different sources – the remains of the great ancient Indus Valley civilization and the religious literature of the Aryans. The first tradition, which provides the material base to the faith, takes us back to the 3rd century BC. The other tradition requires a backward glance at the religious life of the Indo-European Aryans who entered India a century earlier. This source provides Hindus with their religious literature (Hopkins, 1971).

Unlike most other world religions Hinduism does not appear to have originated on the basis of an individual's personal experience with the Divine, or if this is the case, that specific knowledge has been hidden in antiquity. Still, the system has thrived and expanded. The third largest religion in the world, all but 36 million of its estimated 583 million devotees live in India where they make up 79 percent of the population. About 157 000 Hindus live in Canada.

Pedigree

The term "Hindu" derives from what is known today as the Indus River in the northwest of the subcontinent. For nearly 3 000 kilometres, from its tributaries in the foothills of the Himalayas to its mouth in the Arabian Sea, this mighty river acts as a natural boundary to the bulk of peninsular India for those entering from the passes of the Hindu Kush. According to the Vedic Indians, rivers were perceived to have transcendent powers. Tradition offers two possible interpretations of this belief, namely that there actually was a river named "Sindhu," or this term was used to refer to rivers in general (Lipner, 1994).

The two very different backgrounds which merged to form the basics of Hinduism were individually unique. Each offered a separate and distinct contribution to this widespread faith. The Aryan civilization of 2nd century BC believed itself to be superior to its preceding lifestyle and the early Aryan hymns reflected this. They praised the prowess of the Aryans and celebrated the superiority of their gods with their control over nature. Obviously this kind of background posited a very distinct sense of pride for the followers of Hinduism. The Indus civilization, on the other hand, left no literary nor intellectual products behind; yet it provided a treasure trove of physical and material legacy.

The Indus Contribution

A half century ago two large mound sites in western India, revealing two great Indus cities, were excavated. The circumference of these unearthed cities is about five kilometres, and the large citadels and extensive grain storage facilities reveal that they were centres of political and economic activity, possibly governed by a ruling elite. The cities appear to have been well laid-out, but there is little evidence of any strong religious inclination on the part of the former occupants among the various structures. There is, however, much evidence that cleanliness ranked high in their value system, because an elaborate plumbing system has been identified. Perhaps personal hygiene and purification were connected to an as yet undeciphered religious system. Art forms in the Indus civilization appeared to have been highly prized and the remains of a large variety of animal skeletons suggest their importance to the people. There may have been some connection between this phenomenon and the religious system adhered to by these peoples.

The Aryan Influence

When the Aryans arrived on the scene, the Indus civilization was in a weakened state, the cause of which is unclear. The Aryans were a nomadic, mobile pastoral group, marked by a strong militarism. When they entered Indus territory they conquered the cities with no apparent intention of developing them in their accustomed style. They brought a fairly well-defined religious system with them, grounded in their sacred writings known as the *Vedas*. The term "veda" means knowledge or body of knowledge. There are four Vedas or writings, which are believed to be authorless or impersonally originated. Vedic Hinduism either originated, or accepted, four classifications (or castes) of people as Divinely originated – *Brahman* (priest), *Kshatriya* (warrior), *Vaishya,* (laborer and servant), and *Shudra* (the caste of servants and slaves) (Hinnells and Sharpe, 1972). Hinduism also endorsed four human states as divinely-approved, i.e., studentship, marriage, mendicancy and renunciation – these were believed to apply only to the three higher castes (Pereira, 1976).

Early Vedic religion centred around the Divine powers of the gods called *devas*. Some sources suggest that there were about 33 gods in the system, and they were subdivided into three categories – celestial, atmospheric and terrestrial – depending on the area of their work in the three domains; the sky, the atmosphere or on earth. All of the powers of the gods were closely related to the natural world which is the arena in which human lives are mostly affected.

Interest in the cosmic powers of nature is virtually a universal concern among religions, since humankind is governed by and dependent upon the forces of nature for their livelihood. The same is true of

Hinduism. The oldest of the Aryan celestial gods was Varuna, corresponding to the Greek god Zeus, whose job it was to guard the cosmic order. He created the world and established its inherent moral order, called *rita* which means, "the proper course of things." The solar *deva* (god) named Mitra, was Varuna's chief assistant, and the friend and benefactor of mankind. His solar role was shared with other *devas* such as Savitri who represented the sun's ability to stimulate life.

Several other Aryan gods should be explained. Vishnu, for example, was a celestial *deva* and the most benevolent of them all. He is known for having traversed the earth and for having attained "the highest step," which is beyond the flight of birds and beyond the knowledge of man. This is the view of the Vaisnava sect of Hinduism. Indra is the thunder god, Vaya is the god of wind and Parjanya is the god of the rain-cloud. Indra was a very popular god, champion of the Aryan warrior and the model for what a warrior should be. Rudra represented the ambiguous primal powers of nature, and was praised for his powers of healing and protection.

Both Varuna and Indra were traditionally considered champions of the Aryan people, and each dominated their own class of gods. Together they seemed to constitute a divine monarchy of sorts, acting together in controlling the world. As the religion developed, attention was focussed on a third class of *devas,* the terrestrial gods, dominated by the divinized elements of the fire sacrifice: Agni, the god of fire, and Brihaspati, the Lord of prayer. The Aryan fire sacrifice is significant enough to merit a brief explanation.

The Aryan Fire Sacrifice

Fire is a key element in human culture and it is not surprising that many religions have bestowed upon it a place of honor. Among the Indo-European peoples who preceded the Aryans, fire was even awarded Divine status. Some tribes sought to preserve ancient fires, paid reverence to home fires and gave offerings to fire as a personal deity. At its most elementary level, the fire sacrifice was a hospitality rite to the gods. The most important offerings were placed in the fire and conveyed to the other gods by Agni, the god of fire. Later a series of hymns, prayers and rituals evolved to magnify the fire sacrifice. Priests were not perceived to have special powers nor a controlling monopoly on conducting religious rituals because, after all, only the gods could answer prayers. It was believed, however, that priests were skilled agents in inducing the gods to grant requests. This did not limit householders from celebrating rituals in their own homes (Hopkins, 1971). Gradually a distinction developed between *Srauta* rites, using Vedic hymns and necessarily performed by priests, and *Griha* rites, those performed by householders. Common requests during the fire ceremony pertained to health, long life, a prosperous family with many sons or wealth in cattle.

As time went on the ceremonies offered by the priesthood took on an increasing complexity, and the ceremony of the fire sacrifice was seen to have power in its own right. Domestic ceremonies, however, remained simple, and focussed on such events as the new moon and the full moon, the seasons, and the first fruits of the harvest. Special family events were also featured such as the birth of a son, the building of a new house or marking the various stages in a child's life.

Three fires were eventually elaborated in the *Srauta* rites; the first was mainly used for the preparation of food, the second in which the sacrifices were placed, and the third as a means of warding off hostile spirits or receiving special offerings for departed ancestors.

Role of Priests

As the centuries passed the office of priest took on elevated importance. Some of the early religious poets were believed to have special knowledge and powers and their gifts came to be recognized in special ways. The creative powers of this group evolved so that they came to be called *Brahman,* or conveyors of special truth. As holders of special knowledge, these individuals were viewed as fulfilling a unique divine purpose. They were given special education and expected to live according to the highest moral standards. Only a person purified and ritually prepared could be entrusted with *Brahman* power (Hopkins, 1971). Today, as always, Brahmans do not necessarily fill the office of priest, however; indeed most Brahmans are not. A Brahman priest is a specialist in certain kinds of rituals, rites and knowledge pertaining thereto. For example, the priest may be called upon to perform certain rites in connection with life cycle rituals. When these performances are undertaken the priests will be in consistency with the spirit of the great texts and reveal a significant knowledge of them (Babb, 1975).

Principles & Precepts

There are four distinct aspects of Hinduism that assist in developing an understanding of its basic make-up: (i) its teachings or doctrines (*mata*); (ii) its duties, obligations or guidelines (*Dharma*); (iii) the nature of devotion required of a believer (*Bhakti*); and (iv) the definition of the way of salvation (*Marga*).

Like most other major world religions Hinduism is both a way of life and a highly organized social and religious system. Despite this comprehensive nature, Hinduism does not require that its patrons submit to a predetermined list of precise beliefs, not even to a specific idea of a Supreme God who is personal, transcendent and holy, and who reveals Himself and who acts in history. Hinduism is free from dogmatic affirmations about the nature of God, and the core of religion is never believed to depend on the existence or non-existence of God, or on whether or not there is one God or many gods (Organ, 1970). It is perfectly possible to be a good Hindu and still be a monotheist, a polytheist or even an atheist. One's beliefs about the existence and or nature of the God or gods is of no particular significance (Zaehner, 1966). This renders Hinduism as an apparently incoherent religious complex, sometimes appearing rife with inherent contradictions. To the devout Hindu, however, this apparent dilemma is of little significance. A catalogue of systematized beliefs is not that important, practice is.

Hindu Dogma

Hindus sometimes pride themselves that their religion is free from dogmatic assertions. There is no common creed. For the most part this is true, but there are also a number of beliefs inherent in Hinduism which appear to be generally endorsed and never questioned by adherents. Principle of these is the idea of the transmigration of souls, which is thought to be a self-evident truth and which all Hindu sects accept. This belief further presupposes that the condition into which an individual may be reborn in their next life is a result of good or bad actions performed in the present life. This brings up the notion of *Dharma* or obligation. *Dharma* includes both morally right behaviors and ceremonially right behaviors; it covers every aspect of life. It is closely related to *marga* and implies a total training of the will towards the attainment of spiritual rightness rather than the fulfillment of rightness via single acts. The place of *bhaktii* or devotional love is less clearly delineated. It *is* expected that a devotee will manifest some degree of faith and emotion in regards to revered truths, but mere emotionalism would be frowned upon (Organ, 1970).

All of this is not to suggest that Hinduism is not a very finely-tuned religion. Hindu theology, in fact, has a long developmental history, having passed through three major epochs – origins, development and flourishing. The first stage occurred from about 1300 to 600 BC, with the chief themes of poetry and inspiration. Systematization of these ideas did not occur until much later. From about 600 BC to AD 1000 the system developed structures through a refinement of logical and exegetical techniques. After AD 1000 the various subsystems of belief flowered into a comprehensive unity. In fact, the formation of Vedantic schools persisted until after the 18th century (Pereira, 1976).

Basic to Hindu theology is belief in canon law which operates like natural law. It is where *Dharma* comes in. Hindus believe that the eternal law that governs all human and non-human existence is universal, and although this natural order is difficult to know, it dictates the mode of proper (moral) living. The moral law inherent in the universe maintains all things in accordance with eternal principles. These principles exist on two levels – in the sacred texts and in the hearts and consciences of people. Sometimes the two exist side by side in harmony and sometimes there is tension and conflict (Zaehner, 1966).

Of the various Hindu reform movements of the 19th century, none have been as far-reaching as that of Mahatma Gandhi who exposed the glaring discrepancy between the two *Dharmas,* the eternal law which is so difficult to know and the politically-interpreted form of *Dharma* which during Gandhi's time sought to justify a monstrously unjust social system. Gandhi rearranged the face of Hinduism so that it was no longer possible simply to define a Hindu as one who performs his caste duties and accepts the Vedas as revealed truth. The ancient hard core may remain as a tidal wave of the past, but the dike has a small hole in it – a permanent one. Expectedly, it was no accident that Gandhi met his death at the hand of an orthodox Hindu (Zaehner, 1966).

The new Hinduism of India claims a relevancy to all social ranks and an extensive literature has emerged to substantiate this contention. Some of these publications have even appeared in other than the sacred language of Sanskrit and caused a weakening of traditional Hindu authority. This has put Hinduism into a crisis situation of sorts, in that the system is in need of making significant adjustments to the newly emerging social order.

Hare Krishna

A word must be said about the Hare Krishna movement since many observers are not clear on the distinction between Hinduism and this sect. People often come very quickly to a conclusion about the Hare Krishna since the presence of so many of their followers selling literature in airports across the country has conjured up a specific image of them as deviant youth caught up in a brain-washing cult that is committed to breaking up western families (Knott, 1986). It helps to keep in mind that most public knowledge about the Hare Krishna comes from the media.

The Hare Krishna movement, more properly known as the International Society for Krishna Consciousness, follows the teachings of a 16th century individual known as Chasitanya. This makes the movement at least as old as Anglicanism. Its central belief is that Krishna, one of the most popular Hindu gods, is the god incarnate. Krishna, rather than Vishnu, is the supreme personality of the Godhead. To complicate things the Vishnuite sect of Hinduism see Brahma as Creator, Vishnu as Supreme and Ram (or Rama) as a gracious savior deity. The Hare Krishna position is not such a remarkable deviation from traditional Hinduism since the majority of Hindu temples established by the Indian community – about a hundred of them – are indeed dedicated to Krishna. Many Hindus accept Hare Krishna as one of many alternative ways to follow "the path." True, their mode of dress attracts a great deal of press, but it is the devotees way of making a statement about their faith – shaved heads and pink gowns. Still, if one can get past outward appearances there may be something to learn here.

If that is so, Hare Krishna exists in our society as one of a number of religious options open to people (Knott, 1986).

The Hindu Creed

In sum, the following points characterize Hinduism, even though some of them may appear to be contradictory.

1. Hinduism is both a way of life and a highly organized social and religious system, quite free from dogmatic assertions about the nature of God.

2. The basic criterion for anyone professing to be a Hindu is belief in the efficacy of the Hindu scriptures, *the Vedas.* However, even this is not an absolute requirement.

3. The range of individual freedom within Hinduism is probably not matched by any other world belief system. Unless an individual in India professes to belong to any other religion, the state government considers them to be a Hindu. Inherent in this stance is the presupposition that Hinduism is a collection of religions containing common elements of shared traditions that have influenced each other down through the ages.

4. Unlike Christianity, religious observances and worship do not bring the Hindu salvation *from the world.* The believer is not to be saved from the world; rather, he or she becomes the primary means of supporting the world and improving mankind's existence within it. Thus to fulfill one's calling in the world is the noblest virtue. Not a bad idea that!

5. Perhaps the most controversial and thorniest characteristic of Hinduism has to do with the caste system. There are Hindus who maintain that an adherent's principal responsibility is to live within the system and there to fulfill one's obligations and destiny. The potential of constant rebirth (reincarnation) necessitates a serious sense of obligation to one's station in life. On the other hand, some argue that the caste system is merely a form of social organization and is not central to the main tenets of the religion (Lipner, 1994).

One thing is abundantly clear; the cross fertilization of ideas brought about by the increasingly "diminishing" size of the globe has placed the caste system in a dubious light. As caste lines become blurred in India, so have arranged marriages, which are being replaced by so-called love marriages. Similarly, caste distinctions are giving way to ethnic differentiations, possibly influenced by a rising global interest in multiculturalism.

Practices

The two determining forces which impact on the fulfillment of the requirements of Hindu practice are *karma* and rebirth. *Karma* represents the cosmic assignment that a person receives at birth; the promise of rebirth assures a form of perpetual "conscience" with the implicit hope that betterment may be an individual's lot in the next life. Both of these forces coincide with *Dharma,* namely the inherent universal form of requirement to moral living. *Dharma* requires rationality, responsibility and free will and at least a little bit of emotionality. Obedient souls pursue their assigned *karma,* and as they become enlightened through the ages, they eventually reach the highest elevated caste, the world of the Brahman. Once attained, these souls transcend the cycle of birth.

The doctrine of *karma,* naturally, is quite complicated. On the deterministic side, individuals come into the world with the accumulated *karma* of a beginningless chain of previous existence. The maturing of this *karma* is in many facets beyond the control of the individual, i.e. genetic make-up, sex and other physiological characteristics, or birth circumstances. Essentially one's storehouse of *karma* consists of three kinds: (i) *Prardbha karma,* which represents the elements of life over which one has no control; (ii) *Kriyamana karma,* which is the sum of one's merit and demerits points; and, (iii) *Samcita karma,* which is accumulated *karma* that is not activated. Free will comes into play in terms of how one decides to cope with one's *Prarabdha karma.* You cannot choose your lot in life, but you may have some say in how you will react to it, particularly in terms of attitude. Basically, however, one has to contend with an overwhelming set of predetermined forces. It would be fair to say that Hindus do not expect nor seek "salvation" in this life. They are primarily concerned to just to stay afloat as they continue life's journey, hoping for health, contentment, economic security, success in various ventures and protection from danger – pretty well the concerns of any average person in any average country, regardless of religious affiliation (Lipner, 1994).

Three traditional Hindu festivals are celebrated by the devoted. The first, Diwali, is an annual event and is practically pan-Indian in scope. It lasts five days and is known as the Festival of Illumination. Highlighted by fireworks, this is intended to represent the act of renewal, that is, to symbolize that Divine power has overcome the darkness of the underworld. The second festival is the Purna Kumbha Mela, and while it is celebrated only occasionally, it draws enormous interest. Accompanying daily bathing opportunities are religious lectures and discussions, singing and plenty of fellowship. In 1989 between 15-20 million people made a pilgrimage to the confluence of the Yamuna and Ganges Rivers for healing and spiritual renewal.

The third festival is the annual Durga Punja celebrated in Bengal. It symbolizes the power of the goddess Durga over evil and chaos. The event lasts ten days of which the last five are the most important. During the festival the city is rife with images and decorated sets dedicated to the goddess Durga. Prizes are awarded for the most spectacular display.

Anyone looking for a list of explicit commandments for Hindus to obey will have difficulty. The ideal person to become would be the Brahman, whose scale of values is said to be the model for Hindu society as whole. It is the Brahman who best exemplifies the pursuit of *marga,* or "the path to follow." Mahatma Gandhi himself said that he was a "humble seeker after Truth" and he interpreted the fundamental mandate of a good Hindu to be: "Search after Truth through non-violent means" (Organ, 1970, 5). Following this interpretation, Hindu society appears to be organized around the task of caring for its gods, and a division of labor among the castes is necessary to attain this end. Since gods can only be worshipped by mortals of high ritual purity, this inherent purity must be preserved by lower castes who remove impurity by taking up cleansing activities. The system is oriented towards self-preservation and all members of the community derive benefits from the worship given by the Brahmans to the gods (van der Veer, 1989). Clearly a rationale to ensure perpetuity is built into the very essence of Hinduism.

Peculiarities

Outsiders who undertake a quick survey of religions other than their own are usually struck by uniquenesses and peculiarities. In the case of Hinduism, there are plenty to go around, especially from a western Christian perspective (Ridenour, 1980). Here are several examples.

The Caste System

To begin with, there is the matter of caste, and although many Hindus would say that caste is *not* an integral, nor inherent, part of their religious system, caste differences are rarely missing from any conversation about the faith. A close corollary is the notion of reincarnation, which allows for the possibility of elevating one's station in life through possible rebirths. This belief, of course, is not unique to Hinduism, and it has recently become the subject of much curiosity and attention in North America through what has come to be known as "New Age" religion. Essentially promoted by a number of high media figures, this movement has targeted a number of traditional "spiritual" beliefs such as reincarnation, and thereby offered them as new items of hope to a religion-thirsty generation.

Strictly speaking, it is impossible to become a Hindu other than by being born into a caste. Traditionally, as described earlier, four castes have been recognized, possibly originating in the Aryan tradition. In days past there was a stratum beneath these four castes known as the arena of the untouchables, that is, persons whose rank was so low that they did not even matter on the human scale of being. Most Hindus accept the caste system as Divinely decreed and would probably argue that one need not believe in the caste system in order to be a Hindu; it is simply a reality – a "given" fact of life. They would probably also argue that every society has its social or socioeconomic layers (or strata), and inequities between the layers inevitably emerge and maintain themselves. Gandhi himself did not wish to see the caste system abolished altogether, possibly recognizing it for its value as a social cement, but he *did* abhor the notion of untouchability (Hinnells and Sharpe, 1972). This practice, in its most severe form, mandated that if even the shadow of an untouchable fell on a Brahman, a rite of cleansing would be initiated immediately. Although still recognized in parts of India, the severerity of caste rules has greatly decreased.

Role of Women

Closely related to the inequality implied in the caste system is the position of women in traditional Hinduism. Suttee (*Sati*), or the practice of widow-burning comes to mind as the most extreme form of discrimination against women. The role of women in marriage in India was traditionally one of submission, obedience and service. Women could not remarry after the death of their spouse. In fact, it was deemed to be the ultimate act of sacrifice and love and devotion if a widow immolated herself on her husband's funeral pyre (Hinnells and Sharpe, 1972). This practice was abolished by law in 1829 but it is still identified by outsiders as a most heinous practice – as though it is still ongoing. Traditionally the alternative to *sati* was a life of perpetual seclusion in the "women's house," a practice not without parallel in other religions, for example, in Judaism.

Animal Worship

Although particularly repugnant to Westerners, the idea of reverence for the cow has always played a striking role in Hindu mythology as well as in the day-to-day religious practice. The roots of this belief are very deep and are possibly founded on the idea of the symbolism of the Divine bounty of the earth – the cow is an alternative symbol of the earth and viewed as the "mother of gods and men." The mother-goddess Aditi is called "the cow," and Hindu literature extolls her as the animal that sums up the whole of creation. In Vedic times there was no prohibition of cow-killing or eating of beef; that belief emerged later. Corollary beliefs also originated, e.g., he who unhesitatingly abandons life for the sake of the cow is freed from the guilt of the murder of a Brahman. It is highly auspicious to be able to die clutching a cow's tail. For lower castes, a cow-shed sometimes filled the function of a temple and became the focus of their daily worship. The five products of the cow – milk, curds, clarified butter, dung and urine – were all used in purificatory rituals (Hinnells and Sharpe, 1972).

A series of myths to support the value of cow worship originated through time and perpetuated from generation to generation. Gandhi suggested that belief in cow protection would take the human being "beyond his species . . . man through the cow is enjoined to realize his identity with all that lives" (Hinnells and Sharpe, 1972, 121). In fact, all things, animate and inanimate, are viewed in Hinduism as possessions of "splendor" (Stroup, 1972). As with any religion, there are special or even sacred objects in its make-up. Hinduism is not unique in this and like any other religion holds fast to its "sacred cows," in this case, literally!

God or gods?

Pursuers of Truth (following Gandhi), might be confused by the proliferation of Hindu gods from which to choose. Philosophically, any dualism between man and god is inadmissable, for essentially man is god. This observation finds an easy parallel in the writings of existentialists like Martin Buber, Gabriel Marcel and Jean Paul Sartre, and in the words of Ayn Rand, inventor of the "Gospel of Objectivism." Compared with Islam or Christianity, Hinduism is much more individually-based and permits an easier process of evolution and involution (Channa, 1984). This does not mean that Hinduism has nothing to do with God or gods; on the contrary, in Hinduism it is possible to have, to do, both – to accept an absolutistic way as well as a relativistic point of view, the one not spurning the other. The relation between God and man is in many ways influenced by the relation between the Supreme Being and the essential self (Dandekar, 1988). In theistic terms one might say that a true believer/follower is one who becomes that which he or she is supposed to become in the Grand Scheme of things. Undoubtedly there are many lesser maxims to which one might subscribe!

References

Babb, Lawrence, A. (1975). *The divine hierarchy: Popular Hinduism in central India*. New York: Columbia University Press.

Channa, V.C. (1984). *Hinduism*. Darya Ganj, New Dehli: National Publishing House.

Dandekar, R.N. (1988). Scattered voices: The nature of God. In Eleanor Zelliot & Maxine Berntsen (Eds.), *The experience of Hinduism: Essays on religion in Maharashtra* (pp. 60-63). Albany, NY: State University of New York Press.

Hinnells, John R. and Sharpe, Eric J. (Eds.). (1972). *Hinduism*. Newcastle, UK: Oriel Press.

Hopkins, Thomas J. (1971). *The Hindu religious tradition.* Encino, CA: Dickenson Publishing Co.

Knott, Kim. (1986). *My sweet Lord: The Hare Krishna movement.* San Bernardino, CA: The Borgo Press.

Lipner, Julius. (1994). *Hindus: Their religious beliefs and practices.* London: Routledge.

Organ, Troy Wilson. (1970). *The Hindu quest for the perfection of man.* Athens, OH: Ohio University.

Pereira, Jose (Ed.). 1976). *Hindu theology: A reader.* Garden City, NY: Image Books.

Ridenour, Fritz. (1980). *So what's the difference?* Ventura, CA: Regal Books.

Stroup, Herbert. (1972). *Like a great river: An introduction to Hinduism.* New York: Harper & Row.

van der Veer, Peter. (1989). The concept of the ideal Brahman as an ideological construct. In Gunther D. Sontheimer & Hermann Kulke (Eds.), *Hinduism reconsidered* (pp. 67-80). New Delhi: Manohar.

Zaehner, R.C. (1966). *Hinduism.* New York: Oxford University Press.

9

Islam

Anyone wanting to get involved with a religion that has ancient roots, very specific beliefs, precisely-prescribed practices and a strong bent towards evangelism should examine the Muslim (Islam) religion. This religion is 800 million strong worldwide, and there are 253 000 Muslims in Canada.

Specifically, the images of Islam prevalent in the Western world are of brutality, fanaticism, hatred and disorder. The very names of noted Muslim leaders of our times – Khomeini, Gaddafi, Arafat – have become symbols of these images (Ahmed, 1988). Some writers contend that the lack of understanding of Islam stems partly from outsiders' failure to understand the inner workings of the religion, and partly from the failure of Islam adequately to explain itself. The blunt truth is, that in the Western world at least, Islam *does* have a somewhat tarnished image.

The history of Islam goes back to the roots of the Biblical Patriarch, Abraham, who had a son, Ishmael, with Hagar, his wife's hand-maiden, allegedly with his wife, Sarai's, approval. Hard to believe, isn't it?

According to the Biblical record:

> So she [Sarai] said to Abraham, "The Lord has kept me from having children. Go sleep with my maidservant; perhaps I can build a family through her (Genesis 16:2).

As the account goes, Abraham had been promised children by the Lord God, and when Sarai did not conceive, she and her husband decided to rush things a bit on their own. Later, after Ishmael, Sarai conceived and gave birth to her own son, Isaac. In a fit of jealousy she chased Hagar and Ishmael into the desert. The Lord God had mercy on Hagar and subsequently elevated her son Ishmael to the position of father of the Arab nations and Isaac became head of the Jewish nation. For most people Islam is perceived as synonymous with Arab cultures, but, ironically, many Arabs initially retaliated against the reforms of the Persian founder, Mohammed. They had no inclination to pray, read the Koran, or give alms. Their conversion to his gospel must be interpreted as one of the greatest shifts of the public mind in human history.

Today the single largest Muslim country is Indonesia and indeed many Muslims are not Arabs. However, there are large communities from the Arab world, the Middle East, and newer communities from places such as Iran and Somalia living in other parts of the world, including Canada. Most Canadian Muslims are located in Vancouver, Edmonton, Toronto and Montreal.

Pedigree

Although information about his early life is scant, the prophet Mohammed was born in AD 570 to a cadet branch of one of the leading families of Mecca. He was orphaned and brought up by an uncle who was engaged in the caravan trade. Mohammed became commercial agent to a widow named Khadija; he married her and they had several children, both sons and daughters, but only four daughters survived.

During his married life Mohammed came into contact with a religious movement which rejected the polytheism of the time and declared that Allah was the only God. On his conversion, Mohammed became convinced of a profound sense of dependence upon the omnipresent and omnipotent Lord. He saw God as the all-powerful Lord and all-knowing Judge of mankind – a God who demanded loyal self-surrender and unconditional obedience. The service He required was a serious life characterized by prayers, almsgiving and temperance. As a result of this gripping experience, Mohammed began to resort a great deal to private prayers and took up ascetic practices. Eventually, the angel Gabriel visited him and told him that he would be the next (and final) prophet of God. Though he enthusiastically shared this message with his wife, Khadija, who encouraged him, he soon fell into despair and depression, and a second visit from the angel became necessary.

Mohammed's home city of Mecca was a wealthy city, almost monopolizing the commercial trade in the area between the Indian Ocean and the Mediterranean. Naturally the extreme commercialism of the centre produced the usual strata of have and have-not social classes, a reality that drew the attention of Mohammed in his early ministry. Like many other religious reformers throughout history, it is said of Mohammed that he had no intention of bringing about a new social order. Rather, his pronouncements were targeted against the evils of a class-oriented society and his preachments caused much concern among the commercial barons of his time (Gibb, 1969).

After a decade of preaching, Mohammed fled from Mecca to Medina with a small group of followers. Here he was welcomed as an arbitrartor and peacemaker among various disputing Arabic factions. Mohammed interpreted the fact of his being welcomed at Medina as proof of Divine approval for his ministry.

Like other religions with a "hero at the helm," Islam is often criticized for making a saint out of their founder. In fact, Muslims have always been aware of, and constantly refer to, Mohammed's human nature and its limitations. They have never seen him as a quasi-Divine or deified being; he was a messenger, singled out by God to deliver his version of the gospel to a people at a given time and place. Even after Mohammed became ruler of Arabia, which happened only two years before his death, he maintained a fairly simple life-style. He never set store by money and estate, he avoided excessive eating and drinking and soft clothing, and strictly committed himself to fasting and watching and praying. He did, however, declare himself to be exempt from those restrictions in regard to the female sex which he imposed on all other Muslims. He was criticized for this, as well as for his tendency to use his prophetic character as a pretext for the establishment of his political power. Islams point out that up to the age of 53, including 25 years of happy marriage, Mohammed maintained a monogamous marriage to his first wife. Only after her death and after he had achieved a new social and political status following his invitation to help the citizens of Medina, did he become polygamous (Abdul-Rauff, 1985).

Mohammed's engagements in war are justified by his followers in the context that his "enemies made him do it." He hated war and conflict, but when war was forced on him, he strove to render it humane. He abolished savage and barbarous practices. He commanded in battle, but scrupulously refrained from personally shedding blood. His strategy was faultless and was always designed to reduce loss of life and keep human suffering to a minimum (Khan, 1980).

Despite these concessions, devout Muslims consider Mohammed to be the "beautiful model" and insist that his way of life must be followed, even to the minutest detail. This is the objective of the most pious. Mohammed is the "seal of the prophets," the last of a long line of people to bear witness to a special message of God (Schimmel and Falaturi, 1979).

After the death of Mohammed, a series of successful religious wars ensued using Persia as the base for campaigns in Central Asia and western India. Later there were campaigns into Spain and France. A century after the death of the great leader his followers were masters of an empire greater than Rome at its height (Hitti, 1962).

Immediately after Mohammed's death the question arose as to who was to be his "representative." These leaders were called Caliphs. The lot initially fell to Abubekr who was involved in a series of vicious wars between opposing factions, and he died in AD 634. He was succeeded by an individual named Amar who led for ten years. Before his death Amar instituted a formalized system of selecting leadership.

Principles & Precepts

Islamics see their faith as based on several very important principles. First of all, Islam is a tradition grounded entirely on a distinct revelation; consequently a sense of the transcendent and the revealed is a potent force in Islamic society. Islamics believe that any philosophy that ignores both revelation and intellectual intuition, thus divorcing itself from the twin sources of transcendent knowledge, cannot truly be called a philosophy. Second, there is the question of the relation between reason and revelation. It is obvious that if the function of the intellect is reduced to reason, and if revelation is limited to the most esoteric and outward level of meaning, then faith and reason can never be truly harmonized.

Islam professes to possess a unified vision of phenomena, that is, it provides a potential unity among all forms of knowledge. It is believed that mankind will never be able to develop a unified approach to the question of *raison d'etre* unless the interrelation between the various fields of knowledge is assumed and pursued. For this reason Islamics can proudly point to a long intellectual tradition in their ranks (Nasr, 1981).

The Koran

The book of sacred writings for Muslims is the *Koran,* a 300 page treatise whose passages begin with the phrase, "The Prophet said." The volume is a record of both the informal utterances and formal discourses which Mohammed and his followers accepted as Divinely-inspired. Orthodox Muslims accept the book as the literal word of God mediated through the angel, Gabriel. They believe that the entire text of the *Koran* was revealed by God to the prophet, who transmitted it to his contemporaries. A vast majority have even entrusted it to memory (Abdul-Rauf, 1985). Non-believers are not as committed, and have real doubts about the value of the *Koran.* Some might even go as far as Carlyle who said of the *Koran,* "It is as toilsome reading as I ever undertook, a wearisome, confused jumble, crude, incondite. Nothing but a sense of duty could carry any European through the *Koran*," (Gibb, 1969, 25).

The contents of the different parts of the *Koran* are extremely varied. Many passages consist of theological or moral reflections. Here the reader is reminded of the greatness, goodness and righteousness of God as manifest in nature, in history and in the revelation of the prophets. In some passages the sacred book falls into a diffuse preaching style, and other passages seem more like proclamations or general orders. A great number contain ceremonial or civil laws, or even special commands to individuals down to such matters as the regulation of Mohammed's harem.

Despite these unique qualities or eccentricities (at least from a non-believer's perspective), the *Koran* is highly regarded by orthodox Muslims. Strictly speaking, the *Koran* should not be touched except in a state of legal purity. It must not be placed at the bottom of a pile of books, and one must refrain from drinking or smoking while reading it aloud. Some passages in the *Koran* bear a remarkable similarity to parts of the Bible, although any derivation therefrom would be denied. Islam boasts no official clergy, it being a lay religion, but certain individuals still emerge as spiritual leaders from time to time, based on their knowledge of the *Koran* and tradition (Hitti, 1962).

Islamic Regulations

Early in his ministry Mohammed developed a series of precepts by which his followers should live. These were drawn from both Jewish and Arabic sources. In particular, Mohammed made specific rules about property and set himself about elevating the status of women and guaranteeing certain rights for them. He retained the right of blood revenge, but reserved for himself the right of permitting it. He initiated a series of activities oriented towards encouraging fellowship and developed a system of alms-giving for the sake of the poor. His vision was that every Moslem would be every Moslem's brother. Gradually, this very practical form of religion developed into a form of cultural practice to the point of formulating the very foundation of an entire social system. In short, Islam became a state religion.

Mohammed quickly encountered resistance from Jews who opposed his reforms. For example, he insisted that Mecca, rather than Jerusalem, be the direction of prayers, and he appointed Friday, rather than Saturday, as the principal day of worship. He also instituted the established feast of sacrifice on the day of the Meccan festival. Naturally, these actions did not please the Jews, and served to intensify a historic religious feud.

Islamic Doctrines

There is currently visible within Islam an international phenomenon of considerable dimension, often referred to by western observers, either neutrally or unhappily, or even with some degree of fright, as the "resurgence of Islam." The movement has multiple dimensions; it may mean the recent increased spread of Islam into western countries, or the revival and strengthening of certain Islamic traditions or values in different Muslim countries. It may also be influenced by the tremendous wealth recently attained by several oil-rich Arabic countries, who have as a result managed to throw their political power around (Rahman, 1979). The reform movement has essentially been an urban movement whose leaders have tended to be state officials, intellectuals, or those fiercely opposed to traditional interpretations of religion (Choueiri, 1990). By studying the pre-industrial phase of European civilization, for example, Islam's exponents have hoped to discover the prerequisites for building viable political structures and a sound economic base.

To a certain extent, all of the above interpretations have some merit. The described events did take place. Defenders of Islam are quick to point out that the "moral revival" in their own ranks is parallelled by a move towards decadence in the West. They claim that Western civilization has become so ubiquitous – declining and decadent forces are rampant – and the West appears not to have benefitted from the moral revival within Islam. Western decadence could result in serious damage to the rest of the world, not only politically or economically, but also intellectually and spiritually if it is not opposed by truth. The *Koran* is optimistic about the future, however, and Islamics are "going with their good book" (Rahman, 1979). Their primary task will be to construct a new social order on a viable ethical basis. Economic well-being and the exploitation of nature for human ends are integral parts of this morality. Technology was made for mankind, not the other way around. Mankind has higher ends than the machine or the marketplace.

Against this agenda, Westerners must cringe when they read the clearly delineated, self-designed (God-designed?) mandate of Islam. A variety of approaches are feasible, not all of them bathed in fear. For example, it should be recognized that the transposition of western political institutions into the Middle East has permanently changed the area's public orientation. The problem is not that an alien tradition has been introduced, but that it has been understood in an imperfect way. Middle Eastern political theorists and practitioners now need to examine the liberal nationalist idea in its entirety, as it was developed in Europe and North America. This would help them develop a constitutional framework for their own national movements and minimize the malpractices and instability that have characterized these systems for three generations. To a certain extent the combination of Islamic and western traditions in the Middle East has already occurred, and the process cannot be reversed. As Taylor (1988) points out, what is subject to change is the way both systems are interpreted. With proper understanding and implementation of the nobler aspects of each heritage, the cross-fertilization may be relatively free from problems, at least in the dimensions that are most compatible.

This optimistic view offers hope for reciprocal learnings, and is a long ways from the utilitarian opposition inferred in the warning of the late Chicago sociologist, William Graham Sumner, "If Communism [Islam] ever hits the country, be sure and get on the committee."

The Bedouin

Although Islam is often perceived as a specifically prescriptive religion, there is room for interpretation of the rules among the ranks. The Bedouin Arabs (or desert wanderers), for example, also believe in one God, Allah, and His prophet, Mohammed, but they live according to some unique norms. A main characteristic of their faith is visiting the tombs of holy persons and ancestors. On site they may slaughter a goat to a holy man and ask him to make representation on behalf of themselves, their children or their livestock. More regular features of Bedouin religion include fervent prayers, seeking the protection of Allah against the dangers of the desert, and showing kindness to strangers and relatives. For the Bedouin, every aspect of daily life, including all human relations, is religiously connected.

The Bedouin take great pride in being able to survive in the desert and, generally speaking, they have little use for cities. The harsh and sometimes unsympathetic desert environment necessitates their being a mobile people, and they essentially divide the year into two seasons.

The first season begins when the first good winter rains fall and some of the groups will till their land, currently by quite modern means. The second season begins after harvest which occurs around the end of April and the beginning of May when the Bedouin move to pasture areas. They are viewed by outsiders as a "camel people," and that beast holds a very special place in their culture. Norms have been developed around the camel's use, virtually establishing it as one of the basic institutions of Bedouin life. Bedouin chiefs are powerful individuals, although they earn respect by persuasion or because of outstanding personality characteristics. They are listened to because of their position. From time to time they may be called on to settle disputes or to provide their people with protection. Because of these kinds of considerations, a certain flexibility is built into Bedouin culture which marks it off as a rather unique variation of Islam.

Practices

The key to being a good Muslim is to seek to emulate the qualities that Mohammed revealed in daily living. Like every prophet he had to possess the qualities of truthfulness, trustworthiness, authentic conveyance of the message and intelligence. No one could imagine that he ever told lies or had been treacherous or stupid. Clearly he must have used every opportunity to share his version of the Divine message, even though subject to ordinary human contingencies (Schimmel and Falaturi, 1979). These are the traits of a devout believer.

The Five Duties

In a more formal sense, followers of Islam must strictly comply with five basic duties which reveal the intensity and devotion demanded of them.

1.   Once in their lifetime, followers of Mohammed must say with conviction and understanding, "There is no god but Allah and Mohammed is His prophet."

2. Five times daily, the believer must pray – at dawn, at noon, in the after-noon, at dusk and after dark. At the muezzin's call the believer should observe the ritual prayers. These prayers are established in form and pre-cept; when the believers pray, they must cover their heads, remove their shoes, and place a carpet under them. They must prostrate themselves con-tinually. A more formal ritual is required on Fridays when a mosque must be visited, the *Koran* is read and set prayers are said.

3. The Muslim must give alms generously; these are prescribed – traditionally so many cattle and so much grain. In countries where Islam is the state re-ligion, tithes are collected by the state. Almsgiving is associated in the *Koran* with prayer and considered a feature of piety.

4. Every Muslim must keep the Feast of Ramadan, although disabled and handicapped individuals are exempt. Moses fasted forty days and forty nights, and so did Jesus Christ. Fasting involves abstinence from food, drink, smoking and conjugal relations.

5. Once, during their lifetimes, Muslims must seek to make a pilgrimage to Mecca. Since this undertaking is recommended for a particular time of year, the effort often unites large numbers of believers in meetings for so-cial and spiritual benefit (Bailey, n.d.). Mohammed probably derived the notion of pilgrimage from what were believed to be heathen sources, but he gave the practice new meaning (Hitti, 1962).

Peculiarities

To begin with, Islam distinguishes itself among the many religions, ideologies, and philosophies by an extraordinary consciousness of norms which are held to be revealed, to possess an absolute nature and universal validity, and to provide human thought and action with an unconditional regulator (Waardenburg, 1979). Islam believes itself to be connected to the one primordial religion which has existed from the beginning of humanity and is in keeping with mankind's nature.

The Doctrine of Unity

One of the unique features of Islam is that unlike western perspec-tives, there is no distinction between secular and sacred. An Islamic state cannot be isolated from society because it is a comprehensive, integrated way of life. The division between private and public, or state and society that is familiar in western culture, is not known in Islam. The state is only the political expression of an Islamic society. An Islamic state evolves from an Islamic society. The ideological foundation of an Islamic state lies in the doctrine of the unity of God and of human life – as a comprehensive and exclusive program of worship (al-Turabi, 1983). In this there is a parallel with North American First Nations' conceptualizations of God, the cosmos and society. There is no dichotomy. The difference is that Islam is politically and perhaps imperialistically-inclined. Aboriginal peoples are more oriented towards an acceptance of things the way they are – including the workings of the universe.

Islam and Christianity

One of the simplest ways to point out the distinctiveness of Islam from a Christian perspective (which is one of the underlying points of reference for this book), is with regards to conceptions of God, the doctrine of the Trinity, the Incarnation and religious pluralism. Christians believe in one Absolute Godhead, divided into three persons, Father, Son and Holy Spirit. As a means of developing at least some kind of "cross-cultural" understanding of these not-diametrically opposed positions, it helps to keep in mind that the Christian doctrine of the Trinity is not a revealed truth, but a theological theory designed to resolve a theological difficulty, principally to avoid any semblance to polytheism. Thus Islam and Christianity both believe in One God as a revealed truth. Second is the question of the Incarnation which for centuries has fostered among adherents the notion of a unique superiority of Christianity as the one and only religion that God has founded in person (with Jesus Christ). Recent restatements of the doctrine of the Incarnation, however, see Divine Incarnation as a Supreme instance of the paradox of grace or of the inspiration of God as Spirit. In this view a literal manifestation of the Incarnation is not necessarily required. Some of these interpretations convey a little more flexibility than has previously been the case and thereby leave open the possibility of genuine inter-faith dialogue (Hick, 1991). No one may change their mind through such encounters, nor should they be expected to, but the very possibility of initiating such a process at least fulfills an objective that every major religion apparently values highly!

References

Abdul-Rauf, Muhammad. (1985). Outsiders' interpretations of Islam: A Muslim's point of view. In Richard C. Martin (Ed.), *Approaches to Islam in religious studies* (pp. 179-188). Tucson, AZ: University of Arizona Press.

Ahmed, Akbar S. (1988). *Discovering Islam: Making sense of Muslim history and society.* London: Routledge & Kegan Paul.

al-Turabi, Hassan. (1983). The Islamic state. In John Esposito (Ed.), *Voices of resurgent Islam* (pp. 242-251). New York: Oxford University Press.

Bailey, Clinton. (n.d.). *The Bedouin: People of the desert.* Printed in the Holy Land by Palphot Ltd.

Choueiri, Youssef M. (1990). *Islamic fundamentalism.* London: Pinter Publishers.

Gibb, H.A.R. (1969). *Mohammadanism: An historical survey* (2nd ed.). London: Oxford University Press.

Hick, John. (1991). Islam and Christian monotheism. In Dan Cohn-Sherbok (Ed.), *Islam in a world of diverse faiths* (pp.1-17). London: Macmillan.

Hitti, Philip K. (1962). *Islam and the west: A historical cultural survey.* Toronto: D. Van Nostrand Company.

Khan, Zafrulla. (1980). *Muhammad: Seal of the prophets.* London: Routledge & Kegan Paul.

Nasr, Seyyed Hossein. (1981). *Islamic life and thought.* Albany, NY: State University of New York Press.

Rahman, Fazlur. (1979). Islam: Challenges and Opportunities. In Alford T. Welch & Pierre Cachia (Eds.), *Islam: Past influence and present challenge* (pp. 315-330). Edinburgh, UK: Edinburgh University Press.

Schimmel, Anne Marie & Falaturi, Abdoldjavad. (1979). *We believe in one God: The experience of God in Christianity and Islam.* New York: Seabury Press.

Taylor, Alan R. (1988). *The Islamic question in Middle East politics.* Boulder: Westview Press.

Waardenburg, Jacques. (1979). World religions as seen in the light of Islam. In Alford T. Welch & Pierre Cachia (Eds.), *Islam: Past influence and present challenge* (pp. 245-275). Edinburgh, UK: Edinburgh University Press.

10

Judaism

Every year thousands of tourists converge on the Holy City of Jerusalem, particularly at Christmas and Easter to commemorate the birth, death and resurrection of Jesus Christ. Tourist buses carrying passengers from all parts of the world flood the landscape during these seasons and the visitors come for the express purpose of visiting important historical sites pertaining to the life of Christ. Jerusalem is said to be one of the most popular tourist attractions in the world.

By Canadian standards, Israel is a tiny country. However, at times it has expanded its territories, especially after the Six Day War of 1967. The City of Jerusalem is the capital as it was in the 400 year period from the Kings of Israel and Judah, from David and Solomon, to Jehoiachin and Zedekiah. The largest Jewish community in the world today is in the USA, with approximately 5.9 million. The second largest is in Israel, with approximately 3.6 million. There are 318 000 Jews in Canada.

Since the historical basis of Christianity has Judaistic roots, it is appropriate that Christians have a good grounding in Jewish history. As a result much of the content of Sunday school curricula taught in Christian churches incorporates stories from the Bible. It might even be appropriate to suggest that some Christians are better acquainted with Jewish history and beliefs than some Jews are!

Pedigree

The names of familiar biblical characters like Abraham, Isaac, Jacob, Moses and Joshua form the Jewish historical hall of fame. It was Moses who brought the people of Israel out of Egypt, the land of bondage. Here they had labored as slaves for 400 years. Moses gave the Jews the ten commandments as well as the various ceremonial, moral and levitical laws.

After freeing the nation from Egyptian rule (whose army, by the way, suffered a quick death in the Red Sea while pursuing the Jews), Moses summoned the Hebrew people and imparted the "stipulations, decrees and laws" that God had covenanted with them (Deuteronomy 4:44). In the years that followed, the nation often strayed from the law and had to be reprimanded and punished. In each instance the Lord God Jehovah also raised up a prophet to warn them to repent and raised up a savior to lead them back to their original purpose. Names like Jeremiah, Ezekiel, Hosea, Amos, Haggai and Zechariah come to mind as individuals who filled these roles.

The story of the Jewish sojourn in Egypt and their successive escape (including their subsequent 40 year period of wilderness wandering) is perhaps best known, but Jewish history is actually much older than that. It all started with Abraham (1996-1822 BC), the father of the faith, who was told by God to leave his hometown of Ur of the Chaldees, beyond the Euphrates River. God told Abraham to depart for a place unknown, a "land of promise" which He would show to Abraham. Abraham took with him his wife, Sarai, and his nephew, Lot. Abraham eventually ended up in Canaan to claim God's promise that his successors would number as many as the stars of the sky and the sands of the seashore.

Abraham was succeeded by his son, Isaac, though he and Sarai were quite advanced in years before Isaac was finally born. Isaac and his wife Rebekah had twin sons, Esau and Jacob (Israel). The elder son, Esau, the "one born first," had rights as heir to the promise of being the patriarch of a great nation. He was cheated by his brother, Jacob, who then claimed that right, and Jacob's 12 sons became the heads of the 12 tribes of Israel. Sandwiched in between are the exciting biblical stories of Joseph, one of the sons of Jacob – his coat of many colors, his being sold as a slave to Egypt, his brush with Potiphar's seductive wife, and his subsequent reunion with the brothers who betrayed him. Joseph then lured his father Jacob to come to Egypt with "all his household" (numbering about 70 souls) and they remained there until a subsequent Pharoah turned them into slaves.

Attaining Nationhood

After escaping from Egypt and eventually reestablishing themselves, the Israelites became a nation with a King (Saul) at the helm. Saul was succeeded by David, the shepherd boy, who was followed by his son, Solomon, the wise, rich king with a thousand concubines. Then the kingdom split into Israel and Judah, and the prophesies of a coming Messiah were traced through the lineage of the Tribe of Judah. Christians acknowledge this Messiah as Jesus Christ; Jews do not.

In the intervening millennia between Moses and Jesus, Judaism was impacted by at least three civilizations, Babylonian, Persian and Greek. During the Babylonian period, great wealth came to many families who also assimilated a great deal of Babylonian philosophy and astrology. Persian thought also affected Judaism, producing a more distinct eschatological concept regarding heaven and hell, including the resurrection and final triumph of the righteous. Greek philosophy aided in the interpretation of the Gospel of Jesus Christ as evidenced by the writings of the Apostle Paul who combined both Hellenistic idealism and fundamental Judaism.

These historical movements converge in New Testament writings and the Christmas story is essentially an intermingling of them. A Jewish maiden, in Bethlehem because of Roman requirements, gave birth to a babe, the story of whose life was told in the Greek language. Even before the sages from the Orient arrived on the scene, Jew, Greek and Roman were all implicated in the culminating event.

Political Divisions

The political history of Palestine is intertwined with its civil, social and religious life. The division of Palestine into three major geographical areas, Judea, Samaria and Galilee, enhanced the growth of several distinctive cultural orientations. Judea, including the Holy City of Jerusalem, was the hub of Jewish culture and also the centre of the restoration. Samaria was home for a vanquished people who had fallen under Assyrian influence and, although they were also descendants of Abraham as well, their purism was severely questioned by orthodox Jewry. Galilee was known as the "district of the Gentiles," where Jews were more liberal in their interpretations of orthodoxy, and included Perea on the eastern side of the Jordan, where Jewish thought had only a little effect.

By the time of Christ, Palestine had developed a series of Jewish sects who dominated the religious and political scenes and promoted a particular doctrine or theme. These groups included:

1. The Pharisees who had as a primary goal the fulfillment of the ceremonial law, and sought hard to live up to the letter of the law. They were a "separatist" people, and gave Jesus a hard time when He made declarations about "the Sabbath being made for man and not man for the Sabbath."

2. The Sadducees were basically an aristocratic party and while they agreed with the Pharisees on the importance of legalism, they rejected the doctrine of immortality, the resurrection, and the existence of angels and spirits.

3. The Essenes held a position to the right of the Pharisees, so far right, in fact, as to comprise an ascetic community that was located in the desert region of the Dead Sea and isolated them from the rest of Judaism. A few decades ago, several biblical manuscripts known as the Dead Sea Scrolls were found in an Essene community, almost perfectly preserved.

4. The Zealots took a position to the left of the Pharisees and were much caught up in politics. The Zealots were interested in the independence and autonomy of the Jewish nation to the neglect of every other concern. A group of zealots was involved in the last fight against the Roman takeover in AD 73 when, under the leadership of Eliezer, son of Yair, they took to

the Mount of Metsada and held that fortress during nearly three years of seige. The historian, Josephus, in his *War of the Jews* described the heroic end of Metsada:

> They then chose ten men by lot out of them, to slay all the rest, everyone of whom lay himself down by his wife and children on the ground and threw their arms around them, and they offered their necks to the stroke of those who by lot executed that melancholy office; and when these ten had, without fear, slain them all, they made the same rule of casting lots for themselves, then he, whose lot it was should first kill the other nine, and after all should kill himself. . . . The dead were about nine hundred and sixty-nine. . . . The Romans could not help but wonder at the courage of their resolution . . . . (Vilnay, 1979, 128).

Against this background it is not difficult to appreciate the thrust of historical Jewish nationalism, even though it seldom takes on the magnitude of the Metsada event. At the same time, when a people believe themselves to be specially selected by Almighty God to fulfill His purpose on earth, one can also understand the possible extent of their social and philosophical, if not political, militancy.

5. The Zadokites operated a community termed "The New Covenant" and were considered part of a reform movement that originated about a century prior to the establishment of Christianity. Their reforms helped prepare the way for Christian inroads by their shaking up the foundations of orthodox Jewry.

6. The Herodians were strictly a political party with religious matters purely a second concern. While the ministry of Jesus was gaining in popularity the Herodians were in constant fear that He might precipitate a nationalistic political movement that would thwart their own designs for the future (Dana, 1951).

Contemporary Developments

After being scattered in various countries for many years and persecuted under Hitler and in the Soviet Union, the tenacious Jews have at long last a soil to call their own. In 1945 an Anglo-American Commission conducted an inquiry and agreed with a 1937 report that recommended the partition of Palestine into two sovereign states. The residents of Palestine, including Jews, Arabs and others, rejected this proposal and subsequent ones, and on 15 May 1948, the British forces, then occupying Palestine, were withdrawn. The State of Israel was immediately declared and recognized by both the United States and Russia. Since then Israel has fought in offensive and defensive wars. Of her involvement in military actions, Jews declare that they fight in a "unique way, one that combines biblical inspiration and patriotism with the intellectual sophistication of indirection" (Schweitzer, 1971).

The role of the Jews in the medieval and modern economic life of the Western world has been the subject of much inquiry, controversy, error and prejudice. In the ancient empires of Persia, Rome, Islam and even in the severely persecuted Byzantine Empire, there were no special occupations from which Jews were either excluded or to which they were confined, and in general they had considerable autonomy. Only in western Christendom, beginning in the 4th century, did occupational segregation become the order of the day. In fact, the common stereotype of the Jews as having some special attribute, or genius for business, basically stems from this segregation. Some observers have even gone so far as to suggest that western capitalism owes its origin and early development to Jews – or in its most extreme form – that the spirit and practice of capitalism reflect, or are synonymous with, the spirit and practice of Judaism.

It is true that in the 16th and 17th centuries the Jews played an important part in the development of the Netherlands and in certain parts of Europe. But the foundations of these economies had already been laid before the Jews arrived on the scene, and subsequent developments would probably have been the same with or without them. In the last part of the 17th century, when the economic hub of power shifted to England, the Jews had nothing to do with it. The notion that Judaism is a highly legalistic and rational religion, and thereby imbues the Jews with a special capacity for the kind of rational and shrewd calculation which leads to the making of profit, simply does not stand up. This is an untenable position because the theory overlooks the profoundly non-rational aspects of Judaism which are as much a vital aspect of the faith as rationalism (Schweitzer, 1971).

On a more positive note it should be mentioned that Jews *are* often at the forefront of leadership and the backbone of support. Jewish Nobel Prize winners have been so prevalent in the 20th century that their numbers are approximately 25 times their percentage in world population. In recent decades 30 to 40 percent of American Poet Laureates have been Jews, rising to prominence in a parallel movement with scientific advances (Douglas, 1991).

Principles & Precepts

Judaism is primarily a culture, albeit a religious culture (Meyer, 1967). Defining it in exclusively religious terms does an injustice to the breadth of its concerns and its capacity to evoke continued commitments from those among their number who have no religious faith. At the heart of the religious tradition is Jewish law, and as with Islam, the law declares the existence of a monotheistic God. Strict observance of the law is believed to be the will of God, and the law is manifold in intent and application. At Sinai, God gave Israel a moral code consisting of ten commandments, which constitute the Decalogue. These are not detailed but give general directions that are easily understood. The first is a commandment to remember who God is and His goodness to Israel. Then come nine commands: two of them are positive, indicating what must be done, and the other seven negative, outlining both the religious attitude of the chosen people and the secular code of morals that should govern human affairs. The corollaries of these principles include 613 obligations – 365 negative and 248 positive which from then on and for all eternity guide the behavior of the Jews and must be manifest in the life of each practicing believer (Aron, 1971; Goodman, 1976).

To give a specific example, orthodox Jews are commanded that before eating bread they must ask a blessing, and before this blessing can be said, they must first wash their hands. As they wash their hands they must recite a blessing over the hand washing. Even the manner in which the hands are washed is prescribed, the kind of utensil used, the order in which the hands are washed, and the number of times each hand is washed (Liebman and Cohen, 1990).

In addition to having knowledge about laws and rituals, ceremonial or civil, there is much more knowledge to be acquired. To illustrate, this is a passage which every well-educated Jewish child knows by heart (Fackenheim, 1987):

> Hear, O Israel, the Lord our God, the Lord is one. And thou shalt love the Lord thy God with all thy heart, with all thy soul, and with all thy might. And these words which I command thee this day shall be upon thy heart; and thou shalt teach them diligently to thy children, and shalt speak of them when thou sittest in thy house, and when thou walkest by the way, and when thou liest down and when thou risest up. And thou shalt bind them for a sign upon thy hand, and they shall be for frontlets between thine eyes. And thou shalt write them upon the door-posts of thy house and upon thy gates (Deuteronomy 6:4-9).

Jewish Literature

Jews are sometimes called "People of the Book." The basis for this title is their dedication to the written word. Jewish beliefs are founded in a library of their own. It goes something like this: the Torah is the whole body of Jewish religious literature including the scriptures, the Talmud, etc. The Talmud is a collection of writings constituting Jewish civil and religious law; the Mishnah is the first part of the Talmud containing traditional oral interpretations of scriptural ordinances compiled by rabbis about AD 200. Its code is divided into 6 major units and 63 minor ones. The Gemara is the second and supplemental part of the Talmud providing a commentary on the first (Goldy, 1990). And there is more.

The Old Testament of the Bible comprises a history of the Jewish nation, and consists of 39 books including the Five Books of Moses (the Pentateuch), the Books of Poetry, the Books of History, and the

Major and Minor Prophets. This constitutes the scriptures for the Hebrews. The other half of the Bible, The New Testament, consists of 27 books including the four Gospels, the Book of Acts, the Epistles and the Revelation. Christianity essentially derives its beliefs from the New Testament. Jews reject the New Testament.

About 400 years passed between the writing of the two testaments, but it would be erroneous to suggest that no literature was produced during that time. Best known of the writings during the intervening period are the Apocryphal Gospels, some of which are included in the Roman Catholic version of the Bible, but not the Protestant Bible. Although the ecumenical Council of Carthage in AD 397 gave the Apocryphal Gospels formal standing, they were still not accepted by many authorities. Themes of these writings suggest religious passion and the pathos of martyrdom, the intense devotion to the law and worship of Jehovah, a commentary on persecution by heathen nations, and descriptions of efforts at compromise made by devoted followers of the faith (Dana, 1951).

Practices

In the generation preceding the birth of Jesus, the Jewish teacher Hillel was challenged by an impudent heathen to state the essence of Judaism while standing on one foot. With exemplary patience, Hillel replied, "What is hateful to you, do not do to your fellow. All the rest is commentary; go, learn it" (Gittelsohn, 1978). Jesus Himself, perhaps reflecting his rabbinical training, made a similar statement when he stated in reply to a question by a Sadducee expert in the law:

> Love the Lord your God with all your heart and with all your soul and with all your mind. This is the first and greatest commandment. And the second is like it: Love your neighbor as yourself. All the Law and the Prophets hang on these two commandments (Matt. 22:37-40).

It may be tempting to think of living out these precepts through individual judgment and brotherly love, but this is not the case for the orthodox Jew. The cycle of holiness for such a person begins upon awakening. It consists of putting on a yarmulke (Jewish skullcap), ceremonious washing and recitation of prayers. These may be recited alone or with the community at morning worship. All males 13 years and over are required to pray 3 times daily, and to wear phylacteries during morning service. Phylacteries are ritual prayer boxes containing biblical quotations that are secured to the forehead and customarily affixed to the left arm by leather straps (Fishbane, 1987). Thus the day goes by, chalking up a myriad of ritualistic enactments designed to fulfill one's obligations to the Almighty.

The religious obligations of being a Jew also include weekly requirements, yearly festivals and sacred days to honor. The annual Passover, for example, is a spring holiday celebrating the Exodus from

Egypt. The festival lasts eight days, during which Jews refrain from eating all unleavened foods and products. A special ritual meal (called *seder*) is prepared, and a traditional narrative (called the *Haggadah*), supplemented by hymns and songs marks the event. The life cycle has similar rites of passage with complex requirements concerning birth, marriage and death. On the eighth day following birth the ceremony of circumcision is held for every male child. This surgery is accompanied by a religious rite symbolizing the entrance of the child into the covenant which God established with Abraham (Gittelsohn, 1978).

Death is considered the liminal moment *par excellence*, dramatizing the ultimate changes of status for the deceased and relatives, and because the occasion of death is one of great anxiety and disrupts social patterns, all the procedures connected with the event are carefully regulated according to fixed custom. Burial usually takes place within three days and "watchers" stay with the deceased and recite psalms. After burial a second stage of mourning begins, and those who wish to console the bereaved will visit their homes and offer solace and prayers (Fishbane, 1987).

Peculiarities

It might be offensive to orthodox Jews to suggest it, but there are other religious or ethnocultural communities who also believe they are a covenant people. The Jewish covenant in Isaiah's text reads:

> I, the Lord, have called you in righteousness,
> I will take hold of your hand.
> I will keep you and will make you to be a
> covenant to the people
> and a light for the Gentiles,
> To open the eyes that are blind,
> To free captives from prison
> and to release from the dungeon
> those who sit in darkness (Isaiah 42:6-7).

The Christian Connection

It is somewhat paradoxical that a unique world religion, believed by its adherents to belong to an exclusive group of people, would birth a "dissident offshoot," which would become the world's most widespread faith, namely Christianity. Christians, of course, foster the fond notion that they have gained access to the Jewish-Divine covenant via the spiritual dimension because "there is no difference between Jew and Greek" (Romans 10:12). Ironically, today some Christians are committed to the salvation of the Jews. At one time Christians even arrogated to themselves the doctrine of the Chosen People – and for the longest time – the very name "Children of Israel." For example, in AD 1095 Pope Urban II, in his famous sermon at Clermont initiating the crusading era, referred to wresting the Holy

Land from the "wicked race of Turks," and said it should be under Christian control. Not only did Christians consider themselves to be the chosen tribe of Israel and deny the claim to Jews, they even espoused a kind of Christian Zionism. The crux of the matter was that Jews and Christians made what seemed to be irreconcilable claims to the same ancient Hebrew heritage (Schweitzer, 1971).

The early expansion of Christianity was tied in with the emergence of the new "congregation of Israel." The new church consisted of God-fearing Gentiles who remained apart from Jewry, and adherents considered themselves "children of Abraham by the spirit" (Kaufmann, 1988). The efforts of the Apostle Paul, a Jewish convert to Christianity, certainly boosted the fortunes of the new church, and his missionary zeal added a series of new depots to the faith.

The Historical Jesus

The central dispute between Christianity and Judaism concerns the person of Jesus Christ. The Christian believes that the Messianic hope has been fulfilled in Christ and the Jew rejects this claim. Many Jews still look for the coming Messiah (Kezwer, 1994). The Christian cannot understand how the Jew can reject the Messiah, and the Jew finds it difficult to comprehend why Gentiles would better understand this than members of their own community. The gap is wide. The Messianic hope has its ultimate foundation in the belief that Jehovah has set apart the Jews as a peculiar and choice possession; His covenant cannot be repudiated. For the Jew, the Covenant incorporates the expectation of the supreme elevation of the nation of Israel. The ushering in of the Messianic age will bring the subjection of the world to the rule of Jehovah and his anointed (Dana, 1951).

In a spiritual sense, Christians share the Messianic hope, some in a literal sense of commandeering an earthly kingdom as joint-heirs with Christ, and others spiritually, in the sense that the possible physical resurrection of Israel has no particular meaning. The bottom line is the acceptance or rejection of the Messiah.

There is another facet to the issue. To the faithful Jew, the country of Israel has always been a reality. This belief overshadows the notion of Judaism as primarily a metaphysical religion; it also has geographical dimensions. Further, Jews do not "believe" in God in the way that Christians generally use that word, but they are directly aware of the presence of God. A Jew may also be a nonbeliever and therefore he or she would experience the nonpresence of God. Beyond that, the Jew needs certainty and the physical presence of Israel, as a nation, helps provide it (Aron, 1971).

It is not easy to differentiate Christianity from its Judaistic roots. Though some might try to elaborate the differences between the two perspectives strictly in terms of law versus grace, the issue is more complex than that. The disciples of Jesus initially remained faithful to the Jewish law and rejected the more liberal views of St. Paul. Jesus accepted the oral law taught by the Pharisees who were the legal rulers of the day. He denounced them, however, for their persistence in always placing the law above human need. When Jesus healed an individual on the Sabbath day, for example, *He* was denounced for His unorthodox, non-legitimate, albeit humane action. He insisted, however, that human need should sometimes take precedence over the law.

The Holocaust

More than any other people the Jews have been a persecuted people. In Israel, to compare the tragedy of other peoples with Jewish tragedy is tantamount to anti-Semitism (Liebman and Cohen, 1990). The story of Jewish persecution is a central element in the Jewish tradition, one that obviously influences American and Israeli Jews to varying degrees. Persecution and compulsion did not descend on Israel in all its diaspora at any one period. Judaism, though often decimated, was never obliterated, and Jews have retained their religious identity in pagan as well as in Christian and Moslem countries. The tale of Jewish slavery in Egypt is recounted at the Passover, the most widely observed ritual practice in the Jewish calendar. Other religious holidays like Purim remind the Jews of the dangers that Gentiles pose to their security. The story of Purim tells how the king's adviser, Haman, tried to formalize a plan to obliterate the Jews in 473 BC (Liebman and Cohen, 1990). Some biblical authorities suggest that the actual events of the Book of Esther, which records the incident, may never have occurred, but in a metaphoric sense the story happened a countless number of times and keeps on happening to this very day (Schauss, 1962).

Specifically, who can disregard the effects of, or remain indifferent to, the Holocaust – or capture the magnitude of the anguish or the depth of horror felt by a survivor of the Holocaust? To the destroyers of the Jews these people were not seen as humans but as "devils" to be tortured and exterminated. To illustrate: the parallels between two periods of history bear this out and the behaviors of the two tyrants involved are too great to ignore. The Babylonian ruler, Nebuchadnezzar (604-522 BC) who subdued the Jewish nation, along with many others, tried completely to annihilate the nation. On a parallel note, nothing less would satisfy his 20th-century successor, Hitler, than the murder of every Jewish man, woman and child. The ancient oppressor bade representatives of every conquered nation bow down to his idol; thus he set the Jewish representatives free to testify against it as it were, thereby *creating* Jewish martyrdom. Similarly, nothing less would satisfy the *modern* Nebuchadnezzar than the murder of Jewish martyrdom (Fackenheim, 1987). Sandwiched in between the rule of these two dictators was the Maccabean period of the 2nd century BC which underscored the readiness of Jews to suffer martyrdom for their faith (Kaufmann, 1988). The hope of the Messiah became stronger as a result of this experience; the extent of human wickedness made the coming of the Messiah necessary (Fackenheim, 1987).

As a covenant people, the Jews certainly appear to have been given a difficult assignment; perhaps their rewards will be equally as great.

References

Aron, Robert. (1971). *The Jewish Jesus*. Maryknoll, NY: Orbis Books.

Dana, H.E. (1951). *The New Testament world* (3rd ed.). Nashville, TN: Broadman Press.

Douglas, J.D. (Ed.). (1991). *New 20th-century encyclopedia of religious knowledge* (2nd ed.). Grand Rapids, MI: Baker Bible House.

Fackenheim, Emil L. (1987). *What is Judaism? An interpretation for the present age*. New York: Collier Books.

Fishbane, Michael A. (1987). *Judaism: Revelation and traditions*. San Francisco: Harper Collins.

Gittelsohn, Roland B. (1978). *The modern meaning of Judaism*. New York: Collins.

Goldy, Robert G. (1990). *The emergence of Jewish theology in America*. Bloomington, IN: Indiana University Press.

Goodman, Saul L. (Ed.). (1976). *The faith of secular Jews*. New York: Ktav Publishing House, Inc.

Kaufmann, Yehezkel. (1988). *Christianity and Judaism: Two covenants* (C.W. Efroymson, Trans.). Jerusalem: The Magnus Press, The Hebrew University.

Kezwer, Gil. (1994). Shalom, bonjour. *Canadian Geographic, 114*(4), pp. 54-64.

Liebman, Charles S. & Cohen, Steven M. (1990). *Two worlds of Judaism: The Israeli and American experiences*. New Haven: Yale University Press.

Meyer, Michael A. (1967). *The origins of the modern Jews*. Detroit, MI: Wayne State University Press.

Schauss, Hayyim. (1962). *The Jewish festivals: History and observance*. New York: Schocken Books.

Schweitzer, Frederick M. (1971). *A history of the Jews since the first century A.D.* New York: The Macmillan Company.

Vilnay, Zev. (1979). *The guide to Israel*. Jerusalem: Daf-Chen Press.

11

Sikhs

The Sikh faith encompasses a number of integrated elements – religious, cultural and geographic. The Sikhs have tried hard to maintain their identity both in India, where they originated, and in North America where many of them have emigrated. The Sikhs would probably label their culture as "Indian," thereby identifying with the land of their origins. To be specific, the Sikh faith originated in the Punjab, a northern Province of India. Currently the Sikhs are involved in trying to have the government of India recognize the Punjab as an independent Sikh state (Johnston, 1988).

Most Sikhs live in the Punjab – about 14 million – and they comprise about two percent of India's population. About one million Sikhs live elsewhere. Of the Canadian population of 200 000, almost half live in British Columbia. The City of Vancouver is home to about 30 000 Punjabis, including Sikhs.

The first group of Sikhs came to Canada in 1897 and by 1907 a total of 2 600 had arrived in Canada. The first immigrants worked in lumber mills and did roadwork, but later, as they grew accustomed to Canadian ways, they intensified their cultural maintenance efforts and made inroads into other sectors of the business world.

Pedigree

Essentially, outsiders see Sikhs as adherents to the culture of India. Religiously, their heritage combines two Indian religions – Hindu and Muslim – even though most Sikhs would probably object to the suggestion that their predecessors tried formally to reconcile elements of the two faiths. According to the devout, Sikhism just happened. The religion does hold common beliefs with both of its parent faiths, but there are also aspects of both Hinduism and Islam which Sikhs reject.

Sikh objections to Hinduism include belief in the caste system which, Sikhs say, projects the notion that some people are better than others. Historically, at least, Hindus believed that humans could be categorized as to their importance in the world, and members of the Brahman class were superior to all others. At the bottom of the various lower levels of the system were the outcasts or untouchables. At the time of Sikh beginnings, in the early stages of the 16th century, about one-sixth of India's population were untouchables. The Sikh gurus postulated that all people are equally important in the scheme of things, and they rejected the doctrine of reincarnation which they saw as a placating concept to keep the lower castes in their place. A related Sikh belief is that no one form of religion is better than any other. All religions are equally good, with the exception of those which regard one person as more important than another (G. Singh, 1992, 7).

It was the vision of the third Sikh Guru that encouraged the abolishment of the Hindu practice of Purdah, which required women to wear a veil in public, and the practice of Sati, which involved the self-immolation by women upon the death of their husbands. The Sikhs found this practice detestable (Johar, 1988). Since the 16th century Sikhs have regarded women as equal with men and they are to be treated accordingly.

Another Sikh challenge has been to work out amicable relations with the dominating religions of Hinduism and Islam. Relations between Hindus and Muslims in the 16th century were not cordial. The Muslims, in districts where they ruled, addressed Hindus as non-believers, and did not allow them to have access to the same opportunities as their own people. In fact, Muslims considered it a "sacred" act to harass and mistreat Hindus, even if by force. The Hindus, in turn, called Muslims foreigners. Into this dualism of belief systems, Guru Nanak, the originator of Sikhism, came with his message of equality, peace and democracy.

The Vision

When Guru Nanak began his work he had no intention of beginning a new religion, even though he was bothered by some of the foibles of both Hinduism and Islam. His initial consultations with his followers comprised an informal fellowship of believers. These meetings gradually developed a more formal structure as the decades unfolded. Religious persecution eventually influenced a more fervent stance on the part of the membership and spurred on the formation of a militant Indian freedom movement. Although North American Sikhs see themselves primarily as a religious body, they have a history of political militancy which reached its full fruition at the time of their tenth and last leader (guru). Most orthodox Sikhs today try to distance themselves from acts of political extremism and violence.

Guru Nanak ushered in the Sikh faith premised on a single belief – there is one God only. He questioned the idea of there being different names for Supreme Gods – Vishnu, Brahma or Shiva for the Hindus and Allah for the Muslims, and argued that people should not be called nonbelievers just because they call God by a different name. It was this observation, accompanied by practices which the leading religious officials of the day conceived of as heresy, that launched the birth of Sikhism.

Guru Nanak was born on 15 April 1469. His father, Kalyan Chand (sometimes shortened by his biographers to "Kala"), was the revenue official for the village of Chukarkana. The family priest, who came to cast the child's horoscope, told Kala that his son would "sit under canopy, and both Hindus and Turks would pay him reverence" (H. Singh, 1983, 13). As a child Nanak found friends among both Hindus and Muslims. At the age of seven, he surprised his teacher by writing a poem in Punjabi posing the question, "who is truly learned?" At age 11 he was given the sacrificial cord which signified that he belonged to a high caste, and an appropriate ceremony was observed.

When Nanak was 27 years old, he heard the call of God. He travelled to the four corners of India and beyond, and visited the sacred places of the Hindus, Muslims and Buddhists. After holding discussions with men and women of various nations, religions and creeds, he publicly denounced the caste system and the futility of idol worship. When his ideas had incubated for 24 years he began to proclaim that mutual regard and respect among all peoples comprise the only foundation for a true religion. For him, religious pluralism was a fact of life (Neufeldt, 1987, 269). The right to life, the right to equality and the right to worship are God-given gifts to all (G. Singh, 1992, 8). The simple principles which he elaborated and which he adjured his followers to adopt included:

> 1) practice love, not hollow rituals; 2) deeds alone are valued, not empty words; 3) live honestly; 4) physical renunciation is of no value; and, 5) service is the only form of true worship (Johar, 1977).

When his gospel became formalized, Guru Nanak set about establishing congregations. A congregation (Sangat) was a formalized worship centre where singing and preaching occurred. One person was appointed to take charge of the service. These meetings were sponsored so that everyone, regardless of caste or former religious allegiance could worship together. He also initiated the practice of "Pangat" which involved the sitting together of all worshippers in a common meal. This practice continues in Sikh congregations to this day.

After visiting the high places of religion in Indian and Arabian countries, Guru Nanak spent about 18 years in a small village named Kartarpur (now in Pakistan), which he built with the help of his father-in-law and his disciples. He was revered by his followers, Muslim and Hindu alike. Before he passed away he appointed Bhai Lehna as the second Guru and re-named him Guru Angad Dev.

Passing the Mantle

The *second* guru, Angad Dev (1504-1552), was the son of a shopkeeper. After hearing Guru Nanak preach Angad Dev knew what he wanted to do with the rest of his life. In 1532 he handed the reins of his business over to his nephew and made him head of the family. He moved to Karparpur so he could study the faith in more depth. After seven years of study he was named the second Guru and relocated to his home area at Khadur Sahib to establish a Sikh centre there. One of his major contributions was to develop and teach the Gurmukhi script in which the hymns of the faith were written. This was the beginning of the religious literature for the Sikhs. He also developed the free community kitchen, started by his predecessor, and insisted that food be furnished free of charge to all who came to worship, regardless of their caste, class or race – rich and poor alike. Through the work of Guru Angad, Sikhism became a populist movement. Before his death he named Baba Amar Das (or Amardas), then aged 73, and about 25 years older than himself, to be his successor.

The *third* guru, Guru Amardas (1479-1574), was appointed to his role at the age of 73 and served for 22 years. During that time, however, he added structure to the Sikh movement by establishing 22 preaching centres called "Manjis," and assigning men *or* women to head them. In one instance a husband and wife team headed a Manjis (G. Singh, 1992, 9). He introduced a series of reforms in keeping with the growing crescendo of the Sikh movement, particularly elevating the position of women. He established the concept of the common well with steps leading to the bottom of the well. He then welcomed everyone to use the water and stressed that everyone should engage in the simple act of getting water in the same way. He made Pangat (the common meal) a requirement for assembly, insisting that when people eat together they also bond. It was his position that the untouchable class would not be seen to be abolished except through some direct and visible (and compulsory) means. Some high caste believers, including the emperor, objected to forced integration at worship and decided to harass the guru. After listening to the guru's logic, however, the emperor became convinced of the guru's wisdom and changed his ways. The emperor then offered to allocate state funds to help finance the costs of the community kitchen but the guru refused. He believed that voluntary contributions alone should fund the service (G. Singh, 1992, 10).

Amardas' reforms effected major changes in Indian culture. Before his death he obtained a piece of land on which he envisaged the establishment of a headquarters for the Sikh movement with a temple for worship located in the centre of a pool. The temple was to be a place where God's virtues were to be preached and sung. Before his death he completed plans for the Golden Temple at Amritsar, as it is now known, and named a successor.

The *fourth* guru, Guru Ramdas (1534-1581), oversaw the establishment of the foundation of the Golden Temple at Amritsar (which means "pool of Nector") in 1577, just three years after he took office. His ministry was basically taken up with the construction of the temple, which was completed through volunteer labor. He also supervised the construction of nearby dwellings, which at first were built of clay and later of bricks. He envisaged that a great pool would be dug around the temple to demonstrate an openness to all people. Before his death he named his son, Arjan, as successor.

The *fifth* guru, Guru Arjan (1563-1606), saw the completion of the Golden Temple. The foundation stone of the Harimandar, the sanctum sanitorium in the centre of the pool, was laid in 1589. The temple itself was built with four doors, facing in the four directions to signify that people from all parts of the world were welcome to come and worship. As the work neared completion a famine occurred in the region and an epidemic of smallpox broke out. The guru turned his attention to caring for the sick, touring surrounding areas and offering words of encouragement and hope.

In summing up Guru Arjan's contributions one would have to include the completion of the temple as a central place of worship, and the assembly and formalization of the Sikh scriptures. These include the writings of holy men from all over India, including Muslim and Hindu, plus those of previous gurus. He was careful to include writings from individuals representing all castes as well. The criterion for including a work was simply that it seem to be from God. The guru accepted all prevailing names for God as equally valid, and promoted the idea that all languages were valid in offering praise to God.

Guru Arjan became the first martyr of the Sikhs, and his death marked a turning point for the movement. He was tortured to death by orders of the Muslim emperor, Jahangir, on 30 May 1606, and was succeeded by his son.

The *sixth* guru, Guru Hargobind (1595-1644), led his people in a martial turn after the death of his father. Though his followers were pacifists, he began to advocate the idea that they stand against injustice and tyranny, even if it involved military action. He took it upon himself to wear two swords which were regarded as symbols of spiritual as well as temporal vestiture. Though he did not advocate violence, he did signal to state rulers that the Sikhs would defend themselves if unjustly attacked.

The Sikh movement continued to expand with the death of their martyr, Guru Arjan, and the military emphasis added by Hargobind seemed to provide an element of security in the minds of the adherents. The Muslim leader, Emperor Jahangir, had the guru arrested and placed in Gwalior, far away from the Punjab. A mass appeal to the emperor motivated him to release the guru, but Hargobind refused to leave his prison unless some 52 princes who were incarcerated with him were also freed. The emperor recanted, and let the guru and the princes go; then he subtly arranged for an attack on the guru but the Sikh forces ably defended the life of their leader.

Guru Hargobind never returned to Amritsar after his arrest and neither did any of his four successors. Instead, he established a centre at Kiratpur, a long distance from the Muslim areas of influence, and near the Himalayas. Before his death in 1644 he appointed his grandson, Har Rai, to be his successor.

Guru Har Rai (1630-1661), was the *seventh* leader of the Sikh faith and became known as the tender-hearted guru (Pashaura Singh). Although he never fought in any battles, he kept a force of 2 000 horsemen at his disposal. During his ministry the throne of Delhi was taken by Aurangzeb, who in an effort to show his military strength, executed his own brothers, arrested his father and then turned on the various religious movements (G. Singh, 1992, 15). He began terrorizing the Sikhs in Punjab, ordering many tortures and killings. Finally, he sent for the guru, but Har Rai mistrusted Aurangzeb and instead sent his son, Ram Rai, to see the emperor. Apparently the two attained a mutual rapport to the extent that Ram Rai's father, Guru Har Rai, thought that his son, Ram Rai, had misrepresented the Sikh teachings. He thus excommunicated his son and forbad his disciples to have anything to do with him. Before his death, Guru Har Rai appointed his younger son, Harkrishan to be his successor. Thus the emperor's plan to discredit Sikhism failed. (G. Singh, 1992, 1). Later on, however, Ram Rai, became the leader of a smaller sect of the Sikhs.

Guru Harkrishan (1656-1664) became the *eighth* guru, even though he was only five years old at the time. When he heard of the appointment, Emperor Aurangzeb invited the new guru to Delhi. His plan was to make the visit look like the guru was submitting to the emperor. The emperor's messenger, however, was a devoted Sikh, and intervened. Though the guru was only a young child he was made to understand the nature of the proposed visit and he acted accordingly. When he arrived at the quarters assigned him by the emperor, the guru refused to go to the palace. The emperor was naturally miffed by the refusal, but he tried to act as though nothing unusual had happened. He stated publicly that the guru, who was only a child, had come to the palace to play with his son. He then sent his son to meet the guru.

A smallpox epidemic took the life of the young guru, but on his sick-bed he uttered words which were interpreted to mean that he was appointing his grandfather's brother, Teg Bahadur, as the next leader. This appointment was delayed to frustrate Emperor Aurangzeb, and though the emperor tried to thrust Ram Rai upon the Sikhs as their next leader, the people failed to respond. In addition, several relatives of the guru tried to draw attention to themselves in such a way as to be construed as successors to Harkrishan. When their campaigns failed, Guru Teg Bahadur, took office and rallied the people. An attempted assassination on his life failed.

As the *ninth* guru, Teg Bahadur (1621-1675), faced the difficult task of keeping a hostile national government at bay. He toured the eastern regions of the Indian subcontinent and preached a gospel of reconciliation. He settled his headquarters at Anandpur Sahib, married and had a son. When he heard about the emperor's campaign to convert Hindus to Islam he sent a message to the emperor suggesting that the latter concentrate on converting the leaders and the people would follow. In the meantime a delegation of Hindus approached the guru and asked for his protection against the emperor. They pointed out that their people had previously received such protection at the hands of the sixth guru and asked him to perpetuate that practice. He encouraged the people to stand firm in their faith and never to give up hope. In the meantime the emperor grew angry about the guru's suggestion about converting leaders instead of followers and ordered the arrest of the guru.

The martyrdom of Guru Teg Bahadur in 1675 was staged by the emperor as a public display of his own importance. He ordered the beheading of the guru, an event which was watched by thousands of the citizens of Delhi. Many of the guru's followers were commanded to renounce their faith and when they refused to do so, they were tortured to death. The years that followed caused a wave of intense disappointment and frustration in the Sikh community which was relieved only by the eventual defeat and death of Emperor Aurangzeb in 1707.

The *tenth and last* guru, Gobind Singh (1666-1708), was only nine years old when his father died, and he was delegated to assume the responsibilities of that office. The future of the Sikh movement was uncertain after the death of the emperor, and no one knew what the attitude of his successor might be. Some of the new guru's followers were given training in self-protection and they looked to the guru for direction against almost inevitable persecution. The guru stated: "when all peaceful methods fail to change the mind of the wicked, it is justified to pick up the sword to save one's own honor" (G. Singh, 1992, 18).

Perhaps it was the fearless and resolving tone of the guru's words that deflected confrontation, and the guru went about his ministry among the common people. He engaged the services of 50 scholars to translate Sikh classical literature into Punjabi. These scriptures, as they came to be known, comprise writings from Muslim, Hindu and other sources. Guru Gobind disagreed with the Hindu notion that certain Muslim writings should be avoided because of their origins. He wanted to show his disciples that there was no place for such narrow thinking in his philosophy, and *any* saintly person belonging to *any* religion is worthy of respect (Johar, 1988). Subsequently the scriptures became a vehicle for determining Divine guidance for the believer.

Guru Gobind Singh laid great emphasis on the development of the individual. Individuals together constitute society. If individuals experience success or failure, the community gains or suffers as well.

Individuals have a two-fold responsibility to work not only for their uplifting but also for the good of the community as a whole. Basic to this two-fold development are the practice of such values as truthfulness, justice, generosity, detachment and discipline (Mansukhani, 1976).

Political Pressures

In 1704, Anandpur Sahib was surrounded by the joint forces of the Delhi emperor, the enemy rajas and the governors of Lahore and Sirhind. After several months of failure the leaders asked the guru to leave the town and preach elsewhere. He was promised safe passage and his captors hoped that if he left they could claim at least a moral victory. When the guru and his men left they were attacked by the combined forces but they managed to escape. The guru placed his ceremonial plume on one of his followers who was then killed by the enemy. The enemy thought they had killed the guru who really escaped (G. Singh, 1992, 21). The guru's two older sons, Ajit Singh and Jujhar Singh, and 30 Sikh soldiers were killed. The guru's wife and two younger sons were caught by the enemy and brought to Sirhind where efforts were made to convert the two children. When these efforts failed the boys were put to death.

Eventually Emperor Aurangzeb discovered that Guru Singh had escaped. The guru sent the emperor a letter pointing out that the emperor's actions would eventually be punished, and the Sikh faith would never be stamped out. Aurangzeb apologized for his actions, but he died before he had opportunity to meet with the guru. After his death his sons fought over the throne, and the guru sided with the oldest son, Bahadur Shah, and provided him with military aid. He subsequently became the Emperor of India. The new emperor promised to punish those who had previously sought to kill the guru and eradicate Sikhism, but he failed to keep his promise. The guru therefore assigned a man named Banda Singh Bahabur to go to Punjab and punish the guilty parties. Shortly after Banda Singh's departure for Punjab, the guru was fatally attacked by assassins. In the meantime, having installed the holy scriptures as the official source of leadership and inspiration, there was no concern about naming a successor. He bequeathed his mission to his followers in a public ceremony and named his corporate successor, Guru Khalsa Panth. The believers were now corporately the gurus of the Sikh faith. Some observers have called this the most significant development in all of Sikh history (P. Singh, n.d., 3).

The People as Guru

In 1699, at a gathering called by Guru Gobind Singh, he asked for a faithful volunteer to give his head (be beheaded) for the cause, and when an individual came forward, the guru took him to a tent and returned a little later with a blood-stained sword. Many of his congregation, assuming the worst, and fearing that the guru had gone mad, fled from the scene. Without telling his people that the blood was from a slaughtered goat, and as a further test of faith, the guru asked for another volunteer and then for three more. When the fifth one had served his purpose, all five were returned alive to the people (G. Singh, 1990, 286). The guru then prepared a special drink called "Amrit," and the five were asked to participate in a show of consensus and equality. The five volunteers were named, "the five beloved ones," and were given the last name of Singh. After that, all present were asked to drink the Amrit and become one with the movement.

Amrit is a drink of water sweetened with sugar and blessed by stirring it with the double-edged sword. Its enactment is parallel to baptism in other religions. The guru baptized the five beloved ones, and then they in turn baptized the guru. This democratic practice established once and for all the principle of spiritual equality in the faith (Mansukhani, 1976). From that time, all formal baptized members of the Sikh faith take the last name of Singh. In baptism they agree to abandon their previous religion and the practice of all rituals and to denounce the caste system. They are then known as Khalsa or Panth. Every Sikh has the authority to bring in new initiates by serving and presiding over their participation in Amrit.

The Struggle for Unity

Like most other religious communities, Sikh have many subdivisions among them. Perhaps the most publicized division is between baptized (Khalsa) and non-baptized Sikhs (Glazer, 1980; McLeod, 1989). For the Khalsa, there is only one interpretation. While they tolerate and respect other religions, their patience is thin when it comes to distinguishing among their own numbers. They vehemently take issue with the statement that whereas all Khalsa are Sikhs, not all Sikhs are Khalsa. But there *are* many other Sikh sects, like the Udasi, for example, who are the followers of the teachings of the elder son of Guru Nanak, Sri Chand. This group controlled the Sikh shrines and temples in the Punjab until the 1920s (Jain, 1990).

Baptized Sikhs say that they are under obligation to wear the five "K's" but their unbaptized colleagues proffer a number of arguments to the contrary. They claim that the wearing of the five "K's" was a temporary commandment of the tenth guru, and it is no longer applicable today. Others claim that conformity to any kind of external form of appearance would be contrary to the teachings of the gurus. After all, religiosity or piousness is not measured by such temporal means. Spirituality is a condition of the heart. Still others point out that the first guru, Guru Nanak, himself questioned the usefulness of particular outward appearance from the conviction that one does not become a better person through external garb (Jain, 1990). Perhaps the bottom line answer to the question of who is a Sikh emanates from their own history. Guru Nanak and his early successors left no doubt as to which of the fundamental beliefs was most important, namely the doctrine of the Divine Name. The Divine Name is the substance of truth and the one assured means of liberation from the cycle of transmigration (McLeod, 1989). Essentially, this requirement means making a statement of awareness of the existence of the Almighty God; beyond that, and subject to interpretation, the doctrine loses its apparent simplicity.

Principles & Precepts

While many religions have at their basis a theological speculation about creation, the Sikhs have no such interpretation. The commandments of their faith are practical, and target a down-to-earth application.

A Practical Theology

First and foremost, the primary criterion to being a faithful Sikh is to earn a livelihood through hard labor and honest means. Sikhs should not be parasites on society; they should seek to be gainfully employed. Those who do not work obviously rely on others to feed them, and this is not acceptable. Above all, whatever kind of vocation is assumed, the underlying principle is that wages be earned through honest means, and not through exploitation or deception.

Second, Sikhs are to keep in touch with the Divine. This is primarily done through attitude and meditation. The only way to God is through love. This universal love must embrace the entire creation of God, and must extend to every living creature. "Those who love God's creation are merged in the Lord" (Mansukhani, 1976, 39). A worshipful stance implies a constant awareness that God is both Creator and companion. He provides guidance to those who seek Him. It is also a form of worship. In one's search for spiritual growth it is possible to discover the will of God for one's life. Since all of life and, in fact, the whole world is in God's hands, it behooves believers to discover the truths that pertain to their own personal journey and thus fulfill the will of God for them. In short, individuals are the executors of His will.

Meditation is not accomplished through any specific technique, and a variety of means are quite effective – reciting the scriptures, singing, sitting in a quiet place or simply thinking about one's relationship to God. Meditation, therefore, is not an art, but an attitude.

Third, is the guru's order to assume responsibility for others. This begins with wishing others well and continues to the logical projection of being willing to give one's life for the sake of others. Sikhs are to regard all people as equals. They are expected to share their homes and their food with those in need. They are to help the wounded in battle, regardless of their military affiliation.

Sikhs are commanded to share with others on the grounds that all human beings are members of a greater family. This family includes all races, religions and nations. Sharing the fruits of one's labor is a responsibility and must not be done through pride or as a means of drawing attention to oneself. To provide for others, particularly those with less means, is a "family" responsibility in the same way that a parent takes care of a young child. This implies the kinship of all people.

It may be a moot point, but some analysts have questioned the extent of Sikh commitment to the principle of equality of all peoples. Sikhs claim that the founders of their faith laid the foundation for a new type of society in India, then quite foreign to her (Gill, 1975). Still, it should be noted that on the issue of caste, for example, some discrepancy between stated goals and practice appear obvious. Though the notion of caste was denounced by the various gurus, its implementation was not simply straightforward. Interestingly, all ten gurus came from the mercantile caste which had high status in Punjabi society. This fact is noted with some regret even by Sikhs today, and descendants of lower castes often bewail the fact that no lower caste individuals ever became gurus. An even more perturbing note, however, is the suggestion that all of the gurus arranged the marriages of their own children with members of their same caste. (McLeod, 1976). A way out of this dilemma, perhaps, is to suggest that the matter of caste was not important to the gurus, and the above occurrences may simply have been coincidental.

Fourth, is the command to moral living. Married Sikhs are to be faithful to their partners and not commit adultery. In addition, moral living has application to other facets of living as well; Sikhs are forbidden to lie, steal, cheat, or criticize others unjustly. They are not allowed to smoke, drink or use intoxicating drugs. There is some debate about meat-eating among orthodox Sikhs. Some suggest that Sikhs should be strict vegetarians and even avoid eggs. Sikhs who avoid beef but eat other meat are often influenced by the Hindu reverence for the cow. Those who do eat meat, however, usually obey the command not to partake of "Kutha" meat, that is, meat which has been slaughtered by involving Muslim religious rituals. The Muslims call the meat, "Halal" (G. Singh, 1992, 33).

Fifth and finally, Sikhs are to avoid the worship of idols or pictures and they are to be knowledgeable of the Sikh scriptures (Guru Granth Sahib). The formal regulations regarding the scriptures are as follows. First, during the day the scriptures are kept at the altar of the temple under a canopy. Before they are read, a whisk (or wand) is waved over the scriptures as an expression of respect for royalty or Divinity. The temple priest is to keep the scriptures in a separate room during the night. Early in the morning the priest will remove the scriptures from the separate room and install the book under the canopy. There he will wave the whisk and arbitrarily leaf through the book in an attempt to identify a scriptural thought for the day. The passage of scripture on which he places his finger becomes his spiritual theme for the day.

There are times in the year when the scriptures are read aloud in entirety and in a continuous fashion. Individual members of the congregation will take turns in reading for a few hours at a time and will be relieved by others throughout the day.

Baptized Sikhs may choose to keep a copy of the scriptures or a portion of the scriptures in their homes. If they do so, the same rules apply. The scriptures are to be housed in a separate room (a closet will do) and they are to be put away at the end of the day and consulted early in the morning for a spiritual thought. The daily recitation of a passage of scripture will offer a spiritual context to one's thoughts and actions and remind the believer to avoid forbidden and undesirable behaviors.

When Sikhs enter their temples they take off their shoes and wear a headcovering. They show reverence to the scriptures by standing before the canopy under which the scriptures are placed and bowing their heads to the ground. Then they take their place in the congregation, and the service, led by an ordained priest, commences. There is singing, prayers and a sermon. Afterwards a common fellowship meal will be served, usually downstairs, and everyone is welcome to participate. Non-Sikhs are always welcome at Sikh worship services, and from time to time curious visitors from various religious persuasions have availed themselves of the opportunity.

The transfer of the office of guru to the people included a corollary requirement, namely that of the "uniform of the believer," which consists of the five "K's." Few religious forms of attire have caused as much controversy in North America. The five symbols include:

1. *Kesh* or uncut hair, which represents simplicity of life, saintliness, wisdom and devotion to God. It is practiced as a symbol of purity.

2. *Kanga,* is a wooden comb designed to keep the hair tidy. This was initiated in opposition to the recluses who allowed their hair to become matted in defiance to the world. Use of the comb also implies physical and mental cleanliness. The old (hair) is weeded out and replaced with the new. Spiritually, this means that believers need constantly to comb their minds inwardly and keep them free from impurities.

3. *Kara,* is a steel bracelet which is a symbol of belonging to the Guru. It is an ethical symbol of responsibility. It acts as a handcuff to remind the believer not to misuse the hands to commit sin.

4. *Kirpan,* is the sword of knowledge and to wear it is to signify that the individual has used it to curb the root of personal ego. The sword also represents the Sovereign power of God who controls the destiny of the world. It is a symbol of self-respect and honor.

5. *Kachh,* is white underwear consisting of short breeches, a symbol of purity in morality, and a check against extra-marital relations (Sikh Community of Calgary, 1986).

For a century after the death of Guru Gobind Singh, the Sikhs suffered persecution from the new Indian rulers, the Mughals. At the end of the 18th century the Sikhs succeeded in establishing rule in the Punjab and began a campaign to unify the country. Maharja Ranjit Singh (1780-1839), served as the Sikh sovereign and presided over part of a 40 year Sikh reign which ended with the Anglo-Sikh War of 1848-1849.

The Growing Edge

Sikhs in Canada are active in carving out a niche for themselves in the various sectors of society. Many operate successful businesses and their cultural organizations are thriving. New temples are being constructed and several heritage langauge schools (which teach the Punjabi language) are thriving. Sikhs are entering the political scene and gaining a foothold in other areas as well. In the meantime, the Sikh community is also very much under the watchful eye of the media and the Canadian Intelligence Service. The publicity surrounding the Air India disaster in June 1985 and the shooting of a Punjabi cabinet minister who was attending a family wedding on Vancouver Island in May 1986, and other recent events have hurt the image of the Sikhs (Johnston, 1988).

Like other religious or ethnic communities, the Sikhs have their share of internal disagreements. A series of articles in a 1992 issue of the *World Sikh Journal* are concerned with a misrepresentation of Sikh beliefs in a doctoral dissertation written by S. Pashaura Singh at the University of Toronto. Singh, a former temple priest in Calgary, wrote a thesis entitled, "The Text and Meaning of Adi Granth," that consisted of an analysis of two documents which, according to some Sikh scholars, have dubious origins (Mann, 1992, 29). Having read the manuscript, members of the national Shiromani Gurdwara Parbandhak Committee, which is dedicated to promoting Sikh scholarship, demanded that Pashaura Singh appear before them in a hearing to defend his work. However, another writer in the same issue of the *World Sikh Journal* commendably noted that Singh was probably a well-intentioned man, dedicated to defining Sikh roots. Thus the Sikh community should not seek to make an example of him: "Let this matter not become like the Salman Rushdie [affair] for that does not become us" (I.J. Singh, 1992).

Internal disputes notwithstanding, Sikhs do not believe that their particular interpretation of faith constitutes a single path nor the only door of access to ultimate reality. In other words, God reveals Himself to mankind, in terms of the constitution and faculties of the human mind, and in accordance with the needs of the age. Religious dogma has little place in Sikhism; God is seen as possessing infinite attributes and aspects and no religion can claim to have the full and final cognition of God or of reality. God is perceived and experienced under such aspects as are relative to the endowments of the seeker (Ahluwalia, 1983).

On the positive side are favorable economic and political developments in the Punjab. These happenings serve as a special source of inspiration for the Sikhs – the goal of attaining national independence (Koehn, 1991). While this contributes toward a stronger Sikh identity, it also perpetuates the uniqueness and separateness of Sikhism in Canada. Any adversity faced by the Sikhs in Canada will bolster that reality and serve to illustrate one of the polarities of Canadian multiculturalism, that of being separate but (hopefully) equal.

Peculiarities

Many world communities who define socio-religious identity in terms of a geographic landspace are engaged in struggles to gain national independence. The Sikhs have such dreams for the Khalistan in the Punjab in India, and in the last two decades their struggle has frequently erupted in hostilities.

The New Nationalism

Under the leadership of the late Prime Minister Indira Gandhi, the Government of India made no attempt to assist the Sikh vision towards obtaining a separate national identity. Instead the government introduced a number of economic restrictions to the Punjab in an attempt to steer investments to poorer states (Koehn, 1991). The prime minister then ordered the destruction of the Golden Temple and justified the order on the basis that it was the only option left for her to get rid of the terrorist element in the Punjab. On 5 June 1984 the Golden Temple was attacked and by the next day 554 Sikh warriors lay dead and 121 wounded by Indian forces. The army casualties numbered 92 and 300 wounded. In addition the army captured 1 592 prisoners from the temple and 3 000 others from neighboring communities in the Punjab. Naval divers were employed to recover armaments and dead bodies from the sacred tank, and many priceless paintings were destroyed (G. Singh, 1990, 762-763). Since the Golden Temple represents the fountainhead of the Sikh faith (Anklesaria, 1984), its damage spurred efforts towards achieving the development of a separate Sikh state.

Reaction of Sikhs around the world towards the destruction of the temple was one of shock and horror. Interestingly, although 10-12 percent of the Indian army were Sikhs themselves, most of them remained faithful to the army. However, on 31 October 1984, Prime Minister Indira Gandhi was assassinated by two of her trusted Sikh bodyguards. In December of the same year, new elections were held (except in the Punjab), and Gandhi's son Rajiv was elected prime minister. After assuming office he made the situation in the Punjab a priority item and withdrew his troops in an effort to restore peace.

Since the destruction of the temple, the violent act of the state against the sacred temple has served to unify the various factions of Sikhism in the Punjab into a form of ethnic solidarity. They have also served to mobilize nationalistic dreams towards a conception of reality. Sikh patriots are now trying to influence the congress of India as well as to impact their economic oppressors (Koehn, 1991). In the meantime, life in the Punjab goes on at a relatively healthy pace. The annual agricultural output has been increasing, and the Punjab per capita income is the highest in India. The province continues to provide 60-65 percent of the wheat production of the country as well as vast crops of rice. Sikh leaders say that they hope the day will come when the Punjab will separate politics from religion so that the gospel of the gurus can flourish. When this occurs, perhaps attention can be paid to the economic distress of the underprivileged sections of society. This would be a fitting tribute to the original teachings of the gurus (G. Singh, 1990).

Encountering Prejudice

Despite the existence of many politically-framed statements to the contrary, prejudice towards certain groups in Canada is a stark reality. Sikhs, perhaps more than any other group besides Aboriginal peoples, have been targeted for such inhumane treatment. Foremost in the campaign to thwart Sikh assimilation is public antagonism towards the Sikh "uniform," particularly the practice that loyal Sikhs are not to cut their hair (Kesh) and they are required to carry a ceremonial sword (Kirpan). Growing long hair (including beards) necessitates the wearing of headgear like the turban which was long ago adopted by the Sikhs as a means of keeping their hair in place. A great public outcry was evidenced in Canada a few years ago when the Supreme Court of Canada handed down the decision that Sikhs would be permitted to wear their form of headgear as an approved part of the uniform of the Royal Canadian Mounted Police. A similar campaign was launched against younger Sikhs who wore small versions of the ceremonial sword to school. Opponents decried the kirpan as a dangerous weapon and demanded that it be banished from school premises.

It is difficult to understand why the Sikhs have had to be targets of such severe forms of public disapproval when it is primarily a question of differences in costume that sets them apart from the rest of society. For the most part, Sikhs live much like other Canadians. They are employed in traditional Canadian forms of business enterprises and in the workplace. They are good businessmen and work hard for their livelihood. They live in standard-type homes, engage in regular forms of socializing and, like other Canadians, attend the church of their choice. Sikh temples look little different from church buildings constructed by other faiths, and they tend to be very well maintained. Sikh organizations have contributed heavily towards Canadian national relief causes including Steve Fonyo's Miles for Millions, the Mexico Earthquake Relief, the Ethiopian Relief Fund and the Interfaith Food bank, to name a few. Still, in a survey conducted among Sikhs in Vancouver, 52 percent said that they had virtually no contact with other Canadians and only 10 percent said they had a lot (Johnston, 1988). The evidence is clear that Sikhs are often targets of a form of racism which is virtually without any justifiable foundation. It also tends to enlarge their social distance from other Canadians. The Canadian lack of acceptance of Sikhs originates from personal insecurity, jealousy and intolerance on the part of their critics. In Canada, it seems, too many of us still operate on the premise that differences in religious practice (including wearing apparel) are nationally threatening.

References

Anklesaria, Shahnaz. (1984). Fall-out of army action: A field report. *Economic and Political Weekly*, *19*(30), 1186-1188.

Ahluwalia, Jasbir Singh. (1983). *The sovereignty of the Sikh doctrine: Sikhism in the perspective of modern thought.* New Delhi: Bahri Publications.

Gill, Pritam Singh. (1975). *Heritage of the Sikh culture: Society, morality, art.* Jullundur, India: New Academic Publishing Co.

Glazer, Nathan. (1980). Toward a sociology of small ethnic groups, a discourse and discussion. *Canadian Ethnic Studies, XII*(2), 1-16.

Jain, Sushil. (1990). Sikh or Kahlsa? *Canadian Ethnic Studies, XXII*(2), 111-116.

Johar, Surinder Singh. (1977). *Handbook on Sikhism.* Delhi: Vivek Publishing Company.

Johar, Surinder Singh. (1988). *The Sikh religion.* Chandni Chowk, Delhi: National Book Shop.

Johnston, Hugh. (1988). The development of the Punjabi community in Vancouver since 1961. *Canadian Ethnic Studies, XX*(2), 1-19.

Koehn, Sharon D. (1991). Ethnic emergence and modernization: The Sikh case. *Canadian Ethnic Studies, XXIII*(2), 95-116.

Mann, Kharak Singh. (1992, fall/winter). GNDU manuscript 1245: A post 1606 collection. *World Sikh Journal, 12*, 29-34.

Mansukhani, Gobind Singh. (1976). *Guru Gobind Singh: His personality and achievement.* New Dehli: Hemkunt Press.

McLeod, W. H. (1976). *The evolution of the Sikh community*. Oxford: Clarendon Press.

McLeod, W. H. (1989). *Who is a Sikh? The problem of Sikh identity*. Oxford: Clarendon Press.

Neufeldt, R. W. (1987). The Sikh Response. In Harold Coward (Ed.), *Modern Indian responses to religious pluralism* (pp. 269-290). Albany, NY: State University of New York Press.

Sikh Community of Calgary. (1986). *Sikhs in the Canadian mosaic*. (Available from Sikh Community of Calgary, Alberta).

Singh, Gopal. (1990). *A history of the Sikh people, 1469-1988*. New Delhi, India: World Book Centre.

Singh, Gurbakhsh. (1992). *The Sikh faith*. Vancouver, BC: Canadian Sikh Study and Teaching Society.

Singh, Harbans. (1983). *The heritage of the Sikhs*. New Delhi, India: South Asia Books.

Singh, I. J. (1992, fall/winter). The test and meaning of the Adi Granth. *World Sikh Journal, 12*, 8-9.

Singh, Pashaura Bhai. (n.d.). *The Sikhs*. Calgary, AB: Guru Nanak Center, Sikh Society.

PART THREE

The Christian Cafeteria

The diversity within Christian groups is immense, and the differences emanate with regard to virtually every aspect of faith including theology and doctrine, governance, attitudes toward other groups and religious practice. The approaches of the various denominations also vary with regard to the amount and calibre of training required for clergy, concept of the Scriptures, explanations of spiritual gifts (healing, speaking in tongues, etc.), and attitudes toward other faiths and denominations.

Most of the major Christian denominations adhere to the common lectionary, although Baptists and Pentecostals generally reject its use. The larger church groups also require both university and seminary training for clergy, while evangelical groups often look for leaders who have been "called of God," with or without formal training of any kind. Fundamentalist groups and evangelicals are often open in their scorn for the major denominations, which are frequently referred to as being "part of the world" in sermons. Conservative denominations have little to do with the National Council of Churches or Interfaith movements such as the Canadian Christian Festival of Faith. In many instances they regard each other with suspicion and "sheep stealing" (the attempt to win members from other churches), is rampant.

The major Canadian denominations tend to be hierarchical or quasi-hierarchical in governance patterns and the relevant vocabulary includes such words as conference, diocese, presbytery or synod. Smaller, evangelical churches may utilize the office of "superintendent," but because of limited size and resultant familiarity, it is often difficult for these officers to function objectively in making administrative decisions.

The dualism in Canadian denominationalism between mainline and fundamentalist churches also features a middle ground occupied by churches with a heavy ethnic link. These include Christian Reformed Churches, Doukhobors, Anabaptist groups like Amish, Hutterites and Mennonites, Moravians and probably Quakers. Without at least a little analysis it is sometimes easy to confuse these groups with evangelicals, who are more readily identifiable by their zeal in seeking to attract new converts. These churches tend to be quite zealous about spreading their faith, and many of them take great delight in "winning souls" with previous connections to major Canadian denominations.

12

Christianity

The calendar used in North America commemorates the birth of a Jewish child who became the object of worship for the most widespread religion in the world – Christianity. Historical sources are in agreement that Jesus Christ did not deliberately start a religion. In fact, He spent most of His short lifetime wandering around His home area of Galilee with a small group of followers, questioning the relevancy and criticizing the inflexibility of the religion of His day. He also left no written works. What happened to religion (*His* religion) after Jesus died, as recorded in the New Testament, may not necessarily have met with His approval. It was the Apostle Paul, a convert to Christianity, who changed his name from Saul and devoted his energies to spreading the Gospel by establishing churches, who really organized Christianity. His letters to church leaders make up much of the New Testament and constitute the primary source for determining Christian doctrine.

Pedigree

During the 1st century when Christianity burst forth, opposition religious leaders of other belief systems, feeling somewhat flustered by its popularity, viciously attacked it. They reported that Christians were cannibals because they "ate the flesh of Christ in their Sacrament." The critics spoke of the oedipal immorality of the Christians, that is, the Christians apparently practiced incest at their worship services. They also tried to argue intellectually against Christianity by attacking the authority of the New Testament and indeed the whole Bible (Aland, 1985). Some of their arguments still sound quite contemporary.

The persecution of Christians began almost immediately after Christ's death. In the fourth chapter of the biblical Book of Acts, the apostles Peter and John were hauled up before the Jewish Sanhedrin and ordered to stop preaching. Similarly, in AD 41 Herod Agrippa ordered the death of James the brother of John and the arrest of the Apostle Peter. From AD 58-60 the Apostle Paul served a prison sentence aswell. However, despite heavy opposition, for the next four centuries, Christianity flourished. Most adherents were "ordinary people," the poor, the lowly, the undereducated and the politically powerless. This may be inferred from St. Paul's consolation to the Corinthian Church:

For consider your call, brethren; not many of you were wise according to worldly standards, not many were powerful, not many were of noble birth; but God chose what is foolish in the world to shame the wise. God chose what is weak in the world to shame the strong, God chose what is low and despised in the world, even things that are not, to bring to nothing things that are, so that no human being might boast in the presence of God (I Cor.1:26-29).

In its early development Christianity was centred in such cities as Jerusalem, Antioch, Ephesus, Corinth and Rome. It was a religion born of variety. Each church location was typical of a different aspect of Christianity, and, as may be judged from Paul's letters, each congregation struggled with varying kinds of problems and challenges. The church at Jerusalem reflected the historical development of Judaism; the church at Antioch represented Syrian Christianity; and the church at Ephesus represented the mysticism of the Phygians. The church at Corinth revealed the subtle activity of the Greek mind; and the Church at Rome manifested a penchant for discipline and legalism (Foakes-Jackson, 1898).

The political and social background of early Christianity is largely a Hellenistic product. Even within Palestine, the society in which Jesus and his followers lived was directly the result of contact with the outside world. We sometimes overlook the fact that Christianity originated within a "very religious" world, and it helps to keep in mind that the religions of the Roman Empire in the 1st century AD were not as secular as they are sometimes portrayed. The strength and extent of Judaism at that time, both in Palestine and in the Diaspora, is a well-known fact, but the Gentiles were hardly less religious in their own way than the Jews. Paganism, on the other hand, being less stipulative in membership, offered people the help of a different strata of worshipers. Religion was a subject of general interest and occupied a large place in the lives of ordinary folks. Thus, Christians, instead of being among the first advocates of religion to enter this territory, were really among the last (Case, 1960). From the start it appears that Christianity was not necessarily an innovator or liberator, but an interloper.

The Early Church Fathers

A number of names come to mind when the lineage of great ideas in developmental Christianity is traced: Justin Martyr, Clement of Alexandria, Ignatius of Antioch, Origen, Tertullian, Dionysius the Great, Cyprian of Cathage, and Irenaeus of Lyons (Cruttwell, 1971; Wagner, 1994) – familiar names to readers of church history. A brief glance at their importance to the cause shows clearly that all of the elements of theological wrangling – apologetics, polemics, attack and defence – were already in place. Sounds familiar, doesn't it?

Justin Martyr, though well educated in Greek philosophy, converted to Christianity, travelled widely preaching the Gospel and was eventually martyred. His *Apology*, written at Rome around AD 163 is the earliest defence of Christianity that has survived. Themes he addressed in his writings included refutation of criminal charges against Christians, a defence of Christianity against Judaism and the development of a philosophy of Christian religion.

Clement of Alexandria (AD 150-213) set out a creed for Christianity through a steady appeal to Scripture. He is remembered as an important witness to the virtual completion of the New Testament Canon. Similarly, Origin, who was a student of Clement of Alexandria, was responsible for setting out the Rule of Faith for Christianity by blending in a liberal dose of Platonism. He established that the only agent of redemption was the Son of God, who is the perfect image or reflection of the Eternal Father, though being distinct, derivative and subordinate.

Ignatius of Antioch (AD 30-109) was the third bishop of Syrian Antioch and is believed to have been martyred. Seven of his letters (epistles) are included with the writings of the church fathers, including Ephesians, Romans and Smyneans. Two frequent themes in his works are warnings against the doctrines of Docetism (the doctorine that Christ was too Divine to have suffered agony and death, i.e., he only seemed to) and a plea to respect the authority of the office of bishop in the local church.

Tertullian (AD 160-230) was a native of the Roman Province of Africa and of pagan parentage. Converted to Christianity, he read widely in law, literature and philosophy. Although somewhat inclined towards asceticism, he became known as the prosecutor of paganism.

Cyprian of Carthage (AD 200-258) is considered by many as the greatest churchman of the 3rd century. Born into a wealthy family, he was converted to an ascetic type of Christianity and later became Bishop of Carthage and head of the North African clergy. His writing themes include the theory and practice of ecclesiastical administration and discipline.

Dionysius the Great (AD 200-265) began as an unknown writer, and became the first Bishop of Athens and a martyr in Paris. For a thousand years, from AD 500 to 1500 he was the principal influence of Christian theology.

Finally, Irenaeus of Lyons (AD 130-190) bishop in Gaul, devoted his literary energies against paganism and heresy. His principal target was Gnosticism, and his writings were widely used by the early church and regarded as the fullest account of influential figures of the anteNicene Church.

The work of the early church fathers established the base on which the faith would be promulgated in the centuries that followed. From a conservative perspective, the principles which they endorsed and embellished with their commentaries included: (i) the Scriptures would be the ultimate authority for determining and stating truth; (ii) the Ultimate God created the cosmos and the cosmos is good; (iii) God made the cosmos through the Logos (the Word), who was active in creation and superior to all things in it; and, (iv) the authority of the Scriptures and the authority of the church are inseparable (Wagner, 1994). It did not take long before the latter statement grew to be a vital watershed in the development of great divergences in the early church.

Major Church Epochs

Christianity got a major boost after the Apostolic period with the conversion of the Roman Emperor Constantine in the 5th century. One of his major acts was to establish Christianity as the state religion. In AD 325 he issued a general exhortation to his subjects to embrace Christianity. Poor Constantine; he appeared not to have taken the human factor into consideration. He thought that a religion of brotherhood, love, understanding and forgiveness could be mandated, and he did everything he could to see that these virtues would be implemented. Almost indifferent to doctrinal differences, Constantine tried to settle the Donatist controversy by arbitration. He convened the Nicene Council for the adjudication of the controversy between Arius and Alexander, and even moved his capital city to the newly-constructed city of Constantinople or New Rome (Newman, 1953). Still, there are some who would say that Constantine actually set Christianity back by his actions; he should have let it loose to become itself. But wait, there's more. . . .

The coronation of Charlemagne in AD 800 paved the way for the idea of a Holy Roman Empire. Charlemagne liked the idea because he had designs of enlarging his empire through any means including marriage, alliance or conquest. Conquered peoples were required to join the church, and he also aided the church in its growth by organizational aid and endowments. The great dream came to an end in the reign of his successor, Louis the Pious, who placed his three sons in high office. When this plan did not work, Louis was forced to abdicate. In the middle of the 10th century, Otto the Great tried to revive the empire, but failed sadly. He ruled at a time when the investiture between religious leaders and civil rulers was being severely contested. This battle continued for many years.

In AD 1054 an event occurred that produced a separation between the four European patriarchs and the Roman patriarchate which exists to this day. Pope Leo IX, inspired by the ideals of a reform theology, demanded that the Patriarch of Constantinople, Michael Cerularius, acknowledge the supreme jurisdiction of the Holy See. This did not please Cerularius and Pope Leo died without seeing his wish come true. The period of the Great Schism, as this was called, was actually the result of centuries of disagreement with the Eastern patriarchs who had had difficulty with papal supremacy for some time. Cerularius was excommunicated, but the rift between East and West became permanent (Jackson, 1984).

Perhaps the ultimate pinnacle of disunity occurred with the papal split (or schism) of the 14th century. At its peak it was a spectacle of two popes (sometimes three), alternately excommunicating and anathematizing each other in a manner that was by no means edifying. In an effort to rectify the situation, in 1304 the University of Paris formulated a plan of reformation which called for the disposition of both popes and the election of a new one. When the former popes did not resign, and a new one was elected, it appeared as though there were now three in office. After a ten month reign, the elected pope, Alexander V, died in office. The situation was eventually concluded in AD 1417 but western Christianity was divided into two churches. One pope in Avignon was supported by France, Sardinia, Sicily, Scotland, Savoy, Castille, parts of Germany, and a portion of the Hapsburg lands, while the other pope in Rome had the support of central and northern Italy, Flanders, England, part of Germany, and other smaller areas. However, the pope was no longer sole ruler of the church; a council was now in control. The council eventually appointed one heir to the position of pope and the church was slowly reunited.

There were other problems in the ranks. There were rumblings of theological discontent among theologians. The "proletariat" wanted an enhanced voice in decision-making and their concerns were made public in the preaching of John Huss, John Wycliffe, Jerome of Prague and other forerunners of the "protesting reformation."

The Reformation

The Christian church took a major turn in the road in the early part of the 16th century with the occurrence of the Protestant Reformation. This development eventually gave the world the Anglican, Baptist, Methodist, Presbyterian and other Protestant denominations. Depending on the sources one reads, there were an awesome number of reasons why the Reformation happened. Primary among these was the situation with regard to the papacy. At the dawn of the 16th century the church had not yet recovered completely from the schism which was concluded by the stipulation that power was now vested in councils instead of popes. The church was in a state of spiritual disarray and no strong leadership had emerged to wipe away the cobwebs of disunity. Moreover, feudalism was declining, dissident groups were on the rise, and a new thirst in learning was evident. There had been a number of earlier attempts at reforming the church, but none of them had been successful, perhaps because the reformers lacked strong enough convictions, picked the wrong time to act, or simply lacked a common vision. In any event, there *were* deficiencies in the church. With the advent of the printing press, which helped to publicize these deficiencies, it was easier to get antithetical ideas around.

Although the name of Martin Luther certainly stands out with his challenge to church authorities about fixing things up in the establishment, like most social movements, the Reformation was preceded by a series of 15th century protests by "unhappy campers" like the Oxford Reformers, for example – Colet, Erasmus and Reuchlin. Before that there were the voices of John Wycliffe and John Huss. Simultaneous to the work of Luther and shortly after, we have John Eck, Ulrich Zwingli, and later John Calvin and John Knox. A radical left wing group known as the Anabaptists soon emerged and became the predecessor camp for the Mennonites and Hutterites and later (in 1693) the Amish. This movement produced names like Menno Simons, Jacob Hutter, Felix Manz, Georg Blaurock, Hans Denck, and Conrad Grebel. I shall have more to say about them later.

The fact that the Reformation occurred in Germany is also interesting. Most certainly it might have happened elsewhere, but Germany was ready for it. There was an air of disillusionment with the church. Critics were not too concerned with the outward appearance of the church, but instead wanted more theological substance and more stress on the spiritual roots of the Christian life. Those in authority had underestimated this concern, perhaps because they had been in power for too long. When Martin Luther arrived on the scene he was a man for the times, a man of the people, an agitator in the grandest style, and clearly one of the most popular speakers and writers that Germany has ever produced. He was a brilliant and profound theological thinker, a strong-willed man and an orator *extraordinaire* (Ritter, 1966). This combination was plainly unique; the Reformation simply *had* to happen and it had to happen in Germany.

One of Martin Luther's concerns, perhaps the primary one in nailing his 95 theses on a church door, had to do with indulgences (Hillerbrand, 1964). The belief at that time was that when an individual sinned, the Sacrament of Penance could be enacted for the forgiveness of sin. However, indulgences were also required, such as the performance of optional works of merit – prayers, almsdeeds, visits to church or helping the sick. Still, these did not take away the promise of eternal punishment, only temporal guilt. Luther's concern was that indulgences were being applied as means to absolve the sinner of eternal punishment; in his view, only God could do that. He argued that the church could only remit the ecclesiastical penalties it imposed; it could remit neither guilt nor Divine punishment. These are in the hands of God alone.

When the Protestants split with the state church they did not do so *en masse* but rather as a series of disunified groups of dissidents. Consequently, in light of their new-found freedom to develop fresh identities and creative belief systems, they took full advantage of the situation. Soon it was evident that there were many disagreements among them with regard to doctrine and practice. The Anabaptists represented one such group, and another was polarized in the teachings of John Calvin who, following Zwingli's disillusionment with the Anabaptists, gained a following with these beliefs: (i) the supreme role of Scripture in revelation; (ii) Divine revelation comes through *both* reason and Scripture; (iii) the total sovereignty of God to the point of the doctrine of election (i.e., only a select number of believers will be saved); and, (iv) the church must not only be dependent upon the state, it must rule the state.

A controversy emerging from Calvin's strict stance emerged over the doctrine of Arminianism versus Calvinism. James Arminius (1560-1609) opposed Calvin's doctrine of election, which may be interpreted to mean that God alone decides who is worthy of salvation and He arbitrarily (Divinely) picks His "favorites" as the elect. Arminius suggested that the grace of God *is* resistible and individuals *can* walk away from salvation if they choose to do so. Calvin contended that because God foresees all things, He also decides who *will* be saved. Arminius opted for the idea that God may know all things, but He leaves some decisions for people to make on their own – including acceptance or rejection of the gift of salvation.

As the Protestant Reformation spread across Europe, the Roman Catholic Church did not take its growth lightly. In fact, a counter-Reformation was launched and targeted the reconversion of those who had bought into Protestantism. One Catholic order, the Society of Jesus (Jesuits) became policy-makers for the Catholic Church and entered into the task of destroying the Protestant movement with great zeal and energy (Newman, 1953). Founded in 1534 by Ignatius Loyola, a Basque nobleman, and approved by Pope Paul III in 1540, their approach was to demean the claims of the Protestant theologians with superior knowledge and well-crafted arguments. All highly educated, the Jesuits took vows of poverty, chastity and obedience and entrusted themselves to a rigid central authority with "perfect" organization. The Reformation was never stamped out, and a series of religious wars broke out which were resolved only through political peace treaties.

Modern Denominationalism

With the advent of Protestantism there was no stopping the enhanced appetites of lay people to seek additional theological and political power in the church. The age of modern denominationalism was ushered in, and the tendency to split up or break-away and form even more denominations began and continues to this day. As each new church organizes itself, the tendency to add new numbers of devout through energetic missionary efforts has also intensified. From a North American standpoint at least, this objective has often been practiced to a greater extent in "foreign" mission territory rather than in the homeland, perhaps because of better results elsewhere.

As the Christian Church became transplanted in North America, the recurring patterns of growth and development and splintering continued in the new land. In 1728, for example, a great religious awakening took place among the Presbyterians, and resulted in many conversions. The preaching of evangelists like George Whitefield and Jonathan Edwards was credited for the sudden interest in turning to religion, but the results of mass evangelism were not applauded by all. Although the numbers attracted to Christianity generally increased, further church splits also occurred. By the beginning of this century there were already more than 100 Protestant denominations in North America.

Principles & Precepts

Christianity began simply enough. The plan was to further the teaching of Jesus Christ, the "founder" of the faith. His teachings may be summarized in a single statement with dualistic imperatives – a command to love the Lord our God, and to love our neighbor as ourselves. On those two planks, Jesus said, rest the whole of Christian practice. When missionary Paul and his cohorts caught this vision and acted on it the going got a lot tougher. This is because Paul and Peter and John started writing letters to some of the congregations they helped to establish, and those letters found themselves into the Canon of Holy Scripture. The letters then comprised the source for doctrine-making.

Jesus taught principles for daily living; Paul and his colleagues explicated very specific beliefs to adopt, and very precise doctrines to follow. When *their* followers got a hold of the writings and were given some kind of "authority" to explain them, the scene got *very* complicated. The result? Lots of different denominations.

Down through the centuries fresh looks at old scriptural passages have continually birthed new church organizations. Like other world religions, Christianity has had its regular share of newly-enlightened individuals who have laid claim to fresh understandings, all of them allegedly inspired by Divine assistance. As a result of this, it is virtually an impossible task to try to explain the beliefs of the various varieties of the Christian Church. A myriad of doctrinal creeds and subcreeds exist. Still, by way of introduction and in an attempt to offer the reader at least a modicum of help, the approach taken here is first to show the differentiating creeds of Roman Catholics and Protestants. Then a brief catalogue of Canadian Protestant denominations is offered.

Roman Catholic Beliefs

To begin with, Catholics and Protestants have a lot in common, although most adherents within both camps will probably not be aware of this. Protestants should be delighted to note that Catholics believe in the Trinity – the Godhead of three Persons, the Father, the Son and the Holy Spirit. God is the Creator and Father of Jesus Christ; the Son is the Savior, and is both God and man. He is the ultimate revelation of God. The Holy Spirit dwells in mankind and offers gifts to those who seek them – gifts for the sanctification of the believer and charismatic gifts for the help of others. So far, so good.

The Catholic Church believes in the doctrine of grace, that is, through unmerited favor God has chosen to initiate the plan of salvation which is available to all. Catholics believe that the Church was founded by Jesus Christ and it constitutes the body of Christ on earth. They believe in the Bible as the Word of God *and* in the efficacy of church tradition. They believe in original sin *and* in personal sin, that is to say, everyone inherits sin from their first parents, Adam and Eve, *and* everyone also sins personally. Catholics believe in seven sacraments (most Protestant churches recognize only two, Holy Baptism and the Eucharist – also called The Lord's Supper or Holy Communion). Belief in Sacraments rests on the premise that man is a mind-body or sense-spirit organism, and the world is a two-level reality in which matter and purpose are related and interpenetrating. The realm of space-time, therefore, is regarded by Catholic theologians as expressing God's will and assisting people to cooperate therewith. Mankind is also a two-level being, and is touched by God and helped by Him through the Sacraments, primarily through materials or visible signs or means (Ferm, 1945). The seven Roman Catholic Sacraments include: Holy Baptism, the Eucharist, Confirmation, Penance, Anointing of the sick, Matrimony and Holy Orders. They also believe that Mary, the Mother of Jesus, is therefore also Mother of God. Believers can pray to Mary, and because she is the mother of us all, she can respond to our prayers *(Handbook,* 1978).

Protestant Beliefs

Risky as it is for a Protestant to try to summarize Roman Catholic beliefs, it is probably even more foolhardy to attempt to summarize what might be called a general Protestant creed. Perhaps a good place to start is from the angle of the act of protesting. At the time of the Reformation, Protestants objected to a series of revered Catholic principles such as the infallibility of the Pope, the idea that church tradition is also a valid source of revelation, the Divine status of Mary, the Mother of Jesus, the right of priests to forgive sins, and celibacy for priests. Although the larger denominations have retained the two Sacraments mentioned, most of the smaller denominations reject all seven sacraments and retain Baptism and the Eucharist as symbolic acts only.

On the positive side, what's left? Well, Protestants would say, "only the essential doctrines." These would include: the doctrine of the Trinity, the Bible as the only inspired Word of God, the priesthood of all believers, the reality of sin and the need for personal redemption, and the church is the body of Christ on earth. It helps to keep in mind that the aim of the original reformers was to reform, not to revolutionize the church. They wanted to keep the faith as an expression of the Gospel, not the organization. They wanted to give first place to the Word of God, not tradition. They also wanted to bring back worship as a meaningful act for both the individual and the community. For them, Christian community must be based on the Gospel which is found only in the Scriptures. Beyond these three points, the original reformers *were* also revolutionary.

The radical component of the 16th century reform movement was to protest against the entire hierarchical and priestly system, in favor of the common priesthood of all believers. They protested against all formal, external authority in religion – against all tradition. They protested against all the traditional arrangements for public worship, all ritualism, and every "holy work." For the most part they also rejected Sacramentalism except in the case of Holy Baptism and the Lord's Supper. Finally, they protested against the double form of morality, and accordingly, against the higher form – against the contention that it is particularly well-pleasing to God to make no use of the powers and gifts which are part of His creation. All positions in life exist by the will of God including marriage, constituted authority and domestic service. All are to comprise service to God (Harnack, 1957).

Catechetical courses among the various Protestant denominations often utilize such items as the Ten Commandments, the Beatitudes, the Apostles' Creed or the Lord's Prayer as documents of faith and study (Feiner and Vischer, 1973; Nestingen and Forde, 1975). Interestingly, both Catholics and Protestants (at least the major denominations), commonly utilize the well-known Apostles' Creed as a representative statement of belief:

> I believe in God, the Father Almighty, maker of heaven and earth;
> And in Jesus Christ his only son our Lord, who was conceived by the
> Holy Spirit, born of the Virgin Mary, suffered under Pontius Pilate,
> was crucified, dead and buried. He descended into hell; the third day
> he rose again from the dead; he ascended into heaven, and sitteth at
> the right hand of God, the Father Almighty; from thence he shall come
> to judge the quick and the dead. I believe in the Holy Spirit, the holy

catholic church; the communion of saints; the forgiveness of sins; the resurrection of the body; and the life everlasting. Amen (*Service Book,* 1986).

Practices

To be a good Roman Catholic one should have been baptized as an infant, become confirmed as an adolescent, attend Mass regularly and receive The Eucharist, and periodically go to confession. In addition the believer should observe the holy days, engage in an occasional fast and retreat, say prayers and engage in corporal and spiritual works of mercy. Corporal works include feeding the hungry, visiting the imprisoned, sheltering the homeless and visiting the sick. Spiritual works include admonishing sinners, instructing the ignorant, comforting the sorrowful, forgiving those who injure oneself, being patient with others and praying for others (*Handbook,* 1978). What Protestant could possibly disagree with this list?

Like most world religions, Christianity stresses doing good to one's neighbor. All Christian denominations, Catholic and Protestant alike, conservative, liberal or fundamentalist, point to the Sermon on the Mount as an exemplary of the code for Christian living:

> Blessed are the poor in spirit, for theirs is the kingdom of heaven. Blessed are those who mourn, for they will be comforted. Blessed are the meek, for they shall inherit the earth. Blessed are those who hunger and thirst for righteousness, for they will be filled. Blessed are the merciful, for they will be shown mercy. Blessed are the pure in heart, for they will see God. Blessed are the peacemakers, for they will be called the sons of God. Blessed are those who are persecuted because of righteousness, for theirs is the kingdom of God (Matt. 5:3-10).

Peculiarities

From the beginning, Christians have been involved in meeting three challenges, those of: (i) living a just and holy life; (ii) growing in the knowledge and wisdom of the Gospel; and, (iii) responding to the Divine order to "go into all the world and preach the good news to all creation" (Mark 16:15a). This has not been an easy assignment, partially because of the difficulty of the challenge, but mostly due to internal friction, disagreements and criticism – particularly among the dissenting Protestants.

The *first* of the three assignments about living righteous lives is supposed to set Christians apart from the rest of society. They are instructed that they are *"in* the world, but not *of* the world," which means they are supposed to behave differently than non-believers. They are expected to live out the Sermon on the Mount, even when their societal counterparts do not. This is a most difficult task, and as history shows, many times Christians have had to be willing to lay down their lives for the cause of Christ – and they have done so. Hopefully, this will not necessarily always be the case for every believer.

The *second* assignment is fraught with theological land-mines. "Growing in knowledge" usually refers to being aware of both the basics and the finer points of one's particular denominational creed. In some cases it often becomes more important to commit to memory the minutia of a belief system than to implement it (Friesen, 1972). For example, if you are a Baptist, you had better believe that adult immersion is the *only* way to be baptized – and you should know *why* it is the only way. If you are a Methodist you should claim to be an Arminian (or minimally a Wesleyan), not a Calvinist. On the other hand, a devout Presbyterian should be able to offer a really good explanation of the Calvinist doctrine of election. And a fundamentalist should have at the ready a full eschatalogical explanation about the efficacy of a pre-tribulation, pre-millennial perspective as opposed to a millennial or post-tribulation perspective! Now *that's* spiritual knowledge – or is it?

The *third* Christian challenge is about evangelism – getting the word out to unbelievers. Here, statistical data may be incorporated as a helpful tool in calculating success or failure. In some cases, unbelievers get down-right annoyed at what they define as militancy or egoism which some personal campaigners for evangelism seem to convey. Like Islam, Christianity has its share of "you had better repent or else" types. On the other hand, when claims or inferences about personal righteousness seem to flow along with personal entreaties to get converted, irritation on the part of the hearer is sometimes understandable.

Protestantism, particularly in the ranks of the more fundamentalist churches, is also fraught with the phenomenon of "recycling Christians," that is, believers who leave one church denomination and reaffiliate with another. According to a study conducted two decades ago, in Canada the rate of reaffiliation may be as high as 72 percent. An additional 18 percent of new members come from "birth-type" converts, that is, the children of adherents. This leaves only 9 percent for "real growth," and even then many of the "first-time" converted believers come from mainline denominations (Bibby and Brinkerhoff, 1973; Carroll, et al., 1979). A similar phenomenon may be observed with regard to church growth, with conservative evangelical churches laying claim to some amazing results. A more recent study, conducted 20 years later than the one previously cited, and from the same researcher (Bibby, 1987), suggests that the reaffiliation rate is still at least 70 percent; 20 percent are children of evangelicals and 10 percent constitute "real growth."

Unlike their more conservative counterparts, the mainline denominations are more casual about growth rates, partially because of other crises currently facing their officialdom. The United Church of Canada, for example, has lost about one quarter of a million members in the last two decades, and has spent a great deal of time dealing with such issues as who may be ordained, the secularization of the church, finances, relocation of church headquarters and human rights (O'Toole, et al., 1993). A similar situation prevails with regard to other mainline denominations although membership losses have been less severe (Nock, 1993). The Roman Catholic Church has recently shown a measure of growth as have several smaller evangelical or fundamentalist churches.

Real growth notwithstanding, the orders to evangelize have been given, and most Christians will continue to respond in their own fashion. Christians, it appears, regardless of denominational affiliation, are still determined to expand their numbers (Aland, 1985).

References

Aland, Kurt. (1985). *A history of Christianity* (2 vols.). Philadelphia: Fortress Press.

Bibby, Reginald W. & Brinkerhoff, Merlin B. (September, 1973). The calculation of the Saints: A study of people who join conservative churches. *Journal for the Scientific Study of Religion, 12,* 273-283.

Bibby, Reginald W. (1987). *Fragmented gods: The poverty and potential of religion in Canada.* Toronto: Irwin Publishing.

Carrol, Jackson W., et al. (1979). *Religion in America: 1950 to the present.* San Francisco: Harper & Row.

Case, Shirley Jackson. (1960). *The evolution of early Christianity.* Chicago: University of Chicago Press.

Cruttwell, Charles Thomas. (1971). *A literary history of early Christianity* (2 vols.). New York: AMS Press.

Feiner, Johannes & Vischer, Lukas. (1973). *The common catechism: A book of Christian faith.* New York: Seabury Press.

Ferm, Vergilius. (1945). *An encyclopedia of religion.* New York: Philosophical Library.

Foakes-Jackson, F.J. (1898). *History of the Christian church from the earliest times to the death of Pope Leo the Great, A.D. 461.* Cambridge: J. Hall & Son.

Friesen, John W. (1972). *Religion for people – an alternative.* Calgary, AB: Bell Books.

Harnack, Adolf. (1957). *What is Christianity?* New York: Harper & Brothers.

Hillerbrand, Hans J. (1964). *The reformation: A narrative history related by contemporary observers and participants.* New York: Harper & Row.

Jackson, Jeremy C. (1984). *No other foundation: the church through twenty centuries.* Westchester, IL: Crossway Books

Handbook for today's Catholic: Beliefs – practices – prayers. (1978). Liguori, MO: Liguori Publications.

Nestingen, James A. & Forde, Gerhard O. (1975). *Free to be: A handbook to Luther's small catechism.* Minneapolis, MN: Augsburg Publishing House.

Newman, Albert Henry. (1953). *A manual of church history* (2 vols., rev. ed.) Philadelphia: The American Baptist Publication Society.

Nock, David. (1993). The organization of religion life in Canada. In W.E. Hewitt (Ed.), *The sociology of religion: A Canadian focus* (pp. 41-64). Toronto: Butterworths.

O'Toole, Roger, et al. (1993). The United Church in Crisis. In W.E. Hewitt (Ed.), *The sociology of religion: a Canadian focus* (pp. 273-288). Toronto: Butterworths.

Ritter, Gerhard. (1966). Why the reformation occurred in Germany. In Sidney A. Burrell (Ed.), *The role of religion in modern European history* (pp. 28-36). New York: Collier-Macmillan Ltd.

Service book: For the use of ministers conducting public worship. (1986). Toronto: published for the United Church of Canada by CANEC Publishing & Supply House.

Wagner, Walter H. (1994). *After the apostles: Christianity in the second century.* Minneapolis, MN: Fortress Press.

13

Roman Catholic Church

The Catholic Church is represented in at least 217 countries with a combined international membership of more than 600 million. There are 12 204 000 Catholics in Canada. This easily makes Roman Catholicism the largest Christian church in the country and in the world. According to Catholic historians, their church started at the time of the Apostles of Christ in the 1st century. At that time about 120 souls gathered together for fellowship and so formed the first Christian church (Acts 1:15). During this period of "Primitive Catholicism," the New Testament churches were organized on the basis of one church in every city. In each church there were two groups, clergy and lay people, the former presided over the Sacraments and did the teaching and the latter did the learning. Clergy were chosen for their position by the whole local church and they received spiritual powers through a ritual called the laying on of hands. According to Catholic sources, there were three layers of authority among the clergy – the bishop of the church who was assisted by the priests who were assisted by deacons. The latter group took care of the church's property, distributed alms, helped the poor and widows and orphans, and did other benevolent works (Hughes, 1966). Naturally, Protestants claim exactly the same heritage with minor modifications in interpretation.

The Protestant view of Catholic origins reflects their bias. Pelikan (1959) suggests that the Catholic Church may not have done too well in buying into the prestige of the Roman name, and this connection was not universally applauded at the time. Tertullian, for example, denounced Rome and the Roman empire, but praised the conduct of local congregations. Roman loyalty came easier in the 4th century because the Emperor turned Christian. However, the founding of "New Rome" by Constantine was a failure and it did not auger well for the reputation of the church (Gibbon, 1958). Nevertheless, the connection remained, with some interesting twists and turns, and has been perpetuated to this day.

Pedigree

For several hundreds of years, until the 11th century, in fact, the Catholic historian finds little difficulty in expounding the blessing of God upon the church. By the way, the church was also operating under the umbrella of imperial protection, but things went well. The breaking away of the Eastern Orthodox Church occurred on the basis that the Eastern bishops thought that the Roman Pontiff arrogated to himself powers which did not belong to him. Here sources are not agreed in interpreting the relationship of the Orthodox Church to the Roman Catholic Church. One source says that the Eastern Orthodox Church consists of a number of virtually independent churches, for example, in Russia, Greece and Romania, but is still nominally subject to its ecumenical Patriarch. The Eastern Churches are "unhappily" not in union with Rome, but have a valid priesthood and valid Sacraments" (Meadows, 1969). Another source suggests that Rome does not in fact really assert the doctrine of one true church toward the Orthodox Churches. They are treated as churches within the one true church that are "in rebellion" (McKenzie, 1969). Leroux (1963) suggests that the doctrinal questions initially argued by Orthodox adherents were extraordinarily hazy and it was virtually impossible to discern the truth in the impossible clutter of formulae that resulted. He also suggests that the Orthodox Church lost all of its missionary zeal as a result of the schism and fell under civil authority. Though the action need not be regarded as permanent, a complete reunion between the two fellowships does not appear feasible, certainly not in the immediate future (Leroux, 1963). This admirable spirit of eternal optimism may well need to rely on the eternal hope.

Another need for reconciliation in the Catholic Church arose in the early part of the 14th century when the Church simply had too many popes – three to be exact. Perhaps the simplest way to deal with this frustrating and embarrassing situation would be to beg that it be treated as an error of ancient history and best forgotten by all. A more objective analysis, however, reveals that the "human factor" has always been as alive in the Catholic Church as among Protestant churches. Even when there was a possibility of solution to the three pope situation, "no one seemed willing to compromise" (Holmes and Bickers, 1984, 110). Perhaps the most honest approach is to point out that the matter *was* finally resolved, albeit not without a series of failed attempts (Hughes, 1966).

A generous evaluation of the Reformation by Protestant writers is that it was a tragic necessity. It literally separated millions of believers from what Catholics consider the one true church. Catholic writers tend to be kinder, and suggest that the causes of the tragedy of the Reformation are often oversimplified (Hughes, 1966). They admit to weaknesses and corruption in the church and scandal in the life of those who occupied the upper echelons. They also intimate that Pope Leo X may have been ill-informed about conditions in the North or ill-served by his employees (Meadows, 1960). These admissions tend to support the contention that the human element is an active factor in the Roman Catholic Church.

The Catholic Church has made great attempts in seeking to rectify the split with their "separated brethren" as Protestants are now called – particularly since Vatican II, under the leadership of Pope John

XXIII. The Second Vatican Council, which convened in 1960, high-lighted a movement towards reconciliation that began in 1910. The position emanating from that event may be spelled out in this way: the Reformation must not be viewed as a black-and-white movement; Rome must share the blame in the renting apart of Christian brothers and sisters. The Roman Church is also aware of the bankruptcy of their position regarding the one "true" church. Leaders are showing concern about divisiveness in the church and, despite their historical emphasis on "Apostolic Succession," no longer regard Protestant churches as non-churches (McKenzie, 1969). Beginning with the ministry of Pope John XXIII, the encyclicals emerging from the papal office now reflect much more the world concerns, dealing with such items as human welfare and international peace (Holmes and Bickers, 1984). Attempts towards Christian unity have also been on the agenda (O'Brien, 1964).

Principles & Precepts

The clear advantage in joining the Catholic Church is one's tie to antiquity in the Christian faith. Protestants may not like it very much, but their subdivisions are all without exception "Johnny-come-late-lys" – having originated only since the Reformation. Anyone contemplating joining the Catholic Church will be informed of the Church's longevity and appraised of her credentials. They must be prepared to accept the authority of the church with regard to her teachings and practices.

> Here lies in the great line of cleavage that divides the religious world. As long as the individual clings to the right of private judgment, of sitting in judgment on the truth as revealed by God, and of accepting or rejecting doctrines as they appeal or do not appeal to him, he is at an infinite distance from the church (Grace and Korth, 1964, 263).

One can remain in the mode of respectability and still observe that the Catholic Church believes in a lot of things, probably too many things for the Protestant. At the same time, the prescribed list of doctrines and practices can lend an element of security to the individual. It affords a tie to the longevity of Christianity. The principle of sacramentality is another strong feature in developing this security and constitutes one of the Catholic Church's outstanding contributions to Western Christianity (McBrien, 1981).

> Catholicism has had a continuing experience, unequalled in other forms of Western Christianity, of the presence of God and of grace mediated through symbols to the entire course of ordinary human life (Laplante, 1994).

And again,

> No theological principle or focus is more characteristic of Catholicism or more central to its identity than the principle of sacramentality. The Catholic vision sees God in and through all things; other people,

communities, movements, events, places, objects, the world at large, the cosmos. The visible, the tangible, the finite, the historical – all these are actual or potential carriers of the divine presence (Laplante, 1994, 15-16).

Peculiarities

The Roman Catholic Church stands alone in Christian history with a unique and durable record, and aside from the period of the Great Schism, the period of the three popes and the Protestant Reformation, has had very few instances of dissension. This is not bad for a 20 century existence. However, probably more than any other Christian church in recent history, the Catholic Church has also been the target of criticism in the area of sexual deviance (Kavanagh, 1969). Women have complained on national television about being former lovers of priests or bishops (the Phil Donahue Show), and Native people have brought out into the open their experiences of having been sexually abused in residential schools. Thus the advantage of durability may also be turning into a disadvantage if one considers the matter of individual freedom. Either one is a good Catholic or one is not. The church is never wrong. One accepts the rules and regulations laid down by Rome, not the least of which are the pope's pronouncements on such matters as celibacy of priests and nuns, divorce and remarriage, the status of women in the church (O'Malley, 1988), or birth control. It has been very difficult for church officials to hold their believers to the official line whenever the needs of the economy run counter to her demands (Robillard, 1994). The church authoritatively formulates supernatural truths and breaks them down into rules for daily living (Adam, 1963). Undoubtedly, it was this very expectation that contributed towards the occasional schisms in the church and keeps many Protestants believing that theirs is the better way.

References

Adam, Karl. (1963). *The spirit of Catholicism*. Garden City, NY: Image Books.

Gibbon, Edward. (1958). *The triumph of Christendom in the Roman Empire*. New York: Harper Torchbooks.

Grace, William J. & Korth, Francis N. (1964). *The Catholic church and you: What the church teaches and why*. Milwaukee, WI: The Bruce Publishing Company.

Holmes, J. Derek & Bickers, Bernard W. (1984). *A short history of the Catholic church*. New York: Paulist Press.

Hughes, Philip. (1966). *A popular history of the Catholic Church*. New York: The Macmillan Company.

Kavanagh, Father James. (1969). *A modern priests looks at his outdated church*. Richmond Hill, ON: Simon & Schuster of Canada.

Laplante, Richard. (Summer, 1994). The Catholic school experience: Raising questions around Sacramentality. *Salt, 15*(2), 15-23.

Leroux, Jean-Marie. (1963). *The new people of God: a short history of the church*. Westchester, MD: Christian Classics.

McBrien, R.P. (1981). *Catholicism*. Minneapolis, MN: Winston.

McKenzie, John L. (1969). *The Roman Catholic church*. London: Weidenfeld and Nicolson.

Meadows, Denis. (1969). *A short history of the Catholic church*. New York: All Saints Press.

O'Brien, John A. (Ed.). (1964). *Steps to Christian unity*. Garden City, NY: Doubleday & Co.

O'Malley, John W. (Ed.). (1988). *Catholicism in early modern history: A guide to research* (2 vols.). Ann Arbor, MI: Edwards Brothers.

Pelikan, Jaroslav. (1959). *The riddle of Roman Catholicism*. New York: Abingdon Press.

Robillard, Denise. (1994). The Cardinal's conscience by Leslie Armour. [A review published in 1539], *The Literary Review of Canada, 3*(8), 7-9.

14

Greek Orthodox Church

The year AD 1054 is generally held to be the official date of the rupture between East and West in the Roman Catholic Church. On July 15 of that year, Cardinal Humbert Moyenmoutier laid upon the altar of the church of the Holy Wisdom at Constantinople a decree excommunicating the patriarch, Michael Cerularius. The next day, the gathering of the bishops of the imperial city threw this document into the fire, and excommunicated the papal legate in their turn (Le Guillou, 1962). For some time this particular event was basically ignored because there were other concerns in the church at that time. Besides, as the decades rolled by, many eastern patriarchs kept in touch with congregations in the west and with the pope. This continued for several centuries with many officials on both sides hoping the schism would vanish.

There are 232 000 members of the Greek Orthodox Church in Canada.

Pedigree

The division in the Roman Catholic Church had simmering roots of discontent that date back well before AD 1054. It really started in AD 330 when Constantine moved his capital from Rome to Byzantium and began his vast rule from the new city of Constantinople. The theological differences that arose had social, racial, linguistic, mental, moral and philosophical roots. The East was Greek in blood, speech and philosophy; the West was Latin and based on Roman law. Transferring the base of power from west to east also meant a shift of power and influence. Later political developments that culminated in the crowning of Charles the Great made the Roman Catholic Church virtually coterminous with the Holy Roman Empire. Certainly the overbearing character of the Norman crusaders and the horrors of the sacking of Constantinople in the fourth crusade may well have been the *real* causes of the permanent estrangement.

As time went on the differences between the two views deepened. The Western Church held that the Holy Spirit proceeded directly from the Father, and the Eastern Church adopted the view that the Spirit proceeded from the Father *and* from the Son – *filioque*. There was also a difference in governance; the West was ruled by the pope and the East adopted a system of three patriarchs who were the bishops of Rome (situated in the West), Alexandria and Antioch. Later the bishops of Jerusalem and Constantinople were added. Thus the

Eastern Church became an oligarchy of patriarchs, and today each patriarch in his diocese essentially has the same power as the pope does over all the Western Church. His power is supreme.

After the break with Rome the Eastern Church reached out beyond the imperial dioceses to expand its boundaries. Unlike the Roman Church, however, the East did not keep conquered lands for herself, and when the church eventually lost power in captured areas the people returned to the religions of previous times – those of Arabs, Seljuk and Ottoman Turks and Kurds.

From time to time the leaders of the Roman Catholic and Eastern Orthodox Churches have tried to reconcile, but the primary contention of the Roman Church about affirming the infallibility of the pope has always brought negotiations to a grinding halt. The first negotiation occurred at the time of Pope Gregory IX and the Greek patriarch Germanus. Rome's conditions for merger were the recognition of papal jurisdiction, the use of unleavened bread to be enforced upon the Greeks, and the Greeks were required to burn all anti-west writings. The Greek patriarch refused these conditions. Later, negotiations resumed under the leadership of Pope Innocent IV and Clement IV in which the popes proposed essentially the same terms. These were again rejected by the Greeks with the objection that Rome was trying to inflict new creeds on their church.

The negotiations at the Council of Lyons in AD 1274 were loaded with political implications. Michael Palaeologus ruled in Constantinople while Baldwin II, the last of the Latin emperors, was an exile in Europe. Palaeologus wished the pope to acknowledge his title to be emperor of the East and in return promised submission to the papal supremacy and the union of the Greek with the Latin Church on the pope's own terms. This enforced union lasted only during the lifetime of the emperor. The only other serious attempt at union was made at the Council of Florence. It was really suggested by the politically weak Byzantine empire and their dread of the approach of the Turks. John Palaeologus the emperor, Joseph the patriarch of Constantinople, and several Greek bishops came to Italy and appeared at the Council of Florence – the papal council, the rival of the Council of Basel. As on former occasions, and by their interpretation, the Greeks were at first deceived by false representations; they were betrayed into recognition of papal supremacy, and tricked into signing what could be represented as a submission to western doctrine. The natural consequences followed – a repudiation of what had been done; and the Greek bishops on their way home took care to make emphatic their ritualistic differences with Rome. Soon after came the fall of Constantinople, and with this event an end to the political reasons for the submission of the Greek clergy. Rome's schemes for a union (which meant an unconditional submission on the part of the Greeks) did not cease, however, they were no longer attempted on a grand scale. Jesuit missionaries after the Reformation stirred up schisms in some parts of the Eastern Church, and in Austria and Poland many of the Greeks were compelled to submit themselves to the orders of Rome. The result of these schemes has been what is called the United Greeks. These various unions have commonly arisen from dissensions among the Greeks themselves when a portion of the dissentients have made submissions to Rome. Roman leaders commonly promised to allow them to enjoy their own liturgies and rites of worship, but usually broke their promises. This was done so systematically that the Roman College of the Propaganda prints what it professes to be the old liturgies of the Eastern churches. The liturgies are so interpolated as to bring them surreptitiously into harmony with the western rites. According to some sources this is done on such a grand scale that it is impossible to trust any professedly eastern creed or service-book printed at the office of Propaganda in Rome (Lindsay, 1910).

Principles & Policy

The Greek Orthodox Church has no creeds in the modern western sense of the word other than the Nicene Creed. Here, in the third article they add the term *filioque* (which means "from the Son" in Latin). It then reads, "We believe in the Holy Spirit, the Lord, the giver of life, who proceeds from the Father *and the Son* . . . (Farlee, et al., 1985, 27). Orthodox theologians view the Father as the only source of the Trinity. They say that the Spirit proceeds through – not from – the Son. The Western Church counters that Jesus said that He and the Father are one. The Orthodox Church has rigorously preserved the older idea that a creed is an adoring confession of the church engaged in worship; and, when occasion called for additional adoration, the beliefs of the church were expressed more by way of public testimony than in symbolic books. The doctrines of the church may be inferred from these confessions of faith and may be divided into two classes – the ecumenical creeds of the early undivided church and the later testimonies defining the position of the Orthodox Church of the East, with regard to the belief of the Roman Catholic and Protestant Churches. Orthodox Christians believe in the Bible and supplement its teachings on holy tradition as derived from the decrees of the seven ecumenical councils in their history. The Nicene Creed is recited in all liturgies and in some other services; the seven Sacraments are also practiced. Saints are honored, and angels are revered, but the use of carved images is forbidden (Maloney, 1976).

The faith of the Eastern Orthodox Church during the first eight centuries was the same as that of Rome, although difference of race and theological traditions gradually formed a unique system of theology and a different way at looking at the articles of faith. The real difference between the two churches has to do with rites. Since none of the Eastern churches ever knew anything of Roman liturgy, they followed their own traditions from the very beginning. There has never been a parent-rite from which the later ones were derived (Fortescue, 1911). As the centuries rolled by the forms of public worship, organization, institutions, ecclesiastical discipline and the theological formulations of the matter of Revelation, all testify to the divergent spiritual, psychological and historical influences in the East and in the West. While continuing in agreement on the fundamental line of the understanding of Christianity, Easterners and Westerners nevertheless had shades of difference in their perception of the Christian mystery and their way of expressing it. This was the result of two perspectives which, while being at all times complementary, were too often foreign to one another (Le Guillou, 1962).

Practices

Some have suggested that the most striking feature of Orthodox piety is its essential liturgical character. The life of faith begins and grows, in a specifically ecclesial setting, through living communion in the reality of the Mystery found under its symbolic vesture. The sense of community is very strong among eastern peoples, and though the religion is quite naturally centred on the fundamental truths of Christianity, the various rituals are lived out in an attitude of thanksgiving. The Orthodox Church prides itself in its uniqueness from the West; they have not deviated like Westerners have in trying to adjust to the nuances of contemporary lifestyles. Eastern piety continued to be directed towards essentials, producing an impression of a deeply authentic Christianity (Le Guillou, 1962). Naturally, and like so many other denominations, the Eastern Church claims to be the "direct heir and true conservator" of the original primitive church. Their argument for being a preserving church is at least partially based on the fact that their various national groups – Syrian, Russian, Serbian, Bulgarian, Romanian, Albanian, Greek and Georgian – have endured a bitter struggle for existence. Many times they have been involved in bitter wars fought against Arabs, Tartars, Turkish and Western armies (Mead, 1983).

The worship service in an Eastern Orthodox Church is elaborately ritualistic, but a practical sense of application prevails in the prayers which include local and national concerns. Day-to-day Christianity is to be lived out without undue claims being made about spiritual prowess or achievement. In that sense Eastern Orthodox Christians may truly be the "quiet in the land."

Peculiarities

Infants of families in the Eastern Orthodox church are baptized anytime after they are 40 days old. Orthodoxy adheres to this principle by reminding us that Jesus was presented to God in the temple when he was 40 days old (Luke 2:22-24). This practice is unique to this particular denomination.

The casual student of church history is not likely to be aware of the "protesting or dissenting tradition" within the Eastern Orthodox Church. One is used to expecting that theological squabbles and subsequent breakaways arise out of Protestantism. It is therefore somewhat shocking to discover that there are a number of non-orthodox Orthodox Churches in North America; they include: the Albanian Orthodox Archdiocese in America, the American Carpatho-Russian Orthodox Greek Catholic Church, the American Holy Orthodox Catholic Apostolic Eastern Church (affiliated with the Orthodox Catholic Patriarchate of America), the Holy Orthodox Church in America (Eastern Catholic and Apostolic), the Romanian Orthodox Episcopate of America, the Russian Orthodox Church in the USA, the Serbian Eastern Orthodox Church in the USA and Canada, the Syrian Orthodox Church of America (under the Archdiocese of the USA and Canada) and the Ukrainian Orthodox Church. A few descriptive comments on the latter "subdenomination" may prove useful.

The Ukrainian Orthodox Church

The Ukrainian Orthodox Church numbers about 136 000 in Canada, and their history is unique. In the 10th century, Vladimir the Great, ruler of Kiev, sent investigators abroad to study the doctrines and rituals of Islam, Christianity and Judaism. His "spies" reported that the Eastern Orthodox faith seemed best suited to their country. Consequently, Vladimir was baptized into the faith and ushered in Eastern Orthodoxy as the state religion.

For the next six centuries, the Ukrainian Church was under the jurisdiction of the Ecumenical Patriarchate of Constantinople. Then, in 1686, it was placed under the supervision of the Russian Patriarch of Moscow. This authority was rejected in the revolution of 1917 and three groups emerged following three interpretations of appropriate action. The first group, known as the Ukrainian Orthodox Church was formally organized in 1924. The second group became the Ukrainian Orthodox Church of America Ecumenical Patriarchate, and the third body was known as the Holy Ukrainian Autocephalic Orthodox Church in Exile. It broke with the Ukrainian Church in America in 1951 over a dispute about administrative matters. The major Orthodox churches relate with one another through the Standing Conference of Canonical Orthodox Bishops in America, created in 1960 (Douglas, 1991).

References

Douglas, J.D. (Ed.). (1991). *New 20th-century encyclopedia of religious knowledge* (2nd ed.). Grand Rapids, MI: Baker Book House.

Farlee, R., Tonsager, Steven R. & Jones, Susan (Eds.). (1985). *Our neighbor's faith.* Minneapolis: Augsburg Publishing House.

Fortescue, Adrian. (1911). *The orthodox eastern church.* London: The Catholic Truth Society

Le Guillou, M.J. (1962). *The spirit of eastern orthodoxy.* New York: Hawthorn Books.

Lindsay, T.M. (1910). Orthodox Church. *The Werner encyclopedia.* Akron, OH: The Werner Company.

Maloney, George A. (1976). *A history of orthodox theology since 1453.* Belmont, MS: Nordland Publishing Company.

Mead, Frank S. (1983). *Handbook of denominations in the United States* (7th ed.). Nashville, TN: Abingdon Press.

15

Mainline Protestant Churches

There appears to be some agreement among religious writers as to use of the term "mainline" in referring to the various Protestant denominations. In this context there are about 7 679 000 "mainline" Christians in Canada. These denominations have in common the fact that their beliefs and practices are basically acceptable by members of dominant society. Though they may not be official members of these churches, many people will still acknowledge a nominal relationship to any one of them without obligation or repercussion. Proceeding alphabetically, then, we first describe the Anglican Church of Canada, formerly known as the Church of England and as the Episcopal Church in the USA.

Anglicans

The Anglican Church in Canada adopted that name in 1955 and its history has sometimes been described as unfathomable, if not offensive (Aland, 1986). It began in England with the personal action of King Henry VIII (1491-1547) who called himself the "Defender of the Faith" – as did all British kings. Charles Dickens referred to King Henry as "a most intolerable ruffian and a blot of blood and grease on the history of England" (Hillerbrand, 1964, 298). Essentially, Henry cut off the English Church from the Holy (Catholic) See because it would not give him the divorce he was seeking from his first wife, Catherine of Aragon. Catherine had already borne Henry six children but no male heir; still, she was not willing to go along with Henry's plan to declare their marriage "spiritually wrong from the start" as he suggested. The problems really started with the fact that Catherine had been married earlier to Henry's deceased brother, Arthur. The marriage lasted only six months, until Arthur's death. According to religious interpretations of the time, it behooved Henry to marry Catherine and raise up children to his brother's name and memory (Hillerbrand, 1964).

To settle things his way, Henry had himself made supreme head of the church via the Act of Supremacy in 1534, and anyone who would not declare their allegiance to him was castigated and persecuted. One of the more tragic chapters in the story pertains to the beheading of Thomas More, who disagreed with King Henry's actions. This tale was popularized in the motion picture, "A Man for all Seasons."

Pedigree

When the dust had settled from his divorce with Catherine, Henry went on to have five more wives, none of whom bore him a living son and heir, and he was eventually mourned by several female children from three of his wives. Despite its dubious beginnings, the Church of England made several significant strides after Henry's death. The *Book of Common Prayer,* for example, was published in 1549 and a Confession of faith was formalized in 1553.

After her father died, and her Roman Catholic half-sister's bloody reign (Bloody Mary), Elizabeth I assumed the throne (1558-1603) and continued pursuing the cause of the Reformation. The pope, of course, was unable to recognize Elizabeth's rule while Catherine of Aragon was still alive, which made it easier for Elizabeth to promote the newly-originated national church. In 1559, she reestablished the state church through the Act of Uniformity and deposed the bishops who opposed this action. Later the Articles of Faith were made binding on every clergyman in England. An act of parliament made it illegal for any churchman to disagree with state church policy, and any dissenters were deported. By the end of Elizabeth's reign one-third of all clergy had been removed from office.

As the Church of England developed, a concern for expansion originated, and the Society for Promoting Christian Knowledge was founded in 1698. In the early part of the 18th century a divisive thrust became evident in the preaching of John and Charles Wesley who later established Methodism. The Methodist Church, however, did not formally break with Anglicanism until after John Wesley's death.

By the 19th century the Church of England was informally divided into two camps, the high church and the low church. The high church more nearly represents Catholicism in form and format and the low church shows signs of having incorporated the theology and practice of evangelicalism. Later a free church movement emerged from within the ranks, partially because of their commitment to the principle that it was wrong to collect pew rent.

Anglican (Episcopal) beginnings in North America may be traced to Canada and to Frobisher Bay in the summer of 1578 (Carter, 1975), and to the State of Virginia and the Carolinas in the United States where it was the state religion (Newman, 1953). After its initial services in the northern parts of Canada, the church moved to the East. Sixty years before Confederation, the Provincial Synod of Canada was formed, and battlelines between high and low church forms were in progress (Abel, 1991). The western contingent was formally initiated in 1820 when John West was appointed by the Church Missionary Society.

Progress by the Episcopal Church in America saw the establishment of Philadelphia as a headquarters, where a large amount of property was purchased. In 1785 a convention adopted a revised prayer book, a new constitution and the name Protestant Episcopal Church. A century later the church could boast over a half million adherents. Today there are some forty million communicants across the world (Goodman, n.d.). There are 2 181 000 Anglicans in Canada.

Principles & Precepts

It is difficult for the casual observer to differentiate between Roman Catholic beliefs and those of high church Anglican because at first glance, at least, they appear quite similar. Catholics have seven Sacraments and Anglicans have two Sacraments (Baptism and the Eucharist), and five "lesser" Sacraments – marriage, confirmation, ordination, absolution and anointing with oil (Goodman, n.d.). Anglicans are quite hierarchical in organization and like their Catholic counterparts, call their clergymen "priests," although they *are* allowed to marry. They also have bishops, deans, archdeacons and canons. The Archbishop of Canterbury is their highest office. Other offices include: deans, who are senior priests; archdeacons, who work for bishops; canons, who are really the holders of an honorary title; and commissioned deacons who work in local congregations.

Anglicans believe in Incarnation, the veneration of saints, the inspiration of the Bible, Apostolic Succession and a certain degree of ecumenicity. Anglican leaders believe in teaching a rigorous Catechism before Confirmation, and like many other Christians, utilize the Apostles' Creed as a basic statement of faith.

Practices

When catechetical instruction is undertaken participants are challenged to live the Christian life. They are expected to attend worship regularly, engage in private prayer, read the Bible, practice self-discipline, fulfill the spirit of Christ in daily life, stand up for the faith (to the point of serving in the national army), seek to engage in personal service and practice stewardship. Undoubtedly, this list could also be taught with meaning in most Baptist, Lutheran, Presbyterian or United Churches.

Peculiarities

What then is unique to the Anglican Church by way of practice? Good question, and the answer would probably have to be provided by any non-Anglican Christian coming into contact with the behavior of representative Anglican Christians. Like most European-originated fellowships, the most noticeable things would probably be the ethnicity of the Church. It is essentially a transplanted British institution complete with loyalties and rituals drawn from a deep respect for the monarchy and "the old country." Most Anglicans would probably be surprised to have themselves described as "ethnic," since in Canada that label is thought by them to apply to immigrants from any country save the British Isles or perhaps the USA. Outside of French-speaking Canada, and until very recently, most national Canadian social institutions have reflected their Anglo origins in design and practice (Friesen, 1993). Until the 1960s the older Protestant churches had a great deal of power and prestige in English-speaking Canada. That power has eroded since religious commitment and religious experience have been separated from each other, and because increased individualism and hedonism have diminished the appeal of traditional religiosity (Nock, 1993).

The challenge for the Anglican Church in the closing decade of this century is similar to that of other mainline Canadian denominations – the struggle to remain relevant to the emerging generation; here, they will likely prevail. Thirty years ago Canadian writer Pierre Berton denounced his birth church, the Anglican Church, as a fossilized institution because of a desperate effort to preserve its established identity (Berton, 1965). That challenge is still before the church; recent membership losses on parish rolls, between 1988-90 were over 78 000 people (*Anglican Church Directory*, 1993). Against this loss are the compensating features of increased finances, a lively charismatic youth program, an active Native ministry and an optimistic outlook to the future.

Baptists

Baptists are fond of saying that their form of denominationalism did not emerge from the vision of any one individual except perhaps John the Baptist of New Testament times. Baptists are "heavy on local autonomy," and even congregations within a given Baptist denomination have full autonomy from their conference colleagues. There is a considerable variety of Baptist denominations in both Canada and the USA, some of whose leaders might even object to being included in the "mainline" category of church organizations. In truth it would be fair to include Baptists in all three theological camps – mainline, conservative and fundamentalist. Altogether they number about 663 000 in Canada.

Pedigree

When the Reformation impacted upon Europe in the 16th century, use of the word "Baptist" appeared in scattered settlements in Germany and Switzerland. Actually, the preferred word was "anti-pedobaptist" which means that these groups were opposed to infant or child baptism (Mead, 1983). Some Baptist historians argue that similarities existed between various evangelical Christian groups who fellowshipped during the period between the time of the

Apostles and the Reformation. A few of these groups were Montanists, Novatians and Donatists. Another community, which by the way, is also traced in lineage by other small evangelical denominations, was the Waldenses, or Waldensian Church. The existence of this group can apparently be traced back to the time of the Apostles, quite independent of the Roman Catholic Church. Today there are about 25 000 members in the Waldensian Church mostly located in Italy, Argentina, Uruguay and the USA. They maintain a publishing house, social agencies, hospitals and African missions (Douglas, 1991). Apparently the similarity of their beliefs to that of modern Baptists is sufficient evidence to suggest that Baptist denominations have deep historic roots.

To be specific, there is evidence that by 1643 there were about seven congregations around London, England, who identified themselves as Baptists and drew up a Confession of Faith which would be acceptable to most Baptists today. At about the same time Roger Williams was identified as a Baptist preacher in New England. After getting involved in controversy he made his way to Massachusetts, started a church, and quickly managed to influence others in "the way." The second Baptist congregation started in Newport in 1641, and more followed. Henry Dunster, the first president of Harvard University in 1636, had to resign his post because of his "Baptist" leanings, particularly his opposition to infant baptism (Newman, 1953).

At the beginning of the 19th century there were very few Baptist congregations in Canada; most of them were centred in the Maritimes. Independence from one another and local autonomy seem to have been the order of the day. For example, the Convention of Regular Baptists of British Columbia began in 1927, and the Prairie Regular Baptist Missionary Fellowship started in 1930. The Fellowship of Independent Baptists in Ontario started in 1933, and in 1945 the BC Regulars and the General Association of Regular Baptists in Washington State merged to form the Northwest Baptist Fellowship (Davis, 1980). Later the Southern Baptists entered Canada and a decade ago built a seminary near Calgary, Alberta. Although there are many subgroups among Baptists, at present two-thirds of all Baptist Churches belong to the Baptist Federation of Canada.

Principles & Precepts

One Baptist principle, namely adult baptism by immersion, as a statement of personal faith and a prerequisite to church membership, appears to be held with consistency by all Baptist subdivisions. Some congregations accept members by transfer who have been baptized by other modes, but they cannot become ordained without being rebaptized by immersion. In an attempt to be more specific, however, the following beliefs also appear generally to be adhered to across the various Baptist constituencies: the Bible is the sole authority for man's salvation, faith and practice; baptism is a believer's privilege and must be by full immersion; church and state are completely separate; there are no Sacraments (only two ordinances, baptism and the Lord's Supper); and, church discipline must be practiced in business, family and personal life. Oddly enough, Baptists themselves joke that if there are four Baptists in a room there will be five views on theology. One Canadian Baptist leader even went so far as to suggest that there *is* no Baptist theology (Beverley, 1988). Humor aside, Baptists of all flavors traditionally followed a very precise prescription about such matters as "specific salvation," meaning that adherents should know the exact date and hour of their conversion, adult baptism and Calvinistic leanings in theology (Jackson, 1984). Many of them still adhere to this informal code.

Practices

Baptists are expected to live the Christian life according to a fairly rigid list of expectations. Members vow to do so at the time of baptism and admittance to membership, and a form of church discipline is usually put in place to deal with deviance. Members are expected to attend worship services regularly, tithe their income, and witness to their neighbors about spiritual matters. They should study the Bible, engage in some form of church service and raise up their children in the "admonition of the Lord." Traditionally, nearly all Baptists (with the possible exception of Southern Baptists), have been forbidden to smoke. Other taboos included drinking, playing cards or engaging in other forms of worldliness. Today these restrictions apply mostly in more conservative Baptist organizations.

Involvement in resolving social issue has been a dicey topic among Baptists and even today many congregations are struggling to formulate and define any kind of statement of behavior, corporate and individual, in this regard. There are many arenas in which to tackle this heavy challenge: the ecumenical movement, political theology, female ministry, essentials of theology and new forms of evangelism (Pinnock, 1988).

Peculiarities

Baptists are pretty well unique in their belief that adult believers must declare their confession of faith by being baptized via total immersion. A number of smaller evangelical and fundamentalist churches also hold tenaciously to this particular doctrine.

Lutherans

The Lutheran Church's claim to fame is that her connection to the Protestant Reformation is direct in regard to the individual who is most frequently credited for initiating it – Martin Luther. The title, "Lutherans" was originally just a nick-name tacked onto the actions of Luther's followers in the early days of the Reformation. They preferred to think of themselves as "evangelicals." One of the more conservative groups within Lutheranism, the Missouri Synod, begun in 1847, would probably even object to being listed among mainline denominations. They prefer to think of themselves as more restrictive and fundamental.

Lutheran churchmen today like to suggest that the name Lutheran is probably too restrictive to be given to a movement that is not limited to an era nor an individual, but is as ecumenical and abiding as Christianity itself (Mead, 1983). In fact, Lutheran churches today exist in virtually every country in the world. There are 636 000 Lutherans in Canada.

Pedigree

Divisions in Lutheran theological interpretation resulted almost immediately after the Reformation. Evangelical Lutheranism was on one side and the Reformed tradition, from which Presbyterianism sprang, was on the other. Reformed leaders included John Calvin, Ulrich Zwingli and John Knox. Lutheranism made its way to North America with a first church service at Hudson Bay in 1619 and a colony settlement from Holland at Manhattan in 1623. Today there are almost nine million Lutherans in North America.

The earliest controversy which divided the Lutherans arose during Luther's lifetime and lasted until 1560. It concerned differences about the precise meaning of the terms "law" and "gospel." According to Luther (and the distinction runs through all Lutheranism) law and gospel are two factors which assure the individual of salvation. Law is the rule of life given by God, and accompanied by threat and promise, which counts on fulfillment from selfish desires and so produces contrition. Gospel is the message of salvation and comes after the law has done its work, and soothes. An earlier interpretation suggested that this position means that good works are both necessary and useful to holiness. The opposition said that this position limited the grace of God in salvation, and the argument raged on. Finally, when the Lutherans completed the Formula of Concord in 1577 it drew Lutherans closer together and pitted them more firmly against the Reformed churches.

A number of serious attempts to unite the Lutheran and the Reformed divisions were undertaken in 1631, 1645, and 1661, but to no avail. Some of the stricter Lutherans stayed out of these ecumenical conferences, but the two major bodies simply continued their separate ways.

Principles & Precepts

The story of Luther's rebellion against the Roman Catholic Church is well-known to church historians. His position was that the Roman Catholic Church and the papacy had no Divine right in things spiritual, and the Scriptures, not the priest or the church, had the final authority over conscience. In 1519 Luther wrote his Longer and Shorter Catechisms, and in 1537 drew up the Smalcald Articles of Faith. Later, as mentioned, in 1577 the Formula of Concord was formulated. These documents basically constitute the basis of Lutheran theology today.

Summarized, Lutheran theology rests on Luther's firm beliefs on the priesthood of all believers, and the consequent right of Christians enlightened by the Holy Spirit to interpret the Scriptures according to their own judgement. Perhaps Luther's major contribution to Protestantism was his promotion of individualism in matters of faith. Luther believed in respecting the Bible as the Word of God, and in justification by faith and faith alone. Faith must be individually embraced. In fact, Luther felt so strongly about this principle that he suggested that any book of the Bible that did not explicitly teach that truth should be doubted as being Divinely-inspired (Newman, 1953). This gave him serious doubts about the Epistle of James, for example, which he relegated to the very end of his translation of the Bible. Reflecting his Catholic background, and though he was severely criticized for his stand, Luther also believed strongly in the combination of church and state. Consistent with his stand on state religion, Luther also retained belief in infant baptism. The other Sacrament which Lutherans have retained is the Eucharist; their interpretation is a middle-road position between the Roman Catholic interpretation as an "Act of God" and the general evangelical position that the Sacraments are ordinances only. Lutherans see the Sacraments as channels through which God bestows His forgiving and empowering grace on the church.

Practices

With the exception of The Lutheran Church-Missouri Synod, most of the half dozen Lutheran churches in North America work well with one another. The Missouri Synod group was founded on the basis that it wanted to operate solely on the basis of a "pure and uncorrupted explanation of the Word of God." It is the second largest Lutheran Church in North America. At one time there were 150 Lutheran denominations in the USA, but six of them had about 95 percent of all the members (Mead, 1983).

Lutherans tend to be very loyal to their denomination and to their local congregation. They believe very much in participating in the worship, and in appropriating the Sacraments. They believe that, in the act of salvation, believers are filled with the Holy Spirit. They do not accept the doctrine of the second experience, meaning a separate act of God, for the infilling of the Holy Spirit. Their youth are confirmed as teenagers via catechetical instruction in the Bible, and Lutheran church doctrine and history are taught with great rigor.

Peculiarities

Next to Roman Catholics, Lutherans probably have the most liturgical (formal) services. The organization of the church is similarly quite formal; churches are united in synods which have considerable power. Local congregations, for example, cannot depose a pastor from the ministry because ministers are ordained by the synod. Depending on their European country of origin, Lutherans in North America have also tended to reflect strong ethnic affiliations.

Pentecostals

For the most part Pentecostal churches have emerged from within established churches, and they virtually cover the theological range of identification from mainline to fundamentalist. Still, as one of the larger Canadian denominations, and one that is rapidly assimilating into the domain of dominant societal values, Pentecostalism appears to have "come of age." One example would be participation by pentecostals in the biennial Canadian Christian Festival sponsored by a consortium of church denominations known as the PLURAS group – Pentecostal, Lutheran, United Church, Roman Catholic, Anglican and Salvation Army. Other evangelical churches have participated in some of the activities of the festival, albeit only informally.

Pentecostals are not normally included in the "mainline" category of church denominations, and, theologically-speaking they probably belong in the evangelical or fundamentalist camps. However, in light of their rapidly-increasing numbers and potential for influencing great numbers of Canadians, they may well become one of Canada's future mainline churches. There are about 436 000 Pentecostals in Canada. Equally their successful efforts in overseas mission work, particularly in Latin American countries, cannot be ignored (Aland, 1986).

Pedigree

Who are the Pentecostals? They are revivalist Christians who believe in miracles through the personal work of the Holy Spirit, and they believe that the supernatural can happen anytime, anywhere (Durasoff, 1972). They may draw parallels between their beliefs and practices and those of the New Testament Apostles, but they also admit that for the longest time, not much happened in church history by way of pentecostalism. Some would say that the ministry of Methodist founder John Wesley brought new hope, except that Wesley deviated from the needed mandate. A further development was the formulation of camp meetings which comprised great outdoor revival events. These were formalized with the organization of the National Camp Meeting Association in 1867 in the USA. The issue of interpreting holiness arose soon after, and between 1893 and 1900 about 23 holiness denominations were formed out of the Methodist ranks. Some of these groups have familiar-sounding names in the world of modern-day evangelicals – Christian and Missionary Alliance, Free Methodists and Nazarenes (Durasoff, 1972).

Pentecostalism today is an inclusive term that applies to a wide range of revivalist churches, sects or groups. New names for newly-organized subgroups are constantly springing up, many of them employing diversionary titles such as Community Church, Neighborhood Church, New Life Church, Victory Life, Vineyard Church, etc. The rationale is that non-pentecostal-sounding church names may draw in the unsuspecting visitor who, on experiencing the fellowship of said church, will remain permanently.

There was a time when the pentecostal movement in North America suffered an image problem, probably because of their continuing revivalist practices at a time when society was undergoing a more sedate form of religion. A common nick-name for churches engaging in these kinds of activities was "Holy Rollers," and their meetings included long fiery sermons, loud music, altar calls, divine healing and speaking in tongues. Other evangelical churches also engage in these kind of activities from time to time, and thanks to the charismatic movement of the 1960s which affected several mainline churches (including Roman Catholic and Anglican), the Pentecostals have had less of an image problem. Actually the charismatic line of demarcation does not necessarily help explain things for everyone since some observers say that the charismatic movement has always been around. It has from time to time manifested itself throughout church history (Bouyer, 1975). Nevertheless, pentecostalism in *our* time can be traced to some very specific situations and happenings.

Pentecostal historians like to trace their origins to the time of the Apostles – to the era when the Holy Spirit was poured out on the Apostles (as a second experience) and they began to speak in strange tongues (Durasoff, 1972). Probably the best known pentecostal denomination in Canada is the Pentecostal Assemblies of Canada Church which, in many instances, appears to have become quite mainline in philosophy and practice.

Principles & Precepts

For the most part, pentecostalism is a fundamentalist religion, and clings tenaciously to the old-time doctrines such as the atoning blood of Christ, the virgin birth of Jesus Christ, belief in the literal and infallible Word of God and a very strong emphasis on the work of the Holy Spirit in an individual's life.

Practices

Essentially fundamentalist in practice, members of pentecostal congregations were historically forbidden to engage in all of the "standard" sins – smoking, drinking, going to the theatre, swearing, etc. They were also expected to be very active in their local church and engage very seriously in an individual and corporate program of evangelization. Pentecostals practice adult baptism by immersion only and on occasion celebrate the Lord's Supper. Their clergy often manage the local church through democratically-run congregational meetings although the larger pentecostal denominations are moving more towards some kind of centralized form of church administration. Clergy in these churches are not usually seminary or university educated, but tend to be men (and sometimes women) who are very sure of their Divine call to ministry. Beyond that they may have received training at a Bible school or Bible College for three or four years.

Peculiarities

The one point that separates pentecostalism from other evangelical denominations is their emphasis on the work of the Holy Spirit. Basically Arminian in theology, Pentecostals believe that the "filling of the Holy Spirit" is quite separate from conversion. They admit that it *can* happen at the point of salvation but more than likely is a later, "second experience" of grace. When an individual is filled with the Holy Spirit, he or she will speak in tongues, that is, in a different God-given language of praise. At this point there are some minor differences among Pentecostals. Some will insist that the Spirit-filled person *will* speak in tongues, while others soften their position by suggesting that this experience *should* happen. Further, is the matter of interpretation. Some of the most Biblically-literal fundamentalists will insist that when an individual speaks in tongues, an equally and simultaneously inspired person must be present to interpret the inherent message to the congregation. Some congregations do not adhere to this requirement and suggest that speaking in tongues can also be solely for individual spiritual gratification regardless of who may be listening.

Pentecostals insist that their church also recognizes other spiritual gifts than speaking in tongues, such as healing, preaching, teaching, etc., but in practice it is the gift of speaking in tongues that seems to get all the emphasis and publicity.

Presbyterians

The Reformed tradition dating from the time of the Protestant Reformation is best represented today in the Presbyterian Church.

Pedigree

The Presbyterian Church is another offshoot of the Reformation, this time principally in Scotland. This fact provides an historic authentication to their ethnic roots. After Martin Luther's spotlight dimmed a bit, the Reformation experienced greater success in Geneva, where it drew attention to the work of John Calvin (1509-1564). At a time when major splits were occurring in the movement, John Calvin's influence allowed a galvanizing hold on a significant number of Protestants. Then came John Knox (1505-1572), whose influence aided in the development of a presbyterian character for the Geneva Academy (Aland, 1986). In any event, the Academy became the teaching centre for the Reformation.

All of this is very well and good, and shows the origins of the Presbyterian Church to be much like that of any other denomination. However, if one were to take into account the interpretation of a "good" Presbyterian historian, the origin of the church might be explained in terms something like these:

> The Presbyterian is the earliest type of organization in human history for the worship and service of the true God. [It began] . . . When the Hebrew slaves were led out of Egypt, and kept at school in the desert for forty years, learning of God, as the world's first organized body of His worshippers (Scott, 1928).

Now *that's* a unique history, but accuracy is not the major concern here – interpretation is. This is why it behooves the seeker to check out several different versions of denominational history before identifying formally with its claimed "specialness" with God. It is especially important to be aware of the loyalties of the various writers before necessarily buying into their interpretations. By the way, in response to the claim that the Hebrew slaves were "Presbyterians," a corresponding, but taunting Methodist observation was that the first followers of Jesus were probably Methodists. After all, the word "Methodist" is derived from two Greek words – *meta* – after, and *hodos,* a way (Chown, 1930, 84). The Bible records that St. Paul, "while yet breathing threatening and slaughter against the disciples of the Lord, went to the high priest of the Jewish religion, and desired of him letters unto the synagogues of Damascus, that if he found any of *the way* he might bring them bound to Jerusalem" (Acts 9:1-2, KJV). Tricky business, this church history!

Like most other Reformation denominations, Scottish Presbyterianism spread – to England, for example. During the period of 1648-1660 the English and Scottish Presbyterians managed to gain hold on the British Parliament. Their purpose was to ensure that all Englanders would endorse Presbyterianism as a state religion. As history shows, they lost their bid and many of their clergy were later persecuted under Oliver Cromwell's administration. Some congregations endured, despite heavy opposition, but many clergy also turned Unitarian during this time (Newman, 1953).

As time went on, there were divisions in the Presbyterian Church. For example, in 1743 a group of dissenters broke away to organize the Reformed Presbytery. Later this action was transferred to the United States when, in 1744, they organized the Reformed Presbyterian Church of North America at Harrisburg, Pennsylvania. In 1833 they further divided over the question of whether or not one could hold public office and still serve God. The result was the Reformed Presbyterian Church in North America, General Synod, and the Reformed Presbyterian Church of North America, Old School (Ferm, 1945). Later another half dozen offshoots evolved.

The first American Presbyterian congregation was established around 1740 in New York City, and almost immediately became embroiled in controversy when an argument ensued about the use of a book of hymns by Isaac Watts to replace the traditional book of metrical psalms by Francis Rous. British Evangelist George Whitefield (1714-1770) and his converts saw nothing wrong in promoting variation in worship, but the old guard insisted that nothing be used in worship that could not be justified in scripture (Melton, 1967).

During the early part of the 19th century, Presbyterianism came to Canada so that from 1817 to 1870 there were two church associations in what was then Upper Canada and four in the Maritime provinces. In 1875 the four united to form the Presbyterian Church in Canada. Fifty years later, in 1925, when the majority of Presbyterian Churches in Canada voted to form the United Church of Canada, several presbyteries remained independent, not wanting to participate in what their most severe critics called, "the killing time" (Scott, 1928). The reasons for the Presbyterian pull-out of this church union are many; some Presbyterians argue that they were primarily doctrinal reasons, while others suggest that the Canadian Presbyterians were probably more of an ethnic group than either of the other two bodies involved, namely Methodists and Congregationalists. Today there are 636 000 Presbyterians in Canada.

While the United Church merger talks were nearing completion, a theological controversy erupted in the American Presbyterian Church that kept liberals and conservatives at each other's throats for the next decade. It was a sermon by Harry Emerson Fosdick in First Presbyterian Church in New York on 21 May 1922, that precipitated the controversy, Fosdick making a plea for peace between the two. When the national Presbyterian Church met for its 1923 General Assembly, Fosdick's plea became the central issue of the convention.

In 1924, Fosdick was removed from his pulpit, and there were rumblings of discontent in the ranks of the faculty at the denomination's college, Princeton University. In 1929 the evangelical wing of the Presbyterian Church began a rival school, Westminster Theological Seminary. Within a few years the controversy had run its course and a sort of peace prevailed. However, Presbyterianism also began its long course downwards in terms of membership losses, the reason of which are not immediately clear (Longfield, 1991). Some have speculated that the Presbyterian Church, like other mainline churches, has failed to attract and retain members because of their failure to articulate a clear belief system (Kelley, 1972). Whether this analysis is correct or not is difficult to say, but it does appear that religious pluralism is an emerging reality in the Presbyterian Church.

Principles & Precepts

Unlike its two partners in Canadian church union negotiations, the Presbyterian Church historically operated in governing districts know as presbyteries. These are groups of churches which band together for local policy-making and implementation. Methodists, like their mother body, the Anglican Church, tended to be episcopal in government and Congregationalists have always operated in accordance with the principle of local autonomy.

Essentially Presbyterians trace their lineage to the Reformation, but they claim to be unique in several distinct ways. For example, though their confession of faith is generically Christian, they lean heavily towards the emphasis formulated by John Calvin, in holding tenaciously to the doctrine of the elect. In fact, the City of Geneva, where Calvin expounded the Scriptures, wrote books and provided a confession of faith for his followers, was called "the most perfect school of Christ that ever was since the days of the Apostles" (Henderson, n.d.). The Presbyterians are catholic in the sense that they claim membership along with non-Presbyterians in the one universal Christian church. They are evangelical in the sense that they believe in witnessing to others who, on the basis of conversion, become their own priests before God. They are unique in that they are inextricably bound to other Presbyterians in a common and strict theology popularly known as Calvinism. It has even been suggested that Presbyterian Churches regard the common doctrinal allegiance as the basic aspect of their unity. Calvin's system may be summarized in five points: human impotence (everybody needs God), unconditional predestination (God chooses whom He wants to save), limited atonement (only the elect will be saved), irresistible grace (no one can refuse God's grace) and final perseverance (eternal security for the believer) (Mead, 1983).

Practices

Essentially Protestant in character, Presbyterian believers try to live out Christianity in practical daily life. They are expected to attend worship, read the Bible and be good to their neighbors. Their ministers are highly educated and the church supports military involvement. Their two Sacraments are Holy Baptism and the Eucharist. In 1925 the church generally adopted the Westminster statement (which is essentially a Church of England statement of faith) with only minor modifications. These included restricting divorce for infidelity, denying infant damnation, extending the Sacraments to all who profess faith and who profess to pursue the Christian life, abandoning the exclusive use of psalms, reaffirming belief in the verbal inspiration of the Bible, affirming Christ as the only way to salvation and affirming that salvation is open to all.

In 1960, a committee presented new guidelines for worship to the General Assembly of the Presbyterian Church, which were accepted. The New Directory for Worship revived some Calvinist ideas such as the weekly celebration of the Lord's Supper, a new emphasis in worship on both liberty and orderliness, and more corporateness in confession and in saying "Amen" at the end of prayers led by the minister (Loetscher, 1978).

Peculiarities

If the Presbyterian Church is anything, it is committed to, and actively pursues, accuracy – at least in its own interpretation of the role of the church. Still somewhat ethnically-bound, Presbyterians pride themselves on their form of church government and explicitness of theology (Calvinist). They are proud of their biblical base for theology and what they term their 20th century "dedication to change" (Melton, 1967):

> Never must the church sponsor a blanched, eviscerated, spineless statement of its faith. It must give birth in this revolutionary transition time to a full-blooded, loyally-biblical, unashamedly ecumenical, and strongly vertebrate system of Christian belief (McKay, 1960).

United Church of Canada

In 1925 the "impossible" occurred in Canadian church history. Three Christian denominations of three entirely different doctrinal persuasions organized a truly national church for a new country. Congregationalists, Methodists and Presbyterians birthed the new United Church of Canada that year, and what made it virtually impossible was the fact of their historical credal and organizational differences. The Congregationalists were strong on local autonomy and were "liberal" Anglicans in origin, so liberal, in fact, that most of their original congregations in the United States have since turned

Unitarian. The Methodists were episcopal in government and Wesleyan-Arminian in theology. At the other end of the spectrum were the Presbyterians – governed by the democratic form of the presbytery and Calvinistic theology. That these groups could even *think* of merging, much less accomplish it, would today be theologically unthinkable. About 3 079 000 Canadians call themselves adherents to the United Church of Canada.

Pedigree

It is interesting to briefly examine the three church traditions that make up the United Church of Canada.

(i) *Congregationalists.* The smallest partner of the three-way union, this church traces it roots to the non-conformist, or independent movement in England, at the time of the Reformation. When church union occurred their theological repertoire consisted of: liberty of conscience, a strange mixture of evangelical zeal and doctrinal eccentricity, and devotion to the principle of congregational independence (Saunders, 1985). They paid a price for the latter conviction, of course, and constantly had to deal with the problem of local church interpretation. Even though union talks began as early as the 1880s it took the Congregationalists until 1906 to establish a national organization to participate in the talks. Local autonomy does not easily lend itself to corporate decision-making.

(ii) *Methodists.* In 1736, John Wesley, accompanied by his brother Charles, was sent to America by the Society for the Propagation of the Gospel of the Church of England as a missionary to the American Indians. Enroute the brothers met up with a group of Moravians who seemed to be so on "fire for the Lord," that the experience could not be forgotten. On his return to England, Wesley, caught up with the Moravian evangelical fervor, began preaching it. He was soon chastised by more sedate English state church officials. John and his brother began to hold services in barns, homes, mining pits and wherever they could attract crowds. Thus the first Methodist society was formed in 1739 and attached to a Moravian congregation in Fetter Lane, London. Though Wesley tried hard to remain in the Church of England, he was eventually ousted for his radical preaching. Immigrants bound to America took the new religion with them, and in 1769 the New York Methodists built their landmark church, Wesley Chapel.

Methodism in Canada began in a small way; in 1781 the Rev. William Black, styled as the "Apostle of Wesleyan Methodism," began his work in the eastern provinces. As the church developed it was affiliated with the New York Conference, but became an independent body in 1828 (Hopper, 1904).

Ironically (at least in name), church union talks in Canada began in 1886 when the Synod of the Anglican Province of Canada invited Presbyterians and Methodists to confer on the subject. The Church of England was officially invited to join union talks in 1906, as were the Baptists. The latter group simply declined the offer, but the Church of England was more specific; the episcopate was to be a "given" in negotiations. When this could not be guaranteed, they too pulled out of church merger talks.

Before the Methodists could enter merger talks with a unified front they had to "merge on their own." This required two internal unions. In 1874 the Wesleyan New Connexion united with the Wesleyans of the Upper and Maritime provinces. Ten years later they were joined by the Methodist Episcopals, Primitive Methodists and Bible Christians to form the Methodist Church (Grant, 1967). Now, church negotiations among the three "official" denominations could begin.

(iii) *Presbyterians*. When the last of three congregational votes on the United Church merger was taken in 1924, one-third of the Presbyterians declared themselves by ballot as wanting to stay out of the union. These dissenters are the spiritual ancestors of the Presbyterian Church in Canada today. There were a number of reasons why some chose not to "go into union," the most radical of these was wanting to "stay loyal to the truth" (Scott, 1928). Some Presbyterians feared that a watering down of doctrine would occur with merger, while others simply found it difficult to give up their ethnic roots.

Church Union

In any event, the United Church came to be, and her founders did their best to incorporate Presbyterian basics. For the first 25 years the church experienced real growth (Beaton, 1949). Then a period of stabilization set in after which the membership began to decline.

The governance pattern of the United Church today is essentially Presbyterian. Important local church actions, like the calling of a minister, have to be approved by Presbytery. The offices of bishop and district superintendent (episcopal offices), as senior officials, were abolished. A common complaint about the United Church's composition is that the church has retained Presbyterian dignity and Congregational freedom, but has not done justice to the evangelical emphasis of Methodism. The proceedings of Church courts are usually conducted with a Scottish seriousness, and Presbyterian precedents are more likely to be cited than Methodist. A specific debt to Congregationalism is not so easy to identify, but many United Church people travelling abroad find that it is in churches of the Congregational order that they are reminded most forcibly of home (Grant, 1967).

Principles & Precepts

There is ample reason why the United Church should be thought of as a "mainline" Christian denomination; the church believes most "mainline" things in Christian theology – the plenary inspiration of Scripture, encouragement of a "half-tithe," ordination of "fit" individuals regardless of sexual orientation, the two "standard" Sacraments, active political agitation and a not too-well-defined eschatology. Even their contemporary rendition of the traditional "Apostle's Creed" reflects a penchant for trying to be relevant to the Canadian mainstream:

> We are not alone, we live in God's world.
> We believe in God: who has created and is creating, who has come in Jesus, the Word made flesh, to reconcile and make new, who works in us and others by the Spirit.
> We trust in God.
> We are called to be the Church: to celebrate God's presence, to love and serve others, to seek justice and resist evil, to proclaim Jesus, crucified and risen, our judge and our hope.
> In life, in death, in life beyond death, God is with us.
> We are not alone.
> Thanks be to God.

For the United Church, trying to live the Christian life is more important than "getting it together" theologically (Crysdale, 1966).

Practices

Despite her apparent, "liberalism," the United Church affirms that all Christians are called upon to witness, and participate in, the ministry of Jesus Christ to the world. This ministry of judgment and redemption addresses persons, institutions and the whole culture. Christ calls individuals from dividedness to oneness, from death in isolation to life in the community. The church recognizes that these are times of ferment, and members are called upon to join the national church in the area of theological struggle and the quest for social justice *(Yearbook and Directory,* 1993). The United Church prides herself on being a "uniting church," and in 1968 two additional denominations joined the union, the Evangelical United Brethren Church (situated in Ontario) and two congregations of Brethren in Christ Church situated in Alberta. More than this, however, the United Church has been very active in promoting ecumenism in Canada through the Canadian Council of Churches, the Christian Festival of Faith and through various local Interfaith Agencies. Her leaders have often been "first in line" when it has appeared necessary to remind national government officials about some injustice being done to Canadian citizens.

Peculiarities

If it is true that the United Church has downplayed her Methodist roots of evangelistic zeal, the substituted theological axiom has been a zestful social concern. The United Church has consistently been at the forefront of social change since merger. One of the most severe criticisms of the church has been in this area. The church is accused of being liberal in practice, wishy-washy on theology and too much involved in political concerns. The membership seems to support this orientation. In 1965 the Board of Evangelism and Social Service of The United Church of Canada gave its approval to survey their constituents in this area. The results indicated that while four-fifths of the church's members believed in the Divinity of Christ, one third rejected a literal view of miracles. A majority of the members endorsed national medicare, and indicated strong support for other public measures for social welfare and economic planning. Congregations were generally hesitant about evangelism, but 54 percent had concrete projects of service going on in their congregations (Crysdale,1965). The United Church may not be a theologically traditional church, but her members do seem to care about others.

References

Abel, Kerry. (1991). Bishop Bompas and the Canadian church. In Barry Ferguson (Ed.), *The Anglican church and the world of western Canada, 1820-1970* (pp. 113-125). Regina, SK: Canadian Plains Research Center.

Aland, Karl. (1986). *A history of Christianity* (2 vols.). Philadelphia: Fortress Press.

Anglican church directory, 1993. Toronto: Anglican Book Centre.

Beaton, Kenneth J. (1949). *Growing with the years*. Toronto: The United Church of Canada.

Berton, Pierre. (1965). *The comfortable pew*. Toronto: McClelland and Stewart.

Beverley, James A. (1988). Tensions in Canadian Baptist theology, 1975-1987. In Jarold K. Zeman (Ed.), *Costly vision: the baptist pilgrimage in Canada* (pp. 217-240). Burlington, ON: Welch Publishing Co.

Bouyer, Louis. (1975). Some charismatic movements in the history of the church. In Edward D. O'Connor (Ed.), *Perspectives on charismatic renewal* (pp. 133-144). Notre Dame, IN: University of Notre Dame Press.

Carter, David J. (Ed.). (1975). *The Anglican church in Calgary*. Calgary, AB: Century Calgary Publications.

Chown, S.D. (1930). *The story of church union in Canada*. Toronto: The Ryerson Press.

Crysdale, Stewart. (1965). *The changing church in Canada*. Toronto: The United Church of Canada.

Crysdale, Stewart. (1966). *Churches where the action is*. Toronto: The United Church of Canada.

Davis, Kenneth R. (1980). The struggle for a united Evangelical Baptist Fellowship, 1953-1965. In Jarold K. Zeman (Ed.), *Baptists in Canada: Search for identity amidst diversity* (pp. 237-266). Burlington, ON: G.R. Welch.

Douglas, J.D. (Ed.). (1991). *New 20th-century encyclopedia of religious knowledge* (2nd ed.). Grand Rapids, MI: Baker Book House.

Durasoff, Steve. (1972). *Bright wind of the spirit.* Englewood Cliffs, NJ: Prentice-Hall, Inc.

Ferm, Vergilius. (1945). *An encyclopedia of religion.* New York: The Philosophical Library.

Friesen, John W. (1993). *When cultures clash: Case studies in multiculturalism* (2nd ed.). Calgary, AB: Detselig Enterprises Ltd.

Goodman, M.L. (n.d.). *The diocese of Calgary.* Calgary, AB: The Anglican Diocese.

Grant, John Webster. (1967). *The Canadian experience of church union.* Richmond, VA: John Knox Press.

Henderson, G.D. (n.d.). *Why we are Presbyterians.* Edinburgh, UK: Church of Scotland Publications.

Hillerbrand, Hans J. (1964). *The reformation: A narrative history related by contemporary observers and participants.* New York: Harper & Row.

Hopper, Mrs. R.P. (1904). *Old-time primitive Methodism in Canada, 1829-1884.* Toronto: William Briggs.

Jackson, Jeremy C. (1984). *No other foundation: The church through twenty centuries.* Westchester, IL: Crossway Books.

Kelley, Dean M. (1972). *Why conservative churches are growing: a study in sociology of religion.* San Francisco, CA: Harper & Row.

Loetscher, Lefferts A. (1978). *A brief history of the Presbyterians.* (3rd ed.). Philadelphia: The Westminster Press.

Longfield, Bradley J. (1991). *The Presbyterian controversy: Fundamentalists, modernists, and moderates.* New York: Oxford University Press.

McKay, John A. (1960). *The Presbyterian way of life.* Englewood Cliffs, NJ: Prentice Hall.

Mead, Frank S. (1983). *Handbook of denominations in the United States.* Nashville, TN: Abingdon Press.

Melton, Julius. (1967). *Presbyterian worship in America: Changing patterns since 1787.* Richmond, VA: John Knox Press.

Newman, Albert Henry. (1953). *A manual of church history* (2 vols.). Chicago: The American Baptist Publication Society.

Nock, David A. (1993). The organization of religious life in Canada. In W.E. Hewitt (Ed.), *The sociology of religion in Canada* (pp. 41-63). Toronto: Butterworths.

Pinnock, Clarke H. (1988). Baptists and the "Latter Rain." In Jarold K. Zeman (Ed.), *Costly vision: The Baptist pilgrimage in Canada* (pp. 255-272). Burlington, ON: Welch Publishing Co.

Saunders, J. Clark. (1985). Congregationalism in Manitoba, 1879-1937. In Dennis L. Butcher, et al. (Eds.), *Prairie spirit: Perspectives on the heritage of the United Church of Canada* (pp. 122-146). Winnipeg, MB: The University of Manitoba Press.

Scott, Ephraim. (1928). *"Church Union" and the Presbyterian Church in Canada.* Montreal, PQ: John Lovell & Son Ltd.

Yearbook and directory, 1993. Toronto: The United Church of Canada.

16

Fervent Protestants The Evangelicals

Having outlined the form and practice of Canadian mainline church denominations the task at hand gets more difficult. Partially, the problem stems from our use of language. We do not have adequate words by which to distinguish some of the smaller, more conservative Christian religious bodies in the country. Labels that are sometimes bandied about when these more conservative denominations are discussed include: evangelical, fundamentalist, conservative, and sometimes even sect and cult.

To Differentiate

One of the pioneers in the sociology of religion in the 1930s, Ernst Troeltsch, devised a model for differentiating between "church" and "sect" (Friesen, 1972). He suggested that the *church* tends to be the more universal in nature, possesses a definable organizational structure with a paid ministry, features a fairly stable set of expectations for their membership, and largely accepts the dominant social and political order. *Sects,* by contrast, are small, often locally-run bodies who have no paid ministry, and are either hostile or indifferent to the dominant social and political order. Two decades later, Richard Niebuhr built on this schematic and looked at the process by which churches tended to spawn sects and how sects later tended to grow "respectable" enough to become churches (Nock, 1993). Canadian sociologist, S.D. Clark later applied this formula to this nation in a ground-breaking study of church and sect (Clark, 1942). In following this logic we will attempt to differentiate among fundamentalists, evangelicals, conservatives, sects and cults.

Fundamentalists

The use of language tends to change as time goes on, and in this instance clearer lines of demarcation have recently tended to appear on the religious scene. The word "fundamentalist," for example, brings up the notion of holding fast to something that is very strongly believed. We can obtain a little assistance from history in this context, because there have been times when fundamentalist controversies have broken out and were identified as such. One incident occurred in the early part of this century just prior to the First World War. A number of denominations were involved in it, such as Baptists and

Presbyterians. The issues were whether or not Christ was born of a virgin, whether the Bible was verbally inspired or if it just "contained" the Word of God, and would there be a literal physical second coming of Christ.

Another example of a fundamentalist controversy occurred with the Scopes trial in 1925 when William Jennings Bryan, a conservative Presbyterian, took on lawyer Clarence Darrow in what was later billed as the "monkey trial." The central issue was evolution, and the debate was whether or not it should be taught in public schools in the manner that a young biology teacher named John T. Scopes had done in Dayton, Ohio. Bryan lost the case (Longfield, 1991).

Christian fundamentalists are fond of making definitive statements like those frequently uttered by American evangelist, Jerry Falwell, "The Bible is absolutely infallible, without error in all matters pertaining to faith and practice, as well as in areas such as geography, science, history, etc." (Ammerman, 1987). This kind of pronouncement leaves no room for doubt, argument nor intelligent discussion. This case is closed. Christianity is not the only religion susceptible to fundamentalist claims; most world religions have these folk in their midst – Judaism, Islam, Sikhism, etc. Sometimes, as in the case of Sikhism or Islam, the promulgators identify the epistemology of their faith with geographic implications. Contemporary Islamic fundamentalists are not content to see the formation of an Islamic state under the umbrella of nationalism; it must be based on specific religious principles, *their* principles (Lawrence, 1989). Fundamentalist Sikhs insist that the Punjab must be returned to them for rule. Again, there is no room for doubt, argument nor discussion. The case is closed.

Fundamentalism, coupled with political concerns, can have devastating effects. In Algeria, where a civil war has raged since the summer of 1992, the western press has focussed on the attack of foreigners by the Islamic Salvation Front. But far more devastating has been the attack by the Front on those Algerians they regard as the forces of modernity and thus the enemies of Islam. Several key individuals have been assassinated because of their public stand against the Front; several professors have also been killed. Women and teenage girls in Algiers who have refused the regulations of the state have been murdered by the Front. The press estimates that since January 1992, between 4 000 and 5 000 have been killed on both sides with deaths running about 200 a week (*CAUT Bulletin,* 1994).

The cause of fundamentalism in the United States probably received its greatest publicity in the 1988 failed bid for presidency by evangelist Pat Robertson. A former spiritual colleague of backslidden evangelists Jimmy Swaggart and Jimmy Bakker, Robertson tried hard to disassociate himself from the two and still declare his form of Gospel interpretation as the answer to America's ills. He promoted radical change for America, arguing that the nation should return to her Christian roots, as identified in the original Constitution (Capps, 1990).

After reading the above section one might be tempted to ask the question, why would anyone want to join a fundamentalist group? The answer is at least twofold, one reason being that fundamentalists sound so convincing, so sure of themselves. They also seem to have answers to all of life's questions. This orientation alone may be comforting to people in an age of change, flexibility and relativity. The second reason may have to do with guilt; fundamentalists are fond of promoting it. For people who seem to feel that they need forgiveness (because they have been made to feel guilty), fundamentalism may provide a path to personal autonomy and confidence (Ammerman, 1987). In addition, one must look to the job security this arrangement guarantees to the "providers of forgiveness," namely fundamentalist leaders themselves!

Evangelicals

George Marsden once defined a fundamentalist as "an evangelical who is angry about something" (Marsden, 1990, 22). This does not imply that evangelicals cannot get angry nor that they always avoid militant actions. The difference is in emphasis. Evangelicals are concerned about getting the Gospel out, winning the lost and evangelizing the world. It is true that evangelicals pretty much agree with fundamentalists on the basics of their faith, but they are also considered sectarian because they are exclusive in their membership. If, for example, individuals wish to move from one kind of evangelical church to another they would have to request an official membership transfer from their clergyman or church board. The receiving pastor or congregation would then have to make a decision about the theological validity of the sending congregation. In some cases, though these persons would be welcomed into the fold, they might be restricted from holding high office in the church. They might even be requested to be rebaptized.

Evangelicals are first and foremost Christians, and take no delight in being thought of as archaic, dogmatic or unreasonable individuals. On the other hand, evangelicals refuse to let the world dictate their convictions (Inch, 1978). The basis of being an evangelical includes these tenets: a public profession of faith, believer's baptism and a "living relationship" with Jesus Christ. Evangelicals are proud that they uphold theological orthodoxy and reject the liberal, or modernist, theological views that triumphed in academic theology during the 19th century (Hexham, 1993).

For the past 30 years evangelicals have recognized that a crisis exists in terms of the reality of Christian evangelism (De Jong, 1962). Quite frankly, except for a few denominations, evangelism of the "lost" (unconverted) souls simply has not occurred. As the studies of sociologist Reg Bibby have consistently shown over the past two decades, "real" growth in evangelical churches is rare; most of their "converts" tend to be from mainline churches, other evangelical churches or their own children (Bibby, 1987).

Conservative Faiths

For some reason it simply would not be accurate to classify what we have called "conservative" churches with the evangelicals. These churches differ from evangelicals on several counts. In the first instance, many of them have strong ethnic roots, and they are more moderate in evangelism. With some exceptions, they tend to be restrictive, and refrain from involvement in the Canadian Council of Churches or the Canadian Christian Festival of Faith and do not generally participate in local interfaith projects (Bruce, 1984). With the possible exception of their overseas missionary efforts, they tend to let the world come to them rather than going into the "highways and byways" to win the lost. Anabaptist groups are good example of this orientation – Amish, Hutterites and Mennonites.

Perhaps the differentiating characteristic between conservative and evangelical churches is that the former primarily stress the conservation of the church with evangelism being lower on the list of priorities. They speak of the "brotherhood" or the "community of believers" as though the primary obligation is to keep the saints together. Thus it seems appropriate to deal with these churches in a separate chapter.

Sects and Cults

In the classic sense, the term "sect" applies to any new religious movement that is in opposition to developments in contemporary society and to established church denominations. Sects usually arise within the context of existing denominations and usually take an antithetical stand against the mother church. After all, the situation is apparently so bad morally and spiritually that they have to start again. Normally, involvement in a sect becomes the "key" status of an individual's life, overshadowing such important definers of self as gender, family, socioeconomic status or occupation. Members of a sect tend to be judgmental of other religions whose adherents they often see as "sinners" in need of true salvation (Nock, 1993).

The term "cult" has an even stronger connotation, and its use is often controversial. As an ideal type, a cult is a religious movement in a high state of tension with dominant society and its beliefs. Unlike the sect, which largely remains within the confines of the conventional religion, cults leaders promote entirely new and different "truths" that are not part of the conventional religious tradition (Nock, 1993). For example, an Amish or Hutterite group might point to a particular section of scripture as a basis for their deviating from mainstream Anabaptism, whereas the David Koresh cult of Waco, Texas, boasted a brand new and unusual "revelation." While no one particularly likes think of themselves as belonging to a sect or cult, the truth is that many groups may have started out with that designation. As time went on, however, the group gained respectability and changed its public identity. Also, as newer groups keep bursting on the scene with "newer" revelations, the older ones may pale by comparison.

Against this background, this chapter very briefly examines a number of Canadian denominations which claim an allegiance to evangelical theology and practice.

Baptists (Some)

Although Baptists are also included in the earlier section on mainline denominations, there are at least two conservative Baptist conventions which are still quite concerned about "keeping the faith" and "winning the lost." One of these denominations even includes the word "evangelical" in its official title, the Fellowship of Evangelical Baptist Churches. The other denomination is the North American Baptist Conference which has a strong ethnic (German) heritage. A sign of its gradual assimilation into the dominant theological mainstream, however, is the restructuring of its Bible College in Edmonton from a Bible College emphasis to a university and seminary.

As an aside, Canadian Baptists in the Maritimes tend to be more vocal about evangelism, and place more public emphasis on church growth through witnessing (Beverley, 1980).

Christian & Missionary Alliance

This church has the unique distinction of attracting members from other denominations, possibly because of its lack of specific ethnic roots. Its program offers an unbeat, middle class, "with it" kind of theology and practice.

Pedigree

This group had its origins in a movement dating back to 1881 emphasizing witnessing and foreign missions. Then in 1887, A.B. Simpson, a Presbyterian minister, developed distinctive ideas on sanctification and Divine healing and founded the Christian Alliance for local expansion and the Evangelical Missionary Alliance to promote pioneer foreign missions. These two bodies united in 1897 to form The Christian and Missionary Alliance Church.

Early in its growth period the group suffered breakaways to pentecostal concern groups, but it managed to survive. Initially the organization was intended to function as a parachurch organization but over the decades it has developed into a fullfledged denomination with paid, trained pastors and with Baptist and/or evangelical overtones. Members frequently transfer formal memberships and loyalties between Christian and Missionary Alliance churches and other evangelical congregations with ease. The Christian Missionary Alliances Church numbers about 60 000 in Canada.

Principles & Policy

Essentially evangelical in theology, the Christian & Missionary Alliance Church has had difficulty in holding onto its original stress on the doctrine of sanctification and Divine healing as a provision of the atonement (Douglas, 1991), no doubt partially because of its growth through transfer from other churches of "like faith." The denomination doubled its membership between 1978 and 1987 largely through transfers from other evangelical churches, rural to urban moves and "conversions" from mainline denominations.

The Alliance Church is conservative in theology and has affirmed the accuracy of both the Old and New Testaments of the Bible. God's revelation through Jesus Christ is complete and faith in Christ alone is the only possible way to salvation. The church also practices two ordinances: adult baptism by immersion only and the Lord's Supper.

Practices

The Alliance Church expects its adherents to live out a four-fold Gospel: Christ, our Savior; Christ, our Sanctifier; Christ our Healer; and Christ, our coming King. Interpreted into practice these four truths may be rendered as follows: (i) The Savior alone can offer salvation; therefore faith in Christ and in Christ alone is essential; (ii) Christ alone can cleanse us from sin and through His redeeming grace believers can become sanctified, that is, they no longer are "capable of sinning." (iii) Christ can heal the believer from all ailments, including physical, provided one's faith is strong enough; and, (iv) Christ will eventually return to earth and the world evangelization will hasten the day of His premillenial return.

Peculiarities

The Christian & Missionary Alliance Church has the distinction of being an evangelical body that does not have particular ethnic distinctives other than its Presbyterian beginning. Often people who feel attracted to this denomination do so because of the opportunity to leave their ethnic baggage behind. The Alliance Church tends to be a moderate, middle class WASP church. It fits in well with mainstream society – with people who like to espouse conservative theological lingo. When people of specific ethnic backgrounds *are* attracted to the church they may form their own congregations, e.g., the Chinese Alliance Church in Calgary.

Church of Christ (Disciples)

Pedigree

The Church of Christ (Disciples) as they are known in Canada are called The Christian Church (Disciples of Christ) in the USA. There they also have the distinction of being the largest American-born denomination although their membership in Canada numbers about 5 500. Rather than a denomination per se, these churches comprise a fellowship of independent congregations featuring local policy and organization. In 1804 Barton W. Stone and five other Presbyterian ministers set in motion the wheels of another denomination. In 1809, another leader, Thomas Campbell of Washington, Pennsylvania, along with a group of followers, formally launched the Disciples of Christ Church. Later his son Alexander carried on the leadership and established the rudiments of their basic belief system. In 1832 this group joined with Barton Stone's group and they became one church.

Simultaneously, in Canada, a group of disillusioned Scottish Baptist preachers gathered to form a "real New Testament Church." Within the next few decades this group formally joined with the Disciples of Christ Church (Muir, 1967). In 1891 the group sent out their first missionary, and in 1922 they held their first national conference.

Principles & Policy

The Disciples of Christ believe very much in local autonomy for each congregation. Although they are very similar to most other evangelical denominations in doctrine, the Disciples of Christ tend to associate only with selected evangelical causes; still, they belong to the Canadian Council of Churches. Believing themselves to be a "uniting church," the group initially explored the idea of joining in merger talks with the perceived United Church of Canada prior to 1925, but they soon left on the basis of "significant doctrinal differences." The doctrines of the Disciples of Christ Church have their historical roots in fundamentalist Baptist or Reformed Presbyterian ones, both of which they still appear to value to some degree. They may be said to be proudly "God-centred, Christ-centred and Bible-centred" (Mead, 1983).

Practices

Essentially firmly fundamentalist in theology and practice, the Disciples of Christ recognize adult baptism (by immersion only), and they observe the Lord's Supper on a weekly basis. They are strong on a missionary movement and although their predecessors sought to begin new congregations right from the beginning, their contemporary growth rate has been slowed.

Peculiarities

Although the church claims to be ecumenically evangelical in doctrine and practice, many of their congregations do not accept membership transfers from other evangelical or conservative churches without the individual (adults only) being rebaptized by immersion.

Churches of Christ

Although the Disciples survived the American Civil War without division, in 1906, some of their members withdrew to form the Churches of Christ on the basis that the main body was "getting liberal." The new group, also represented by small numbers in Canada, believe that instrumental music and the formation of missionary societies are unscriptural. They also reject the doctrine of original sin and demand absolute adherence to what they interpret to be the New Testament pattern in all things.

Church of God (Anderson, Indiana)

There are at least 16 North American church denominations that use the phrase "Church of God" in their title, making this one of the most confusing category of churches to decipher. This section deals with the denomination often called the "Church of God (Anderson, Indiana)" where its headquarters are located. Although the church has nearly 175 000 members on this continent, it has only a very limited representation in western Canada.

Pedigree

The Church of God (Anderson, Indiana) began in 1878 by John Winnebrenner, a German Reformed minister in Pennsylvania. Two years later a subdivision of the church was started by Daniel Sidney Warner, a preacher and song-writer who came out of the United Brethren tradition (Oldham, 1973). This group took the name Church of God Reformation as a repudiation of denominational names, and adopted a thoroughgoing evangelical list of doctrines (Douglas, 1991). This body still insists that the Bible is the sole authority for Christian practice as Christians seeking the guidance of the Holy Spirit may determine for themselves.

Principles & Policy

Essentially a holiness church, the Church of God believes in sanctification but repudiates speaking in tongues. Basically evangelical, the church believes in the inspiration of the Bible, the need for repentance and sanctification, and the imminent, personal return of Christ. The church also believes in the unity of all born-again Christians and regards other similar denominations as sister churches. Although viewed as a separate denomination by other churches, Church of God believers say that they are connected to other evangelical believers by a spiritual bond (Warner, n.d.).

Practices

The Church of God requires a basic Christian discipleship of its adherents, urging them to accept and encourage fellowship with other Christians of "like faith." The church also celebrates three ordinances – adult baptism by immersion, occasional celebration of the Lord's Supper and foot-washing which usually precedes the celebration of the Lord's Supper.

Peculiarities

A unique feature of this church is its refusal to keep membership rolls. Theoretically, according to them, every "born again" Christian belongs to the universal "Church of God" and on confession of faith and adult baptism by immersion, they may access all of the rites and privileges of "membership." Naturally, local church "members" know who is a regular and who is not and formal church offices are therefore pretty well kept in-house.

Unlike most other evangelical denominations, the Church of God adheres to an amillennial prophetic eschatology (Heffren, n.d.). They make no pronouncements about the time or details of Christ's second return.

Evangelical Covenant

This denominational name was entered in the record books in 1957. The church's former name was the Swedish Evangelical Mission Covenant Church, giving a clear indication of its ethnic roots.

Pedigree

Around 1870 various groups in Sweden broke with the Swedish Lutheran Church because of a revivalist movement that swept parts of the country. The group wanted to establish "free churches" with local congregational rule. The American counterpart was formed in 1885 by representatives of the new Swedish denomination. The new organization basically maintained Lutheran doctrines but adopted a more pietistic statement – justification by faith as the way to salvation (Douglas, 1991). Its number of adherents in Canada is small, possibly only a few thousand.

Principles & Policy

Although the Covenant Church collaborates with other evangelical denominations, they remain somewhat atypical in retaining the two

Sacraments of Holy Baptism and the Eucharist. They also endorse *both* infant and adult baptism. Officially the church tries to walk the line between fundamentalism and liberalism, alternately cooperating with bodies on both sides of the fence. The church celebrates a congregational form of rule although only the denomination can officially ordain clergy.

Formally stated, the Evangelical Covenant Church claims no allegiance to any creed, but their articles of faith, originally articulated by Theodore W. Anderson in 1936 in his *Covenant Mission,* endorsed the supremacy of the Bible, the necessity of spiritual life, belief in the unity of all true Christians, the autonomy of the local church, and the urgency of the missionary task (Ferm, 1945).

Practices

Basically evangelical in doctrine and somewhat mainline in practice, the Evangelical Covenant Church values highly the principle of personal freedom (reflecting the establishment of the denomination as a "free church.") Personal freedom is to be distinguished from the individualism that disregards the centrality of the Word of God and the mutual responsibilities and disciples of the spiritual community (Mead, 1983).

Peculiarities

The Covenant Church never really outgrew the mainline (Swedish Lutheran) roots from which it sprang, although claims about being evangelical in doctrine might be made. As such, this denomination may actually be able to carry out a very unique mandate – combining the Gospel of two very separate traditions – provided its newly attracted adherents never find out. They may be looking for one or the other.

Evangelical Free

The Evangelical Free Church is a Reformed body with roots in 19th century Scandinavian pietism. Its parent churches were the Swedish Evangelical Free Church organized in the USA in 1884, and the Norwegian and Danish Evangelical Free Church Association, organized in 1909. The two bodies merged in 1950 to become the Evangelical Free Church of America (Douglas, 1991).

Pedigree

Today the ethnic roots of the Evangelical Free Church have virtually been vanquished. Although the denomination meets regularly for mutual inter-congregational business, local church autonomy is highly prized. Local churches prefer to govern their own affairs "without interference from the denomination." Mainline churches in

Christianity tend to utilize larger organizations to facilitate the ministry of the local church, and this group, like many other evangelical groups, fears any form of larger organization. The denomination currently consists of about 880 congregations in the USA with a constituency of about 100 000 adherents. The denomination has about 3 000 members in Canada.

Principles & Policy

Although the trend in the Evangelical Free Church has been to adopt the principles and policies of "mainline" Evangelicalism, at the time of its origins the concept was that anyone confessing faith in Jesus Christ with a commitment to "Christian living" could become a member. Today evangelical Christians freely move in and out the Evangelical Free Church with the same ease that they effect transfers between other evangelical churches of "like faith" – Baptist, Christian and Missionary Alliance, Mennonite Brethren or Plymouth Brethren. The major criteria seem to be a testimony of a "real" conversion experience, adult baptism by immersion and a commitment to refrain from worldly practices.

Practices

In general, there is a growing trend towards blurring lines among evangelical church denominations. Historically, these churches stressed a strong bibliolatry (relabelled the Sacraments "ordinances"), held adult baptism by immersion, and placed heavy emphasis on evangelism of the unconverted. In addition to these characteristics, evangelicals have traditionally identified a list of worldly habits to be avoided – tobacco and drugs, the consumption of alcohol, attendance at movies and even certain clothing styles. As the lines differentiating the various evangelical groups have blurred some of the walls separating evangelical groups from mainline denominations have also come down. This has "necessitated" the formation of still newer groups, all claiming to represent a more biblical form of sound Christian teaching and practice. Like its sister evangelical counterparts, the Evangelical Free Church made similar claims at the time of its beginnings in 1884. Today it enjoys a flexible interchange of members with its evangelical peers but struggles with the shared challenge of resisting modernity.

Peculiarities

Every congregation of the Evangelical Free Church has the right to formulate its own doctrines, but a 12 point doctrinal statement formulated by the denomination in 1950 is incorporated into the bylaws of most congregations.

Evangelical Missionary

The birth of this unique denomination occurred in 1993, but not without a long checkered history of theological discussions, disputes, disagreements and church mergers.

Pedigree

In 1774, William Otterbein, a Baltimore minister in the German Reformed Church accepted a call to a renegade church operating under the auspices of a group called "The German Evangelical Reformed Church." In 1800 this group formally associated with the Church of the United Brethren in Christ. In the meantime, a disillusioned Mennonite minister, Martin Boehm, was expelled from his church because of his involvement in evangelistic activities. The efforts of these men juxtaposed with the ministry of Jacob Albright, a Lutheran Pennsylvania farmer, who experienced a vision from God and began preaching. His ministry influenced the formation of the Evangelical Association in 1803. This name was used until 1922 when the group became the Evangelical Church in America. In between these years there were differences and splits about slavery and membership in secret societies. Still the two major groups, The Evangelical Association and The United Brethren often came together for conferences to share mutual interests, and formally merged in 1946 to become The Evangelical United Brethren Church (Ellers, 1957). In 1968 this denomination merged with the Methodists in the USA to become The United Methodist Church. About 100 EUB congregations in the northwest region of the USA stayed out of the merger and became The Evangelical Church of North America.

Meanwhile back in Canada, in 1825 the United Brethren Church had expanded into Ontario and experienced a measure of missionary success. In 1922 the churches which resulted from these endeavors merged with the Congregational Church and later joined forces to become The United Church of Canada. The Evangelical Church, in the meantime, began missionary work in Ontario in 1836. When the Evangelical United Brethren Church was started in 1946 the Canadian contingent, consisting only of Evangelical churches, also underwent a name change. Their western expansion began in 1927 at Didsbury, Alberta. They took back the name "The Evangelical Church in Canada" when their Ontario compatriots joined with The United Church of Canada in 1968. Then, in 1993 they joined with the Missionary Church to become the Evangelical Missionary Church. The present membership of the denomination is about 5 000.

The background of the Missionary Church is worthy of at least a brief description, partially because their merger with The Evangelical Church was theologically somewhat unusual. Will miracles never cease? The Missionary Church originated in 1969 in the southeast

USA, as a merger of two bodies, the Missionary Church Association and the United Missionary Church. Up until 1947 the United Missionary Church was the Mennonite Brethren in Christ Church, but it dropped all Mennonite association with the merger. What is unusual about the 1993 merger is that the Missionary Church followed a form of local church control in government, and adhered to more Calvinist doctrines and adult baptism. The Evangelical Church was Wesleyan and episcopal and practiced infant baptism.

Principles & Policy

The merger of the Evangelical United Brethren (EUB) Church with the Methodist Church in 1968 required no basic changes in either church government or doctrine. Essentially, the EUB Church *was* Methodist, having adopted that kind of discipline from the time John Wesley preached in the USA. This meant dedication to an episcopal system of administration along with a Wesleyan, Arminian interpretation of theology. Essentially, this was a mild form of American fundamentalism committed to outreach and evangelism. The western Canadian contingent was developed to be an exception in these areas, and when they gained independence from the Methodist Church in 1968, they abolished the office of bishop and took up a more Calvinistic form of theology, peppered with some well-delineated eschatalogical pronouncements. These tended to coincide more with those of other smaller, grassroots Canadian prairie denominations, with which they had association, like independent Baptist churches or the Christian & Missionary Alliance Church.

Practices

The Evangelical Missionary Church has not been immune to the inroads of moderation in religious thought and practice. Although the official doctrines and pronouncements of the church remain essentially the same as they were some decades ago, their youth are joining the mainstream in pursuing "worldly pleasures" like attending movies, listening to rock music or engaging in social drinking.

Peculiarities

Anyone studying the history of this church is faced with a complexity of names, dates and places – and even theological changes. The miracle is that its adherents even know who they are. If the history of this church is any indicator, there is little doubt that even more changes in principles, policy and practices will soon occur.

Free Methodist Church

Unlike its name counterpart, The United Methodist Church, the Free Methodist Church is very conservative in doctrine and practice. There are about 15 000 Free Methodists in Canada.

Pedigree

The Free Methodist Church formed in 1860 after they were "read out" of their mother denomination. The dispute that led to this dismissal was begun by the Rev. Benjamin Titus Roberts who, along with a group of associates, like John Wesley Redfield and I.M. Chesbrough, agitated against the increased liberalism of the church. Early theological emphasis was on freedom of worship, the doctrine of entire sanctification, ministry to the poor and the abolition of slavery. In Canada, The Holiness Movement Church merged with the Free Methodist Church in 1960 (Douglas, 1991).

Principles & Policy

The unique belief features of the Free Methodist Church originate from their historic claim that the church should return to its theologically primitive roots. They still place a great deal of stress on the virgin birth of Jesus Christ, and emphasize His Deity and vicarious atonement and resurrection. No one is received into local church membership without showing signs of, and giving testimony to, their personal repentance, confession of sins and a confessed search for the experience of entire sanctification. Perhaps this influence resulted from the merger of the church with The Holiness Movement Church in Canada in 1960.

Practices

Members of the Free Methodist Church have to "toe the line" on doctrine and practice, including a professed pursuit of complete sanctification. This is accomplished through a second work of grace, which is like a second salvation experience, except that this time it apparently becomes impossible for a person to "sin." The projected interpretation is they don't *want* to sin anymore after this experience. Observers might disagree with the end result of the experience, but then "sin" may also have to be redefined.

Peculiarities

Unique among Evangelical churches is that the Free Methodists place holiness in the centre of their mission mandate: "The Mission of the Free Methodist Church is to make known to all people everywhere God's call to wholeness through forgiveness and holiness in Jesus Christ, and to invite into membership and to equip for ministry all who respond in faith" (Douglas, 1991, 342).

Mennonite Brethren

The Mennonite Brethren Church was formed in Russia in 1860 as a result of a religious revival that swept through the established

Mennonite community at that time. As part of the Anabaptist movement of the early 16th century, the Mennonites fled to Russia in the 1770s when Catherine the Great offered them free homesteads. While in Russia the Mennonites experienced a series of subdivisions brought about by a variety of reasons and social forces. The Mennonite Brethren Church was formed almost directly as a result of the influence of a Lutheran Pietist preacher named Eduard Wuest.

Pedigree

On 6 January 1860, a group of church elders from a Mennonite Church in southern Russia drew up a statement of secession from the larger body on the basis that they wanted to build a "pure" church more in keeping with the principles of the Bible. They adopted a more lenient form of Arminian theology than their counterparts, with leanings towards a more Calvinistic or Reformed interpretation of Scripture. They also adopted adult baptism by immersion as the only acceptable mode. Their first "reenactment" of adult baptism occurred as follows:

> On a day of the second week of September, a wagon load of Brethren drove to the water. First, we knelt by the water in prayer. Then we stepped into the water. Jacob Becker baptized brother Bartel, and then Bartel baptized Becker. The latter then baptized three sisters by immersing them backwards three times (Dyck, 1967, 215).

Sometimes accused of harboring a superior attitude towards their Mennonite counterparts, the Mennonite Brethren have traditionally insisted that new converts who had been baptized by any mode other than immersion be rebaptized (Epp, 1974). There is some sign that this practice is being substituted by acceptance of members from other Mennonite persuasions, but these individuals can probably not apply for ordination. This issue is currently under debate. Since 1860 there has been other evidence that differences between Mennonite Brethren practices and that of other Mennonites in Russia developed and have remained to this day.

About a century after they migrated to Russia, the Mennonites witnessed an erosion of their promised religious freedoms and sought out a new homeland. Some of the first Mennonite Brethren came to North America in the 1870s and settled in both the USA and Canada.

Principles & Policy

The Mennonite Brethren Church is probably the most evangelical (in doctrine), yet "mainline" (in practice) of Mennonite groups. Its official theological explications are soundly fundamentalist, its connections and practices are distinctly cultural (Mennonite) and with the exception of its strong exclusivity, the practices of its members are very much like those of most Canadians. The church supports a very large domestic and foreign mission program. The Canadian membership stands at about 25 000.

Practices

Publicly, almost all Mennonite groups are known for their pacifism, biblicism, rejection of modernity and desire for isolation. The Mennonite Brethren have tried to overcome their traditional preference for isolation, but, like other Mennonite groups, their ethnic ties have remained strong and made them seem unsociable. In a few isolated cases the Mennonite Brethren in Canada have managed to attract members without previous ethnic ties to the Mennonite community.

Peculiarities

As Anabaptists the Mennonite Brethren are quite unique, and resemble a form of ethnic fundamentalism. Their doctrines are virtually the same as those of conservative Baptists, or Christian and Missionary Alliance Churches, though they claim to be very evangelistic-minded. They are possibly the only Mennonite group to insist on baptism by immersion and the only Mennonites to endorse the doctrine of dispensationalism (Toews, 1975). This unique doctrine originated with an Englishman, J.N. Darby, who helped spawn the Plymouth Brethren (see section on Plymouth Brethren, p. 200). It is not clear how this particular theological concept infiltrated Mennonite Brethren Church thinking, but it was probably accepted because it fit in with their orientation towards exactness or literalism in Scriptural interpretation.

Nazarenes

The theological and doctrinal foundations of the Church of the Nazarene lie in the preaching of the doctrines of holiness and sanctification as taught by John Wesley in the 18th century revival in England (Mead, 1983).

Pedigree

This church in the USA represents a 1908 merger of three earlier established religious bodies with definitive roots in the Methodist Episcopal Church. The three merging denominations were known as the Central Evangelical Holiness Association (begun in 1890), the Church of the Nazarene (begun in 1895), and the Association of Pentecostal Churches of America (begun in 1895). In the next seven years five additional smaller denominations or groups also joined this denomination. Use of the term "Pentecostal" was carefully avoided after 1919 in order not to be associated with other denominations employing the name (Ferm, 1945).

Shortly after their formal convention the Nazarenes began expansion work in Canada. In the West their first church was founded in Calgary, Alberta in 1911. The current Canadian constituency membership stands at 9 000.

Principles and Policy

The Nazarene Church adheres closely to the original Wesleyan ideology, although its main doctrines are built around the concept of entire sanctification as a second work of grace. Like Free Methodists, Nazarenes believe that once salvation has occurred, the believer is to strive for a "second cleansing," which results in a complete and permanent purging from all sin. This may be easier to believe than practice, but I am sure that there are better explanations of this somewhat paradoxical declaration within the confines of orthodox Nazarene literature.

Nazarenes hold to the value of two ordinances – baptism (usually by immersion), and the Lord's Supper. Although local churches have a degree of independence in terms of government, elected superintendents represent a form of centralized government. Represented in every state of the USA, the church also has missions in 60 different world areas.

Practices

Nazarenes are fairly strict evangelicals in the sense that they promote the "standard" fundamentalist requirements – no smoking, drinking or swearing, no attendance at movie houses, no gambling, no excessive adornments and plenty of church participation (Smith, 1962). These requirements do not make the church so unique from other evangelical churches; their members sometimes transfer to other similar evangelical denominations with a minimum of adjustment.

Peculiarities

Unique among Evangelicals, the Nazarene Church is the only denomination to build both its doctrinal statement and its list of expected behavior patterns for believers on a *single* doctrine. Spreading the doctrine of "scriptural holiness" has occupied such preeminence throughout the history of the denomination that its adherence and commitment to mainstream evangelical Christian doctrine has not always been recognized either by observers nor by their own members (Douglas, 1991). Essentially the church occupies a theological position at the right wing of the holiness movement.

Plymouth Brethren

Strongly representative of the evangelical/fundamentalist sector of Christianity is the Plymouth Brethren, who today feature a fairly wide gamut of church policy and practice within their camp. Their institutions range from groups who worship in local "meeting houses" or "Gospel Halls" (*not* churches), to those who comprise contemporary evangelical, theologically moderate, congregations.

Pedigree

The characters referred to in the Plymouth Brethren archives around the turn of the last century include John Nelson Darby of Trinity College in Dublin; Benjamin Wills Newton of Exeter College in Oxford; George Mueller, a German who founded an orphanage in Bristol, England; Henry Craik with the Church of Scotland; and Norris Groves, a missionary to India. The basic distinctive of the church at its beginning was to take the scriptures literally, rather than to formulate doctrines or follow ecclesiastical traditions.

In 1845 personal differences between John Darby and Benjamin Newton developed – matters having to do with prophecy and ministry. By 1849 Darby and a group of followers had split off to form a new group. Darby and his "Exclusive" followers believed that the church was in a state of disrepair and the teachings of the New Testament were no longer being followed. He also instituted the weekly practice of breaking of bread (Holy Communion), but only as an ordinance.

Darby was a prolific writer and propagated his views in several different countries including Switzerland, France and North America. He also translated the Bible into German, English and French. After his death in 1881, however, his followers subdivided into an almost ludicrous number of factions and essentially discredited the movement, particularly in the 1950s and 1960s (Teulon, 1983; Douglas, 1991).

The "Open Brethren" were more successful in terms of growth and tended to follow the teachings of Mueller and Groves. Their tolerance towards others and their less restrictive attitude on doctrine obviously helped them attract a larger following.

Principles & Policy

The "open" Plymouth Brethren today still stress literalism in biblical interpretation and cling tenaciously to dispensational interpretations of eschatology. They emphasize evangelistic preaching, weekly communion, adult baptism by immersion and local autonomy in church government. In essence it is hard to tell the difference in practice between open Plymouth Brethren churches and Baptists, Christian and Missionary Alliance Churches or other evangelical groups.

The doctrines of the Plymouth Brethren are basically evangelical except for an unusually strong attachment to Calvinism (not necessarily the doctrine of the elect), and a premillennial, dispensational interpretation of prophecy and eschatology. Essentially, this means that they are unduly concerned about predicting the time of Christ's second return. Their most conservative faction, known as "Exclusive Brethren" hold to more rigid forms of doctrine, especially forbidding participation in the Lord's Supper to any outsiders. In this instance the definition of "outsiders" is quite exclusive – *very* exclusive!

Practices

As the development of "liberalism" advances in evangelical churches generally, the Plymouth Brethren do not remain unscathed. Traditionally, they did not have recognized clergy, but "spirit-filled" laymen spoke to the local congregation as they were moved to do during religious meetings. Gradually, as the "lot" continued to fall on the same people week after week (males only), it eventually became possible to announce in local newspapers who would be speaking the following week. Today, paid "pastor-teachers" (not ministers), serve as parish clergy.

Peculiarities

Many Plymouth Brethren congregations have probably endured a greater shift in religious policy and practice during the time of their existence than most conservative denominations. Originating as an ideal type of sect (sociologically defined), many of their congregations have made the transition to fullfledged "church" in every sense of the word. They have fairly elaborate buildings, paid pastors, church boards, membership lists, formal statements of doctrine, locally-established policies and mission programs. So well disguised is their restrictive religious history that in some cases their recently-converted adherents do not even know that they are attending a "Plymouth Brethren Church." Naturally the very strong bent of the church towards localized governance makes it difficult to calculate their actual numbers in Canada.

Salvation Army

The Salvation Army is an international, nonsectarian and evangelistic organization, historically known for its street corner services and its dedicated engagement in humane causes. Today the Salvation Army works in 85 countries with 25 000 officers who preach the Gospel in some 112 languages at 14 511 evangelical centres. They also operate more than 3 000 social welfare institutions, hospitals, schools and other helping institutions (Farlee, et al., 1985). The Salvation Army has about 112 000 formal adherents in Canada.

Pedigree

The Salvation Army is rooted in the Methodist Church and rose out of the preaching of William and Catherine Booth. Active in mission work in the mid-1800s in the slums of East London, the Booths were motivated by the philosophy that people would listen more closely to Gospel preaching *after* their basic needs had been met. Thus the Booths left the formal ministry and devoted themselves to operating "soup kitchens" for the needy folks of the slum areas through a mission they organized, "The Christian Revival Association." By 1868 they had developed 13 preaching stations with an average of 150 weekly services. In 1878 the name of the association was changed to "The Salvation Army" (Douglas, 1991).

The Booths never intended to start a new denomination, but wanted to work alongside established churches. However, they discovered that many of their converts who came from poor socio-economic areas did not fit in with established middle class congregations (nor were they particularly welcomed), and the Booths felt that spiritual growth and development for the new converts was essential. Subsequently they began to develop separate meeting houses for the new adherents (Mead, 1983).

Principles & Policy

Coming out of the Methodist tradition gave the Salvation Army a distinctive Wesleyan flavor with a heavy holiness emphasis. This combination of theological perspectives places them fairly safely in the midst of evangelicalism in North America today, albeit their very strong orientation towards alleviating problems of human welfare would probably separate them from most other evangelical groups. With many of these churches it tends to be the Gospel first and human welfare second – sometimes quite a distant second.

Remarkably, William and Catherine Booth devised a unique plan (or organization) for their compatriots – the army model. Even the creed they established was labelled "Articles of War." Complete with a full plethora of army offices and titles (William Booth himself carried the office of "General"), the Salvation Army has consistently carried its ministry through a philosophy of concern to all areas of human need.

Practices

The Salvation Army believes strongly that Christians must be active, but not necessarily as preachers or missionaries. Their emphasis is more in the social sector, but not to the neglect of preaching salvation or teaching doctrine. Representative areas of concern for the Army include: centres for alcoholics, food distribution centres, homes for battered women, residential centres for elderly people, day-care centres, prison-gates homes, homes for the physically challenged, missing persons searches and, best of all, the annual Christmas bell-ringers who collect for charity.

Peculiarities

The conversion techniques employed by the Salvation Army from the beginning were unique. Many Canadians will remember these as part and parcel of the Salvation Army movement – revival meetings in unusual places including outdoor crusades, use of musical instruments such as tambourines and cymbals, the adaptation of popular song tunes to religious themes, colloquial preaching forms and requiring public witnessing of every convert (Ferm, 1945). By now the Salvation uniform is recognized by virtually every North American and stands for help and sustenance – physical as well as spiritual!

References

Ammerman, Nancy Tatom. (1987). *Bible believers: Fundamentalists in the modern world.* New Brunswick: Rutgers University Press.

Beverley, James A. (1980). National survey of Baptist ministers. In Jarold K. Zeman (Ed.), *Baptists in Canada: Search for identity amidst diversity* (pp. 267-278).

Bibby, Reginald W. (1987). *Fragmented gods: The poverty and potential of religion in Canada.* Toronto: Irwin Publishing Co.

Bruce, Steve. (1984). *Firm in the faith.* Brookfield, VT: Gower Publishing Co.

Capps, Walter H. (1990). *The new religious right: Piety, patriotism, and politics.* Columbia, SC: University of South Carolina Press.

Clark, S.D. (1942). *Church and sect in Canada.* Toronto: University of Toronto Press.

De Jong, Pieter. (1962). *Evangelism and contemporary theology.* Nashville, TN: Tidings.

Douglas, J.D. (1991). *New 20th century encyclopedia of religious knowledge* (2nd ed.). Grand Rapids, MI: Baker Book House.

Dyck, Cornelius J. (Ed.). (1967). *Introduction to Mennonite history.* Scottdale, PA: Herald Press.

Ellers, Paul H. (1957). *These Evangelical United Brethren.* Dayton, OH: Otterbein Press.

Epp, Frank H. (1974). *Mennonites in Canada, 1786-1920.* Toronto: Macmillan.

Farlee, R., Tonsager, Steven R. & Jones, Susan (Eds.). (1985). *Our neighbor's faith.* Minneapolis, MI: Augsburg Publishing House.

Ferm, Vergilius. (1945). *An encyclopedia of religion.* New York: Philosophical Library.

Friesen, John W. (1972). *Religion for people.* Calgary, AB: Bell Books.

Heffren, H.C. (n.d.). *The mission of the Messiah* (rev. ed.). (Printed by the author).

Hexham, Irving. (1993). Canadian Evangelicals: Facing the critics. In W.E. Hewitt (Ed.), *The sociology of religion: A Canadian focus* (pp. 289-297). Toronto: Butterworths.

Inch, Morris A. (1978). *The evangelical challenge.* Philadelphia: The Westminster Press.

Islamic fundamentalists target Algeria's intellectuals. (1994, Sept.). *CAUT Bulletin, 41*(7), 11.

Lawrence, Bruce B. (1989). *Defenders of God: The fundamentalist revolt against the modern age.* San Francisco, CA: Harper & Row.

Longfield, Bradley J. (1991). *The Presbyterian controversy: Fundamentalists, modernists, and moderates*. New York: Oxford University Press.

Marsden, George M. (1990). Defining American fundamentalism. In Norman J. Cohen (Ed.), *The fundamentalism phenomenon* (pp. 22-37). Grand Rapids: MI: William B. Eerdmans Publishing Co.

Mead, Frank S. (1983). *Handbook of denominations* (7th ed.). Nashville, TN: Abingdon Press.

Muir, Shirley L. (1967). *Disciples in Canada*. Indianapolis, IN: The United Christian Missionary Society.

Nock, David A. (1993). The organization of religious life in Canada. In Hewitt, W.E. (Ed.), *The sociology of religion: A Canadian focus* (pp. 41-66). Toronto: Butterworths.

Oldham, Dale. (1973). *Giants along my path*. Anderson, IN: Warner Press.

Smith, Timothy L. (1962). *Called to holiness: The story of the Nazarenes: The formative years*. Kansas City, MO: Nazarene Publishing House.

Teulon, J.S. (1883). *The history and teaching of the Plymouth Brethren*. New York: E and J.B. Young & Co.

Toews, John A. (1975). *A history of the Mennonite Brethren Church*. Hillsboro, KS: Mennonite Brethren Publishing House.

Warner, D.S. (n.d.). *The church of God or what is the church and what is not*. Anderson, IN: Gospel Trumpet Co.

17

Conservative Protestants

The line of demarcation between evangelical and conservative churches primarily has more to do with their approach to outreach. Conservative churches often struggle to maintain strong ethnic ties while at the same claiming to being open to new converts. When proselytes *do* join these fellowships they sometimes find it necessary to learn a great deal about local denominational distinctives, but they will also find it difficult to network effectively without a great deal of interaction and knowledge, in order to feel like fullfledged members.

Amish

Almost everyone has heard of the Amish people. These are the people who farm with horses, use horse-drawn buggies for transportation, and practice a unique and traditionally agrarian lifestyle (Hostetler, 1989). Several million tourists check out this information for themselves each year in Lancaster County, Pennsylvania, (and in 20 other states where they reside) as well as in Waterloo County, Ontario. The visitors are enamored with the Amish way of life and often view them as museum mystiques instead of ordinary folk. The truth is that the lifestyle of the Amish is essentially a way of life which all North Americans engaged in a century or more ago.

Pedigree

There are approximately 145 000 Old Order Amish living in 21 American states and 2 800 reside in Ontario (Hostetler, 1993). They have experienced rapid population growth since the original meager band of 5 000 first made their home in America 300 years ago. Long a part of mainstream Anabaptism, in 1693 the Amish broke with the main body of Mennonites in Switzerland. One of their leaders, Jacob Amman, expressed concerns about the moral and spiritual deterioration of congregational life. Amman complained that the Mennonite Church was moving towards modernity; in particular he denounced a trend towards modern dress and the failure of church leaders to practice severe church discipline. He also insisted that the ordinance of Holy Communion (the Eucharist) should be celebrated more frequently than annually (as was the custom), and the religious ritual of foot-washing should be reinstated.

Amman's concerns sparked a conference which forced a direct confrontation among the ministers of the Mennonite conference. The result was that of 69 clergymen who took sides in the division, 27 sided with Amman, 20 of them in Alsace. This area eventually became the European headquarters for the Amish movement (Friesen, 1993).

Principles & Policy

Amish distinctives became evident from the beginning. A decidedly conservative emphasis in the new church decreed that married men wear beards and Amish clothing styles were frozen in time. Buttons, for example, were banished, and clothing was fastened by a hook-and-eye technique. The belief was that buttons represented a repugnant form of modernity and influenced wearers to show off by yielding to the temptation to don fancy forms of buttons. In congregational life the Amish observed a very strict form of excommunication and exercised shunning. If a believer sinned, he or she would be banished from church and community life, until the guilty party showed signs of repentance. The Amish also opted for an independent form of local church government. Except for a very constricting interpretation of humility, in other ways the Amish fairly well share basic Anabaptist beliefs, i.e., complete separation of church and state, pacifism, refusal to take an oath and rejection of all Sacraments including infant baptism. All church traditions not grounded in a strict, literal interpretation of the Bible have been rejected (Harder, 1949). Ministers are selected by lot and any baptized male who is nominated by a local congregation can be eligible for the ministry. The service of selection goes something like this; a bishop will preside and prayers will be said and songs will be sung. Then each nominated candidate is given a Bible and told to look up a particular passage. The selected candidate will realize that he has been chosen when he finds a slip of paper in his Bible indicating so. The paper has been placed in the Bible by the bishop beforehand.

Practices

The Amish prefer to reside in close proximity to one another, and their communities are subdivided into districts called *Ordnung* whose governing authorities determine the exact nature of lifestyle for their particular jurisdictional area. Essentially Amish speak three languages: English to outsiders, High German in church services, and Pennsylvania Dutch (German) for everyday discourse. An example of variation within *Ordnung* pertains to the growing of tobacco which some Amish pursue in Pennsylvania and Ohio. In some districts members are allowed to grow tobacco and to smoke; in others they are allowed to grow the plant but not permitted to smoke; still others forbid both growing tobacco and smoking. Amish leaders never worry about what outsiders may perceive to be inconsistencies in their lifestyle; they simply follow the dictates of their collective conscience in formulating regulations, and they expect implicit compliance from their constituents. The alternative is to be excommunicated, shunned and ostracized.

There are essentially three basic categories of Amish, the most intriguing of which are the Old Order Amish who cling to the traditional, 16th century agrarian lifestyle. Second, are the Beachy Amish (also called Church Amish, Amish Mennonites or Weavertown Mennonites), who originated in 1927 under the leadership of Bishop Moses Beachy. They eschew a more modern form of lifestyle and allow the use of electricity, telephones, tractors and automobiles, although their cars must be subdued in color. This group consists of about 90 congregations although they have not *officially* formed a separate church denomination (Hostetler, 1993). The third group are sometimes called "New Amish," who represent a variety of departures from the Old Order (and often from each other), clearly influenced by modern forms of evangelical Christianity. They may keep plain garb, but allow cars, electricity, formal meeting houses and other more modern religious practices. Yes, you can join an Amish church, although you may have to serve a year's probation before you are fully accepted. On occasion an individual or two may have joined an Amish fellowship, but such an act requires a diligent study of, and commitment to, a series of quite constricting requirements.

A constant form of struggle for the Amish has to do with their youth. Before young persons are baptized and join the church, which usually occurs just before marriage, they are allowed and even encouraged to "run around." This time period is given to running with "wild gangs," wearing "English" clothing, and even giving in to worldly pleasures such as driving cars, drinking or smoking. When it comes time to marry, however, these the things of the world are put away, and the newly baptized individual assumes a more mundane lifestyle. The difficulty of this practice emanates from the fact that many Amish youth find themselves buying into some degree of worldly lifestyle and when the time comes they choose not to join the church. Instead, they may unite with a conservative branch of the Mennonite Church. They will not be shunned for this behavior unless they have already been baptized.

Peculiarities

Do Amish people believe in evangelism? Yes, they do, but they probably represent the most cloistered form of Anabaptism in that any effort to unite with a congregation must be undertaken by the would-be convert. He or she must adhere to all demands made by the local parish. Outsiders are usually viewed with a degree of suspicion until their intentions are established. The Amish have had more than their share of patronizing viewers.

Always concerned about the biological repercussions of inbreeding, due to a very limited constituency for finding marriage partners, the Amish do worry about expansion. There have been instances of outside conversion, but these are rare. One such instance occurred several generations ago when an Englishman named Proudfoot joined. His name was promptly translated into the German equivalent as "Stolzfus." Geneticists have studied the ensuing impact of new blood input with great interest. Meanwhile the Amish have to contend with more than their share of curious tourists and onlookers.

Brethren in Christ

The Brethren in Christ Church is not particularly well-known in Canada even though their predecessors arrived in Ontario as early as 1788. They are sometimes also called "Tunkers" or "Dunkers" from the German meaning "to dip," and sometimes called "River Brethren." This nickname grew out of their preference for baptism by immersion.

Pedigree

The Brethren in Christ originated in Lancaster County, Pennsylvania, and grew out of the revivalist movement of the second half of the 18th century. During those meetings members of a Mennonite group gained "new light" about spirituality and decided to start a new organization. One of their new insights pertained to baptism; they decided that believers ought to be baptized by the mode of immersion instead of sprinkling or pouring. They also did not wish to link baptism with church membership as was the standard practice. After consulting with a number of Mennonite and German Baptist ministers, none of whom would re-baptize them with this mode, one minister suggested that the leaders of the group baptize each other and start their own organization. This they did, and thus in 1780 the roots of the Church of the Brethren were planted. By the time of the outbreak of the Civil War the formalization of the Brethren in Christ Church was complete (Sider, 1988).

The Canadian chapter of the Brethren in Christ began shortly after the church's origins. In 1780 the lure of available agricultural land in Upper Canada proved too strong to resist. By 1788 several families made their home in what eventually became Waterloo County in Ontario; westward expansion began in 1906 in Saskatchewan. Today the denomination has fifty congregations, most of them in Ontario, and most of them very small in number. Their combined membership in Canada and the USA is about 14 000.

Principles and Precepts

Essentially the doctrines of the church are Anabaptist but the denomination appears to be adopting evangelical traits as the need for new members becomes obvious. They believe in most of the basic evangelical fundamentals such as the virgin birth, the verbal inspiration of the Bible and the need for Christ's death and resurrection as atonement for salvation. The officially stated supreme purpose of the church is worldwide evangelism.

Practices

The Brethren in Christ Church is largely in the hands of local governing boards but they do have districts and a general conference. Officers include bishops, ministers and deacons. They tend to be rigorous in doctrinal accuracy and conservative in church and daily practice (Mead, 1983).

Peculiarities

The Brethren in Christ lived with the name of "River Brethren" for a century before their new name took hold. Currently they are still confused with various other "Dunker" groups in the USA. They are one of the strongest of Anabaptist groups to advocate pacifism. In addition, though changes are in the making, they tend to be conservative in methods of evangelism thus rejecting revivalist tactics. They promote temperance and encourage modesty in dress.

Christian Reformed

The Christian Reformed Church in America is the oldest Protestant church in the USA with an uninterrupted ministry.

Pedigree

The Dutch who settled in New Amsterdam organized their first congregation in 1628. Like almost all other ethnic churches the Christian Reformed Church has clung to its roots (Dutch) in both language and culture (Farlee, et al., 1985). This is evident from the list of names which manage the various facets of the denomination including church officials, publications and educational institutions.

In 1857, a small group of Dutch immigrants in western Michigan broke with the main body and formed the Christian Reformed Church in North America. Their first choice of name was "The True Holland Reformed Church" but as time went on they eventually settled for their present name. The issues influencing departure from the Reformed Church in America were: tolerance of Lodge memberships in the larger body, their use of hymns, a lack of regular catechism preaching and lax church discipline (Douglas, 1991). The new church continued to grow, largely through continued immigration from the Netherlands, although a sizable gain was made in the 1880s when discussions about the issue of lodge membership brought in a sudden transfer of members.

Principles & Policy

Historically, the Christian Reformed Church has always affirmed a solid Calvinistic orthodoxy including belief in the infallibility of the Scriptures, human reprobation, Christ's atonement and the requirement of a personal confession of faith for membership. Justification is attained solely through faith in Jesus Christ. Worship services are semi-liturgical in nature. The church accepts Infant Baptism and the Lord's Supper as Sacraments, strongly emphasizes the family as a nurturing agent, and urges school attendance at denominationally-run private Christian schools. In many cases, church members attempt to locate close to private schools for the convenience of their children. The denomination's best-known schools, not surprisingly, are Calvin College and Calvin Theological Seminary located in Grand Rapids, Michigan. The denomination has 85 000 members in Canada and carries on an effective worldwide mission program.

Practices

Essentially "mainline" in practice, the Christian Reformed Church holds tenaciously to specified doctrines as outlined in the Belgic Confession (1561), the Heidelberg Catechism (1563) and the Canons of Dort (1619). These are imparted to youth via a strong catechism program offered in the local church. There are few restrictions on personal forms of Christian practice, in the sense that common evangelical taboos are not forbidden, i.e. attendance at movies, smoking or social drinking.

Peculiarities

An investigation of The Christian Reformed Church holds several surprises, which to the casual observer probably appear inconsistent. This church holds very strongly to a specified Calvinist doctrinal creed and tries to teach this to its young; yet its expected code of behavior on the part of adherents is quite lax. This is a very ethnic church which basically attracts only a specified audience in Canada; yet the church has a strong mission program in many different countries including missions in America to Aboriginal tribes, Blacks and Spanish-Americans. Although "mainline" in many other ways, on the basis of established doctrinal decrees originated in the USA the denomination does not belong to the World Council of Churches nor the National Association of Evangelicals (Douglas, 1991). This is a very unique theological position.

Congregationalists

Although the Congregational Church officially ceased to be in Canada in 1925 with the formation of the United Church of Canada, there are currently 71 congregations of the Congregational Church back in action throughout the nation. These reemerging churches represent congregations which have broken away from the United Church in protest against "emerging trends towards liberalism" in the parent body. Of greatest concern to the Congregationalists has been the United Church's decision to ordain people to the ministry on the basis that sexual orientation need not be a factor in making the decision to ordain, provided that all other requirements have been met.

Only time will tell whether or not the Congregational Church in Canada will adhere to the established American format for the denomination, revert to its "ancient" Canadian roots or establish new forms of doctrine and practice.

Doukhobors

The 17th century in Russia highlighted a period during which a myriad of new religious groups emerged, all of them disenchanted with the state church, the Russian Orthodox Church. A variety of religious opinions propelled these new groups into public awareness, all of them holding in common the belief that the state church had gone bad (Stoochnoff, 1961). In 1652 Patriarch Nikon decided to reform the Orthodox Church through a series of radical "Greek" changes. The reforms included a revised prayer book, the making of the sign of the cross with three fingers instead of two, the eastward direction for processional marches, the ban on beard shaving, a correction of the name "Jesus" and the singing of the word "Hallelujah." Nikon chose to surround himself with Greeks who favored his ideas, and he appointed them to high office in preference to his indigenous clergy (Tarasoff, 1982).

These changes were far too extensive for Nikon's constituents to absorb and they rebelled against them. It is estimated that about 200 religious factions originated over time, some of them characterized by rather extensive departures from theological orthodoxy and others reflecting only minor changes.

Pedigree

Doukhobor origins cannot be dated with any great precision although it is commonly believed that they identified with the pronouncements of a wandering minstrel of sorts about the middle of the 18th century. The name "Doukhobor" (Spirit Wrestlers) was actually given to them in derision by a Russian Archbishop named Ambrosius. He accused the Doukhobors of fighting *against* the Spirit of God, but they liked the name and adopted it claiming that they were indeed fighting *in, not against* the Spirit of God, struggling against the influences of worldly living. Theirs was a living, active faith, they claimed, not a dead form of religiosity. The name stuck.

The Doukhobors early adopted such beliefs as equality of the sexes, rejection of icons and ordained clergy, pacifism and a disdain for all institutions, arguing instead that communal living was the ideal form of Christian living. Individual property ownership encourages capitalism and materialism they argued; communal living fosters brotherhood and peaceful co-existence, unencumbered by materialism. These beliefs later came up hard against the Russian campaign to militarize the country and the Doukhobors learned quickly that their fears about government intervention in citizen's lives were well-founded.

The Russian campaign to build a police state had its effect among the Doukhobors. On 29 June 1895, they showed their disfavor for increased militarism by burning weapons of all kinds in a series of bonfires in various localities in southern Russia. This event is still celebrated annually as the "Burning of Arms." When the Czar sent soldiers to investigate the incident, some 80 young Doukhobors were placed in jail (Greig, 1977). Insofar as the Doukhobor reaction was concerned, the event merely served to strengthen their belief in pacifism and they sought for new ways to live out their faith without interference. Subsequently emigration became a strongly favored alternative.

The Doukhobors arrived in Canada in 1899. They arrived by boat in Halifax and were transferred inland by train to Winnipeg. Although Canadian officials were not ready for a contingent of 7 500 people of their particular lifestyle to arrive in such a short period of time, they somehow managed to accommodate them in temporary immigration sheds quickly built in Winnipeg for that purpose. Food was issued by government ration, by relief agencies and by kindly neighbors. By 1902 the Doukhobors had proven themselves to be able farmers, but the Canadian public was not ready to welcome communalists in their midst. In 1907 their lands were confiscated because they refused to swear allegiance to the Crown. They relocated to British Columbia in 1912 and started over. In 1937 the governments of Canada and British Columbia combined forces with the Sun Life Assurance and National Trust Companies and instigated a surprise bankruptcy on the Doukhobor commune, the Christian Community of Universal Brotherhood. The action involved about 10 000 people in three provinces owning almost 6 million dollars of property, though their debt load was only four percent. After the bankruptcy was concluded the Doukhobors more or less faded into the woodwork of Canadian society except for a small vociferous faction, the "Sons of Freedom," who for several decades managed to stir the public mind to disfavor with their outbreaks of violence and public demonstrations which included burning public buildings and nude marches. They disagreed with the Orthodox group who followed a hereditary line of leadership, and with the Independents who refused to live communally (Tarasoff, 1982).

Today it is estimated that there are about 30 000 people of Doukhobor descent in the nation although only a few thousand would probably admit to it. After decades of suffering discrimination and persecution at the hands of both public and government, many young Doukhobors have tried hard to assimilate into the mainstream (Friesen and Verigin, 1989).

Principles & Policy

There are four specific Doukhobor beliefs that stand out as religious distinctives: (i) pacifism, to the extent of vegetarianism among the Orthodox; (ii) communalism, if not in a physical sense, then at least as a spiritual consideration (it also translates to include hospitality to others); (iii) the oral tradition, which must be translated into viable means if the traditions are to prevail; and, (iv) a disregard for human institutions, because they too often deteriorate into the pursuit of materialism or reflect a concern for regulation, even spiritual regulation.

It is difficult to expand on the nature of Doukhobor beliefs on the basis of their outward signs simply because Doukhobors do not believe in creeds. The sole exception is the appearance in every Orthodox Doukhobor prayer home of a loaf of bread, a bowl of salt and a jug of water. These emblems are simply meant to affirm the slogan, "Toil and Peaceful Life." They represent hard work, respect for the earth and hospitality to one's fellowman. They are not to be viewed as Sacraments or even ordinances.

A list of Doukhobor basics sometimes referred to by the John J. Verigin, current leader of the Union of Spiritual Communities in Christ (the Orthodox group), includes the following:

(i) We, the Union of Spiritual Communities in Christ, are and will be members of Christ's Church, confirmed by the Lord and Savior Jesus Christ Himself and assembled by His Apostles;

(ii) We believe in the law and faith of Jesus as it is expounded in the ten commandments and is to be adhered to on the basis of obeying God rather than men when these polarities contradict one another;

(iii) We do not recognize any political party nor do we support them because they symbolize the giving of the body and soul to an institution. These we offer only to God; and

(iv) We believe in "rendering unto Caesar" all things required of us by the state that do not contradict the laws of God and the faith of Jesus Christ (Popoff, 1982).

Practices

Doukhobor ideology reflects the absence of emblems, festivals and institutions. Even their revered beliefs, as maintained in memorized psalms and prayers, may be subject to individual interpretation because "every believer is his or her own priest." This belief originates from the assumption that every individual, man, woman and child, regardless of age or sex, has a bit of a the Divine Spark in them. Life is to be lived in accordance with the dictates of that Spirit, never according to the ordinances of man or to a written code of any kind.

Peculiarities

It may sound a bit contradictory, but Doukhobor Christians are pretty well on their own in Canadian Christendom, but they can rely on their own community. There are no corporate creeds to adopt except the principle of hard work, kindness towards others and hospitality. Doukhobors do not make public claims about their faith; rather, they would that the student of their ways simply watch how they fulfill the mandate of "toil and peaceful life." You can learn a great deal more by observation and interaction than you can by listening to unsubstantiated claims and speeches. Not a bad creed that.

Hutterites

An early deviating group from mainstream Anabaptism, the Hutterites broke with their mother church, the Mennonites, around 1530. They were led in their protest to Anabaptist ways by Jacob Hutter, a church layman and a hatter by trade. Essentially Hutterites claim to adhere to Anabaptist principles, that is the inspiration of the Bible, separation of church and state, pacifism, social isolation and refusal to take an oath, but they alone of all Anabaptist groups practice communal living. They base this form of society on the scriptural reference, Acts 2:44. They believe themselves to be the only "true" church because they fulfill *all* of Christ's commandments. They practice adult baptism and the Lord's Supper as ordinances only and renounce infant baptism.

Pedigree

From their beginnings the Hutterites quickly established a system of strict church discipline and order in the church and implemented the principle of common property. Their leader, Jacob Hutter, was martyred in 1535 (Horsch, 1931; Peters, 1965). After his death the pattern of life for Hutterites quickly became marked by fear and flight. Persecution of Hutterites had been under way since the early 1530s, but Hutter's death provided them with a formal mandate to fear the state. Originally the Hutterites fled to Moravia (today a historical place in Czechoslovakia) in order to escape their enemies, but as the years went by the Moravian nobility who were their protectors lost power and the Imperial Government of Vienna took control.

As the 1st century of their history ended, Hutterites became homeless wanderers. They left Moravia and sojourned to Slovakia where the King of Hungary had less military power to protect them than their previous benefactors. Later they relocated in other parts of

Europe and managed to live in peaceful isolation in Russia for over a century between 1770 and 1842. In 1842, the Russian Government decided to relocate the Hutterites. Then in 1864, a law was passed which made Russian the compulsory language in all schools and placed Hutterites under the supervision of the state. A few years later compulsory military service was introduced.

As these infringements on their freedom grew, the Hutterites could "feel the walls closing in on them" and they made plans to escape to America, a new land of freedom. In 1874 about 800 Hutterites left the Ukraine and settled in South Dakota in three colonies, each named after the leader of the colony: Lehrerleut, Dariusleut, and Schmiedeleut. By 1915, the total number of Hutterites had increased to 1 700, the colonies to 17, and 2 of these had been established in Montana (Pitt, 1949; Palmer, 1972). Expansion into Canada also occurred and by the end of 1918 the Dariusleut had developed six colonies (Bruderhof) in Alberta and the Lehrerleut, four. The Dakota Schmiedeleut colony expanded to Manitoba.

By 1971 there were 82 colonies in Alberta with a combined population of about 6 732. The total Hutterite population in North America today is 30 000 souls, living in over 300 colonies, two-thirds of them in Canada, and the rest in the United States (Preston, 1992).

Principles & Policy

The beliefs of Hutterites, with the exception of communalism, are basically Anabaptist, although surprisingly, most evangelicals would find little to argue with in the Hutterite statement of faith. Hutterites believe in missionary expansion (there is a Hutterite colony in Japan, for example), and from time to time a few individuals have joined colonies. The requirement is confession of faith, adult baptism and a one year period of probation.

Practices

From an outsider's perspective, Hutterites live a boring lifestyle. Most of their energies are directed towards the maintenance of their communal farms and the expansion of their system through birth and careful socialization. Their children attend two forms of schooling – that provided by the state (on the colony by special arrangement), and the local German language school. The content and objectives of the latter system are basically religious, consisting of Anabaptist and Hutterite history, basic doctrinal beliefs and the memorization of prayers and hymns. Hutterite leaders believe that their colony school system accounts for a better than 90 percent retention rate among their youth.

Visitors to a Hutterite colony are warmly greeted and proudly shown around the premises. On invitation they may attend daily half-hour worship services, Sunday worship or special services like weddings or funerals.

Peculiarities

Clearly adherence to the idea of communal living separates Hutterites from all other conservative Protestant groups. In 1993 a German-originated communal group of 2 000 souls called the "Hutterite Society of Brothers" attempted to join with the Manitoba Schmiedeleut Hutterites and the move split the Manitoba contingent of about 100 colonies virtually in half. Deliberations are still ongoing. The Hutterite Society of Brothers originated in Germany before World War II, but they were expelled by the Nazis. Subsequently they moved to the USA.

Mennonites

Mennonites comprise the best-known of Anabaptist groups and operate according to a wide variety of denominational names – all of them including the word "Mennonite." There are at least two dozen different kinds of Mennonite denominations in Canada.

Pedigree

The founder of the Mennonite faith was a Dutch Roman Catholic priest named Menno Simons (1496-1561). Although Mennonites claim that Simons never intended to start a separate order, this is essentially what happened. In 1536 he renounced the Roman Catholic Church and aspired to develop a new form of fellowship in keeping with New Testament principles. These beliefs from that time on characterized basic Anabaptist principles including a strong bibliolatry, individualism in faith, pacifism, adult baptism only, separation of church and state, isolation, practice of the "ban" and refusal to take an oath. In spite of the persecution that followed the Reformation, the movement spread to the German-speaking territory around Switzerland, to south Germany and ultimately to many other parts of the world (Smith, 1957).

As early as 1707, some of the Swiss Mennonites decided to immigrate to Pennsylvania, thus starting the flow of immigration that was to bring thousands of people to the new world.

In 1786 a delegation of European Mennonites travelled to Russia to inspect lands offered them for occupation and to verify some other very attractive terms. The Russian offer was too good to turn down and carried only one restrictive clause: Mennonites were not to engage in evangelistic endeavors among native Russians.

Mennonite life in Russia was fulfilling and despite a major split in 1860, caused by a pietistic religious revival, (which birthed the Mennonite Brethren Church), the newcomers adjusted quickly to their new country. However, less than a century after their immigration, the Russian government began placing more emphasis on military power. In 1873 a delegation of Mennonites from Russia visited Canada and the United States to determine the advisability of settlement there. Again the conditions of immigration were generous and the first Russian Mennonites relocated to North America between 1874 and 1880. Currently Mennonites in North America are nearly 200 000 strong.

Principles & Policy

Canadians not familiar with the inner workings of the Mennonite network are often confused by the many varieties of Mennonites and are not aware of the vast sociological differences among them. The two major divisions are the Swiss Mennonites, who migrated from their home country to the United States in the late 17th century and those groups which originated in Europe and transplanted to Russia between 1774 and 1786. These communities have been subdivided for a variety of theological reasons, usually having to do with some aspect of literal Biblical interpretation. The largest Canadian church, which is also a truly Canadian endeavor, is the General Conference Church which has a membership of 28 000.

Mennonite divisions probably occur because everyone is considered equal before God, which means everyone (particularly males, that is), has an equal right to interpret the Bible. This applies equally to theologically educated people or laymen. While each new group claims to interpret Anabaptist principles and the Bible more accurately than their mother group, some interesting divisions occur. Sometimes new groups originate on the basis of new interpretations regarding church architectural styles or apparel, or such matters as the use of electricity in church or the appropriateness of choir robes.

Like other Anabaptist groups, Mennonites accept no Sacraments, only two ordinances – the Lord's Supper and adult baptism. The latter is practiced differently among the various subgroups – immersion, sprinkling or pouring.

Practices

Historically, Mennonites have tended to be friendly but frugal, very mission-minded, particularly in regard to helping programs such as those carried out by the Mennonite Central Committee (an inter-Mennonite relief agency), and strong advocates of the separation of church and state. The church believes in evangelism, but its growth occurs primarily through birth. This is probably due to the fact that when outsiders attempt to join they discover that they must adjust to a lengthy list of cultural requirements as well as doctrinal beliefs.

Peculiarities

Mennonites often refer to themselves as "peculiar people," implying that they are unique sojourners in a temporarily assigned dwelling place. Outsiders would probably agree, but on the basis that Mennonites tend to be conservative, culturally-oriented and clannish. As the German language continues to fall into disuse among younger generations and cultural assimilation continues, it may be that eventually Mennonites will be viewed as one of the crowd – denominationally-speaking.

Moravians

The Moravians sometimes claim that they are the original framers or "charter" members of the Protestant Reformation since their origins date back to the 9th century and the work of Constantine and Methodius among the European Slavs. They also claim a tie to John Huss who was martyred in 1416.

Pedigree

By the middle of the 16th century there were 60 Moravian congregations in Bohemia and an equal number or more in Moravia. There were 40 congregations in Poland. Then, fierce persecution by the Hapsburgs almost destroyed the movement. In 1722 a small group of Moravians found refuge in Saxony, and their name, "Moravian," springs from this period; they were named after the country from which they fled (Mead, 1983). Their American beginnings date to 1733 when a settlement was begun in Georgia. Their Canadian outreach began in 1825 in Labrador under the auspices of the Society for the Furtherance of the Gospel (Hamilton, 1971).

Principles & Policy

Although still somewhat ethnic in terms of tracing their origins, for all intents and purposes Moravians have become theological mainliners. Their scriptural interpretations agree with the Apostles' Creed, the Westminster and Augsburg confessions and the Articles of Religion of the Anglican Church. The American Moravian Church was a charter member of both the World and National Council of Churches.

The highest administrative body of the Moravian Church is the provincial synod. Officers include bishops, clergy and laymen.

Practices

Moravians practice the Sacrament of Holy Baptism by sprinkling, or on occasion by pouring. The Lord's Supper is celebrated at least six times a year. A variety of liturgies are used in worship, and missions have a strong emphasis in the church. In fact, the fastest growing segment of the worldwide Moravian Church is in Tanzania (Farlee, et al., 1985).

Peculiarities

Few church denominations have made as rapid and thorough a shift from pietistic and revivalist roots as Moravians. Once a powerful influence on Methodist founder and evangelist John Wesley, to the extent that he lost any bent he might have had towards Reform theology or high church (Anglican) theology, Moravians have become a church with *no doctrine peculiar to them* (Mead, 1983). In addition, a Moravian bishop named Johann Amos (Komensky) Commenius (1592-1670), is often quoted. He was a significant naturalist educational philosopher (Friesen & Boberg, 1990). His books, *Pansopia,* which was to contain all knowledge of that time, and *the Great Didactic,* which outlined Commenius's educational policy and method, may be found on the shelves of many university and public libraries.

Quakers

The name "Quaker" was given in derision by Justice Gervase Bennett of Derby, England in 1650. He suggested that the Quakers wanted him to tremble ("quake") at hearing the Word of God, and they agreed. They stayed with the name.

Pedigree

A man named George Fox is credited with the origins of the Quaker movement, now also known as the "Society of Friends." It happened in Lancashire, England, during the last stages of the Protestant Reformation when Fox preached among sectarians, seekers, independents and others who were loosely known as "Children of the Light." Converts were persecuted for their faith, but it did not stop them (Ferm, 1945). They simply wanted to live out the doctrines and precepts of Christ and learn to love their fellow man through the power of the Holy Spirit (Bowden, 1972). As the European Quakers migrated to America, Rhode Island became their stronghold until 1681 when William Penn, a Quaker, was granted Pennsylvania by King Charles II.

The Quakers controlled the Pennsylvania legislature until 1756 when they stepped voluntarily out of office because they refused to support a tax to finance a war against local Indian tribes. While they ruled the Quakers adhered to a treaty made with the Indians that they would respect one another and never resort to war. This pact was honored as long as the Quakers were in power in Pennsylvania (Vipont, 1970). When George Fox died in 1691 it is estimated that there were about 40 to 50 000 practicing Quakers in Britain and some 30 000 abroad.

Differences over the slavery issue in America drove Quakers (who were against it) to Canada in the early part of the last century. In 1827 a split occurred over "liberalism," and Elias Hicks led a faction towards a more conservative stance – back to their theological roots. In 1845 another group known as the Wilburites emerged, followed by a now-extinct group, the Primitives, in 1861. As this century became visible, mainline Quakerism could hardly be differentiated from other evangelical movements except that the Quakers remained committed to pacifism, and refused to celebrate the Sacraments in physical form. Their pacifism has remained a primary characteristic differentiating them from most other North American churches. In their 300 year history Quakers have rarely produced first-rate theologians, but in virtually every generation those grappling with the implications of the peace testimony have been truly creative (Barbour and Frost, 1988).

Principles & Policy

The basic premise of Quaker doctrine is a personal relationship with Jesus Christ. Heeding the voice of Christ is an opportunity available to all and has nothing to do with outward forms or ceremonies, rituals or creeds. Every human being, according to Quakers, is a walking church and every heart is God's altar and shrine (Mead, 1983). Traditionally this meant that when the "Friends" gathered for Sunday meeting, instead of hearing a sermon preached, anyone inspired by the Holy Spirit could share their thoughts – men, women or children. Today there *are* some Quaker churches with paid workers although the title of "minister" (usually given by outsiders) is awarded on the basis of the recognized gift of leadership rather than training.

Currently very conservative in theological orientation – almost evangelical, in fact – the Quakers believe that while persons cannot be "perfect" in the Holiness sense of the word, they should *strive* towards becoming Christlike. The point is that it is the process of striving, the intention to *try* to live up to the highest light that matters (Brinton, 1979).

Practices

Despite a membership of only 123 000 in North America, Quakers have made a real difference in societies where they have functioned. They have a long tradition of involving themselves in religious and humane efforts for the alleviation of ills among all groups. They have done so unobtrusively and without fanfare. They have celebrated a quiet evangelical faith. When the first World War ended in 1917, Quakers busied themselves in voluntary work by staffing hospitals, rearing domestic animals for food, building homes and driving ambulances. This kind of down-to-earth mission work was carried on in many countries. At one time it was estimated that the Quakers were feeding more than one million German children every day! Now *that's* religion in action!

Peculiarities

Quakers have sometimes been called a third branch of Christianity – different from both Catholics and Protestants. Catholics depend on the authority of the church, Protestants depend on the authority of the Bible, and Quakers depend on the authority of the Spirit (Brinton, 1979).

Unlike their evangelical counterparts, Quakers basically count on the birth of children to enlarge their numbers although outsiders can join if they insist. The Quakers have never been great proselytizers. Newborn children are considered fullfledged members of the Society of Friends, but this form of growth has severely limited the outreach of the church. Sometimes individuals with previous church-affiliations who consider themselves pacifists join the Quakers.

References

Barbour, Hugh & Frost, J. William. (1988). *The Quakers*. New York: Greenwood Press.

Bowden, James. (1972). *The history of the Society of Friends* (2 vols.). New York: Arno Press.

Brinton, Howard H. (1979). *The religious philosophy of Quakerism*. Wallingford, PA: Pendle Hill Publications.

Douglas, J.D. (1991). *New 20th century encyclopedia of religious knowledge* (2nd ed.). Grand Rapids, MI: Baker Book House.

Farlee, R., Tonsager, Steven R. & Jones, Susan (Eds.). (1985). *Our neighbor's faith.* Minneapolis, MN: Augsburg Publishing House.

Ferm, Vergilius. (1945). *An encyclopedia of religion.* New York: Philosophical Library.

Friesen, John W. (1992). *Religion for people.* Calgary, AB: Bell Books.

Friesen, John W. (1993). *When cultures clash: Case studies in multiculturalism.* (2nd ed.). Calgary, AB: Detselig Enterprises Ltd.

Friesen, John W. & Verigin, Michael M. (1989). *The community Doukhobors: A people in transition.* Ottawa, ON: Borealis Press.

Friesen, John W. & Boberg, Alice L. (1990). *Introduction to teaching: A socio-cultural approach.* Dubuque, IA: Kendall/Hunt.

Greig, Hugh. (1977). *The hope and the promise.* Langley, BC: Stagecoach Publishing.

Hamilton, J. Taylor. (1971). *A history of the church known as the Moravian Church.* New York: AMS Press.

Harder, M.S. (1949). The origin, philosophy, and development of education among the Mennonites. Unpublished doctoral dissertation, University of Colorado.

Horsch, John. (1931). *The Hutterian brethren: 1528-31.* Goshen, IN: Mennonite Historical Society.

Hostetler, John A. (Ed.). (1989). *Amish roots: A treasury of history, wisdom, and lore.* Baltimore, MD: The Johns Hopkins University Press.

Hostetler, John A. (1993). *Amish society* (4th ed.). Baltimore, MD: The Johns Hopkins University Press.

Mead, Frank S. (1983). *Handbook on denominations in the United States.* Nashville, TN: Abingdon Press.

Palmer, Howard. (1972). *Land of the second chance: A history of ethnic groups in southern Alberta.* Lethbridge, AB: The Lethbridge Herald.

Peters, Victor. (1965). *All things common: The Hutterian way of life.* New York: Harper Torchbooks.

Pitt, E. L. (1949). The Hutterian Brethren in Alberta. Unpublished master's thesis, University of Alberta, Edmonton, AB.

Popoff, Eli A. (1982). *An historical exposition on the origin and evolution of the basic tenets of the Doukhobor life-conception.* Castlegar, BC: POP Offset.

Preston, Brian. (1992). Religion: Jacob's ladder. *Saturday Night, 107*(3).

Sider, Morris E. (1988). *The Brethren in Christ in Canada: Two hundred years of tradition and change.* Nappanee, IL: Evangel Press.

Smith, Henry C. (1957). *The story of the Mennonites* (4th ed.). Newton, KS: Mennonite Publication House.

Stoochnoff, John Philip. (1961). *The Doukhobors as they are.* Toronto: Ryerson Press, printed privately.

Tarasoff, Koozma. (1982). *Plakun trava: The Doukhobors.* Grand Forks, BC: MIR Publications.

Vipont, Elfrida. (1970). *The story of Quakerism.* London: The Bannisdale Press.

18

Commonly-Known Sects

It is not without a degree of hesitancy that the term "sect" is employed in describing some religious forms, particularly because the mere use of the term may offend some readers. Nevertheless, in keeping with the literature, there are some religious groups which are often defined as such, and thus this book will respect that tradition. It helps to keep in mind that sects are usually groups that see themselves as being in tension with the wider society, with dominant churches and other denominations (Nock, 1993).

Christian Science

Officially known as the "Church of Christ, Scientist," Christian Scientists are known to attract followers from many "leading" walks of life including many professional people. The church's publication, *The Christian Science Monitor* is respected across the world as an outstanding and remarkably objective channel for reporting world events.

Pedigree

In 1866, Mary Baker Eddy, a young widow from Lynn, Massachusetts, was recovering from a severe injury obtained from a fall on a sidewalk. Deeply religious, she was reading a passage of scripture from Matthew's Gospel, 9:1-8, which tells the story of Christ healing a man stricken with palsy. On that basis Ms. Eddy determined that by faith she would rise up and walk, basing her claim to health on a scientific understanding of how God works. After all, she reasoned, if God is perfect, evil can be destroyed by knowing the truth.

Like most other religious leaders and pioneers, Mrs. Eddy hoped to do her work through existing churches. When this became impossible, she established her first congregation in Boston in 1879, and launched her worldwide organization, the First Church of Christ, Scientist in 1892.

Principles & Policy

Christian Science essentially denies any and all historical Christian truths and doctrines; however, they acknowledge that the Bible is useful as interpreted by Mary Baker Eddy. (This fact establishes the notion of Christian Science being "in tension" with other churches.) Similarly Jesus is endorsed as a "Master" or "Way-shower" and His virgin birth and mission are seen as exemplary. Even His crucifixion, death and resurrection are useful concepts, and held "to uplift the faith to understand eternal Life, even the allness of Soul, Spirit, and the nothingness of matter" (Mead, 1983, 82). In the final analysis, when the true nature of God is discovered and one believes that sin, sickness and death are only illusive concepts of the earthly mind, "true" knowledge will occur. The end result is healthful living.

Practices

The central belief of Christian Science is quite frankly difficult to comprehend. The basic premise is that "God is the Divine Principle of all that really is." Mind and spirit are eternal realities while matter is an illusion; it will eventually disintegrate and vanish. Only God can strip away unreality, and sin and sickness are part of unreality. Heaven is harmony and spirituality, and hell is mortal and carnal belief (Douglas, 1991).

To become a practicing Christian Scientist one must become an Idealist, that is to say, someone who accepts the notion that nothing is real and eternal; nothing is spirit, but God and His ideal; evil has no reality. People are God's spiritual ideal and they belong to an order of beings who should not be sick nor subject to sin, sorrow nor death. These are merely errors of the mind. Deny them and they will cease to exist. Individuals must seek to elevate themselves above the world of false beliefs and entanglements and embrace the world of spiritual reality by affirming faith, self-discipline and spiritual practice (Ferm, 1945).

Peculiarities

Essentially a middle class organization dominated by women, Christian Science today is in severe decline, possibly because of the challenge by the similar, but more "with it," New Age Movement. Besides, not every one wants to be a "philosopher" in faith; people tend to prefer a more practical and "carnal" way of fulfilling their spiritual search.

Jehovah's Witnesses

Members of the community of Jehovah's Witnesses would probably object to being called a sect or accused of being affiliated with a "church." They prefer to be called "witnesses to Jehovah" (God), instead of "Christians," they meet in "Kingdom Halls," and they deny many familiar Christian beliefs such as the doctrine of the Trinity, or the notion of eternal punishment for the wicked.

Pedigree

The Jehovah's Witness movement began in 1868 in Pittsburg, Pennsylvania under the leadership of Charles Taze Russell. A Congregationalist by upbringing, Russell gained an interest in Seventh Day Adventist Church doctrine (including its penchant for prophecy), and later predicted that Christ would return to the earth in 1874 and establish His millennial kingdom. Later he revised his figures and made a prediction for 1914. Although most people are apparently not aware of it, some witnesses say that Jesus Christ *did* return to earth, but only the faithful few know about it.

Early in their history Jehovah's Witnesses were called Russelites, after their leader. Later they were known as Millennial Dawnists or International Bible Students, and then, in 1931 as Jehovah's Witnesses (Mead, 1983).

Charles Russell attracted large crowds with his outrageous predictions at a time when such audiences were easily accessible. During Russell's ministry, the American nation was attuned to themes of revival and predictions about the country's future. The second coming of Christ was a central theme in Russell's preaching, particularly his assignment of actual dates.

Principles & Policy

Central to the theology of this "church," is the belief that God is going to take vengeance on this wicked world and establish a new earth (kingdom) for a select group. This will bring in the age of the millennium, which is a one thousand year period of peaceful reign. A special group of 144 000 will become the "Bride of Christ" and will help Him rule in the new world. The rest will be destroyed but there will be no *eternal* punishment for the wicked as most Christians are taught. When Jehovah's Witnesses make claims they are carefully "grounded on scripture," they mean carefully selected scriptures. They emphasize some passages and deliberately ignore others. Here is a warning to individuals who know they *should* respect the Bible but who are ignorant of its contents, if they choose to argue with a member of the Jehovah's Witness faith! They will be no match for their antagonist.

For the most part, the Witness religion is a negative religion, and there is no doctorine of merciful grace in the faith. Witnesses aggressively condemn the three "tyrannies of our time" – allies of Satan, they call them. These include the false teachings of Christian churches, the tyranny of government and the oppression of the business world. Pacifists in doctrine, Witnesses will not allow their children to pledge allegiance to nor salute any national flag, nor take part in any kind of religious or patriotic instruction classes other than those sponsored by their organization. Baptism by immersion is practiced by this group and through baptism the believer becomes an "ordained minister," commissioned to do God's will.

Jehovah's Witnesses must never accept a blood transfusion, because human personality is located in the blood cells. If one accepts blood from a criminal, for example, one will probably turn to a life of crime! The scriptural basis for this belief is apparently Genesis 9:4 where the reader is informed that "You must not eat meat that has its lifeblood still in it." Knowledge to the contrary may be identified in the halls of medical or scientific or theological learning, but Witnesses are expressly instructed to avoid these factories of worldly knowledge.

Practices

Jehovah's Witnesses meet regularly in Kingdom Halls for spiritual refreshment and instruction. These buildings are plain and small. When their numbers in a given congregation reach 200, they divide to form a new congregation (Farlee, et al., 1985). Witnesses also proclaim their faith publicly through quite fervent avenues – handing out tracts, standing on street corners to sell literature and going door to door to share their message. Their literature comes from the Watchtower Society where volunteers faithfully pump out volumes and volumes of "truth." In this religion "pioneers" are expected to give at least 96 hours per month in volunteer work, and "special pioneers" or missionaries are expected to give a minimum of 140 hours per month. The official journal, *The Watchtower*, has a circulation of almost ten million copies. There are about 148 000 Jehovah's Witnesses in Canada.

Peculiarities

Where does one begin in delineating an unusual, yet dedicated group of religionists? A common point of comparison is usually "mainline" Christianity, and Jehovah's Witnesses feature *many* points of departure. In addition to their repudiation of many basic Christian doctrines, they do not celebrate holidays including their own birthdays. Christmas and Easter are considered pagan observances. A truly devoted Witness will obey the rule not to speak with anyone who, having once been enlightened, denies the faith. This includes one's spouse. This is a religion that demands explicit obedience to its many dictates; its central message consists of constant warnings of even more pessimistic times to come – except for the loyal few!

Mormons

Like several other faiths, the Mormon Church (more properly known as the Church of Jesus Christ of Latter Day Saints), relies on a fairly recent version of added Divine revelation. The "new truth" is an addition to the message of the Bible, and in *this* case, all-American-made. The name "Mormon" originates from the claim that a prophet by that name gave the founder, Joseph Smith, his special message.

Pedigree

The Mormon faith is now adhered to by more than eight million people worldwide and the church is alleged to be one of the fastest growing in the world. There are 101 000 Mormons in Canada.

The Church of Jesus Christ of Latter Day Saints was formed on 6 April 1830, and three of the six organizers came from the Smith family into which Joseph Smith, the Prophet and First Elder, was born. Joseph Smith claimed to have found a set of copper plates in a desert. The plates comprised the foundation of Smith's Divine testimony, and was witnessed by three members of the family. In a sense then, the origin of the church was a "family affair" (Persuitte, 1985).

Joseph Smith was born in the State of Vermont on 23 December 1805, and claimed that an angel visited him and showed him a set of copper plates. When the message of the plates was translated, it comprised the *Book of Mormon,* subtitled, "Another Testament of Jesus Christ." Adherents to the faith claim that the *Book of Mormon* is the key to their faith; it describes the story of the descendants of some Israelites who came to the New World before the birth of Jesus. These early settlers were part of the ten lost tribes of Israel, and Jesus apparently appeared to them in Jerusalem after His death and resurrection.

Mormonism was off to a slow start with established colonies in Ohio, Illinois and Missouri, partially because of opposition to their practice of polygamy and their "outlandish" claims about receiving revelations from Jesus Christ, John the Baptist and various other apostles. Smith himself was killed in a riot at Carthage, Illinois in 1844. Four years later a Mormon leader by name of Brigham Young led the main body of Mormons to Utah where they founded Salt Lake City and secured possession of large tracts of territory (Ferm, 1945).

The *Book of Mormon* is not without its critics. On the positive side is the observation that thanks to the students of Mormonism, we know more about the Joseph Smith family than any other poor farm family of the 19th century. When one reads this kind of religious history (although this was not the main purpose for why it was written), the book provides good detail about life in last century America. On the debit side is the accusation that in writing the *Book of Mormon,* Joseph Smith borrowed heavily from existing religious literature and the Bible, and concocted a book of fraud. Additionally, Joseph Smith aroused the ire of critics from the start, and everyone from newspaper editors to next-door neighbors felt obliged to denounce him (Bushman, 1984).

Principles & Policy

Essentially Christian in principle and policy, Mormons are known for their clean living, missionary work, their sense of brotherhood and neighborliness. Some of their doctrines, however, depart substantially from orthodox Christianity. For example, Mormons believe in two orders of priesthood, Aaronic and Melchizedek, and the knowable activities of several angels, especially the guiding spirit of "Moroni." The church's hierarchy of officers includes an all powerful president, who is capable of receiving additional Divine revelation in his time, two other "high priests," and a host of apostles, patriarchs, elders and bishops. The church also believes in visions, prophecy, the gift of tongues, Divine healing and various other "gifts." When Christ returns to earth he will set up a holy city in the USA, the "ten tribes" will be restored and the Jews will return to Palestine (Ferm, 1945). Mormons also believe in a literal resurrection. They believe that families sealed together in their temples can be together in the hereafter. Hence, they feel a responsibility to research their family lines and perform temple ordinances for their ancestors who have accepted or rejected this work.

Practices

Being a member of the Mormon Church affects every aspect of an individual's life. In addition to a list of "forbiddens," such as smoking, drinking, gambling or even drinking coffee or tea, Mormons are admonished to maintain a deep loyalty to the church. This means a compulsory term of missionary work for youth (without monetary compensation), regular participation in worship, involvement in other activities of one's local church (stake) and a commitment to financial support. The church has a worldwide mission outreach and is heavily involved in a number of educational and welfare programs. Brigham Young University in Utah is the largest privately-operated university in the USA.

Peculiarities

The Mormon religion initially began as a protest against the world of harsh, capitalist individualism, and then through much of this century it gradually became "respectable." In fact, it has increasingly taken on the characteristics of the dominant society which it originally rejected. For example, the practice of polygamy is no longer practiced by the Mormon Church, having been outlawed in 1890 by secular law. Two unique practices remain: baptism for the dead and sealing in marriage for eternity. Baptism and salvation for the dead are based on the notion that those who died without the opportunity of hearing the Gospel cannot possibly be condemned by a merciful God. Thus baptism for the dead is practiced with a living person standing in for the dead.

Marriage among Mormons has two forms: marriage for time and marriage for eternity (celestial). Marriage by civil law allows members to remain in good standing with the church, but celestial marriage, which is for time and eternity, is regarded as a prerequisite for the highest opportunity for salvation (Mead, 1983).

Historically, the Mormon Church has reserved the office of priest for white males only. In June 1978 it was ruled that "all worthy male members of the church may be ordained to the priesthood without regard for race or color" (Mead, 1983, 95).

The Reorganized Church

Although there have been several splits in the Mormon Church since the time of its beginning, possibly the best known is the Reorganized Church of Jesus Christ of Latter Day Saints which was established in 1880 in Ohio and in 1884 in Missouri. The church claims to be the continuation of the original body started by Joseph Smith who, they claim, begat his position to his son, Joseph Smith Jr. From then on, descendants of the first Joseph Smith have headed the Reorganized Church.

Essentially the Reorganized Church of Jesus Christ of Latter Day Saints renounced the teachings of Brigham Young who endorsed the doctrine of polygamy. They also claim that Young brought out new doctrines on the Godhead, celestial marriage, the baptism of the dead and the plurality of gods. These are not accepted by the reorganized body.

Old Believers

During the 17th and 18th centuries the religious community in Russia experienced the birth of a variety of breakaway groups, or "sects," as they were known. The Orthodox Church constituted the state religion, and major changes in structure and ritual precipitated the formation of many dissenting groups (Friesen, 1983). When the state church adopted new forms of doctrine, the Old Believers insisted that the old way was the only true faith. Thus, in their view, they became the only true Christians on earth.

Pedigree

Over the years a number of Russian sects have made their way to North America, one of these being the Old Believers now residing in northern Alberta. Disillusioned with changes initiated by a 17th century Patriarch, Nikon Mordvinov, the Old Believers argued that if the subjects of the church possessed true faith there was no justification whatsoever for any changes in ritual or doctrine. Nikon proposed that certain religious texts be eliminated; the spelling of the name of Jesus be changed from *Isus* to *Iiusus;* the sign of the cross be done with three fingers instead of two; the repetition of *alleluia* be thrice instead of twice during services; the direction of religious processions be aligned *with* the movement of the sun, not against it; and the number of prostrations during worship be changed. According to the Old Believers, even to fuss with a single letter of any word would be to corrupt the faith (Kach, 1984). Subsequently, though few in number, the Old Believers believe that they alone have remained true to the faith.

Disagreements with institutionalized state religion drove the Russian government to exterminate the "heretics" with fire and sword. Consequently, mass burnings of dissidents was undertaken; in fact, between 1672 and 1691, when the movement subsided, 37 human holocausts are known to have taken place (Florinsky, 1955). Small wonder then, that the Old Believers sought refuge in other locations.

The Old Believers somehow survived the next two centuries until Nicholas I took over the government in the middle of the 19th century. He initiated a policy that an "official nationality" be set up in Russia consisting of unity in orthodoxy, autocracy and nationality. Thus the crusade against the Old Believers was renewed. The Old Believers therefore migrated to peripheral areas in the outer regions of Russia (including Siberia), virtually "encircling the earth" in quest of peace. Some of their number eventually settled in central Asia, northwest China, Hong Kong, Australia, New Zealand and South America (mainly in Brazil). In 1967 a group of Old Believers occupied small farms in northern Alberta, near Plamondon. Their journey to Canada took them via Alaska and Oregon.

Principles & Policy

The Old Believers promote simplicity, abstinence from "worldly" habits and strict obedience to their interpretation of Christian practice. Their rural homes are serviced by rural power and sewer systems, and they enjoy some of the modern conveniences which those amenities provide. They preach that religion pervades all of life. It determines the hairstyle that an individual may wear, the kind of food that is eaten, and the nature of interactions between old and young and between the sexes. The persuasiveness of faith is also manifest in the many rituals and fasts that are undertaken as well as abstention from tobacco, dancing, television and other "adulterous" forms of worldliness. They believe that the teachings of the 17th century Russian Orthodox Church comprise the truth and no changes to its traditional form should ever have been undertaken.

Practices

For three centuries the Old Believers have protectively guarded their form of faith and practice. Partially this has been possible through their isolation from other cultures and religious forms, and partially because of the strict penalties for deviance. For example, when an individual "marries out," he or she is shunned. Orthodox members are forbidden to have anything to do with ousted persons.

Adult males make the decisions affecting a given community, though their authority is increasingly being questioned by each successive younger generation. Young people are marrying out in greater numbers and there are signs that the older generation is weakening in their stand to completely isolate their deviant offspring.

Peculiarities

Although many religious leaders claim that their interpretation of the linkage between faith and practice has implications for every aspect of daily living, few are as serious about this connection as the Old Believers. There are rituals for the seasons, and various required cleansings for observed religious festivals. In addition, community isolation helps keep the world at bay and provides a more coercive environment by which to enforce restrictions. There are signs that the younger generation is finding life outside the community quite appealing, and many of them are leaving the fold. There is no record of conversion to the faith of the Old Believers by outsiders, and the community numbers only about 300 in Canada, specifically in Alberta.

Seventh Day Adventists

As another splinter group, this time from the Methodist Church in the USA, Seventh Day Adventism began its spiritual journey in the latter part of the 19th century. One of its "founders," William Miller (1782-1849), never actually joined the Adventist Church, but he preached some of the doctrines that contributed to its origins. An ardent student of the Bible, Miller believed he could predict the day that the world would come to an end. He set the date for sometime in 1843-44, but the record indicates that he was wrong. Miller's failure to come through led to serious fractionalizing in the movement (Douglas, 1991).

Pedigree

William Miller's Bible studies motivated others to pursue a similar habit, for example, Hiram Edson, who claimed to have had a vision from heaven that prompted him to recalculate Miller's predictions about the end of the world. Another leader, Joseph Bates, through *his*

Bible studies, started a new emphasis that Saturday was the proper day to conduct worship and this selection was adhered to by his followers. Finally, it was through the writings of Ellen G. White (1827-1915), that the teachings of Seventh Day Adventism gained form and these have been retained in essence to this day.

Mrs. White, a mother of four children, claimed to have numerous heavenly visions about such topics as salvation, sacred history, doctrine, evangelism, church finances, foreign missions, the organization of the church and the inspiration of the Bible. These she illuminated to her followers through her many writings (Hoekema, 1976). In 1860, the name, "Seventh Day Adventist Church" was officially adopted by action of the general conference in Battle Creek, Michigan. In 1903 the headquarters was moved to Washington, DC.

Principles & Policy

Doctrinally, the Seventh Day Adventists are evangelical conservatives with a sound Protestant recognition of the authoritative nature of God's revelation of Himself, through the inspired doctrines encompassed in the entire Bible. They believe in the fall of man, the need for redemption, creation by Divine fiat, and the atoning work of Jesus Christ. They also believe that the ten commandments are a transcript of the character of God, as exemplified in the life of Jesus Christ and comprise the standard for human behavior in all generations (Mead, 1983).

On the matter of inspiration, Adventists insist that the Bible is their single source of Divine knowledge; they do not claim that the writings of Mrs. White are an addition to the Scriptures. However, it has sometimes been stated that anyone who opposes or rejects the "testimonies" of Mrs. White is branded as a rebel fighting against God (Hoekema, 1976, 29).

Practices

Adventists are urged by the church to live good Christian lives. They make good neighbors, and they are kind, considerate and hospitable. Visitors to their congregations are welcomed but not button-holed or coerced into joining. Adventists observe two rituals: adult baptism by immersion and the Lord's Supper which must be preceded by foot-washing.

Peculiarities

Aside from the unique selection of Saturday as a holy day, the Seventh Day Adventist Church is quite orthodox in practice. Perhaps more than any other denomination, the church is strongly committed to clean living, and their many publications reflect this. Believers are expected to abstain from tobacco, drugs and alcohol, and care for their bodies as the "temple of the Holy Spirit." This also means abstaining from certain "damaging foods" (such as pork), striving to keep involved in "wholesome activities" and getting an adequate amount of sleep.

Adventists are very interested in latter-day prophecies, and though no one makes predictions about the end of the world anymore, the "signs of Christ's eminent second coming" are apparently easy to decipher if they are ardent students of the Bible. There are 52 000 Adventists in Canada.

Unitarian-Universalists

In 1961 the Unitarian and Universalist Churches of Canada and the USA united to form the Unitarian Universalist Association of Congregations in North America. Obviously, there were few doctrinal differences to resolve since both bodies had a long heritage of avoiding and denouncing the formation of doctrine.

Pedigree

The roots of Unitarianism were sown in 1568 in Poland as a breakaway group from the Reformed Church. Simultaneously, independent thinkers connected to the Anabaptists in Switzerland, Hungary, Transylvania, the Netherlands and Italy helped form the foundation of Unitarian thought. In England it found its champions in such leaders as Isaac Newton, John Locke and John Milton. Its American roots developed independently out of the liberal wing of the Congregational Church at a time when the nation was "coming of age." The war with England was over and America was a free country; it was a time when intellectualism blossomed and freely offered its analyses of every major institution (Newman, 1953).

The American Unitarian break with the Congregationalists did not formally occur until 1805 when it became evident that real differences in theological perspective had developed. A formal pronouncement of independence was made in 1865. The group has never expanded greatly and there are currently about 17 000 adherents in Canada.

Principles & Policy

The Unitarian Church has no official creed except that it accepts the "religion of Jesus," holding in accordance with His teaching that practical religion is summed up in one's love for God and one's love to man. The church affirms the oneness of God and rejects the doctrine of the Trinity. The term "unitarian" refers to belief in God as one Person in a unified Godhead, rather than as three persons or a Trinity in the Godhead (Douglas, 1991).

Unitarians believe that Jesus was only human. Human character is perfectible and ultimately, because the essential character of God is love, everyone will be saved. Unitarians disregard the notions of heaven and hell, and reject the infallibility of the Bible. They encourage the widest freedom of individual interpretation, practice a form of fullfledged democratic governance, and pay homage to the principles of science in explaining the workings of the universe (Mead, 1983).

Practices

The expected practices of a good Unitarian are primarily moral and ethical as opposed to being doctrinal, biblical or evangelistic. The mandate for the "believer" is to support the search for truth, to cherish it when it has been identified, and seek to implement the principles of brotherhood, justice and peace. The worth of every human being is to be recognized and affirmed and their needs are respected and served. Above all, the vision of a single world community is to be a primary objective, and cooperation among all people of good will is to be promoted (Mead, 1983).

Peculiarities

Probably the most unique feature of the Unitarian-Universalist creed is that besides mildly encouraging belief in God (which even then is subject to personal interpretation), the church has no creed. In a manner of speaking, it is an "unchurchlike church." Spelled out in operational terms, adherents are encouraged to be highly moral and humane seekers – or however they would like to define themselves.

References

Bellah, Robert N. (1978). American society and the Mormon community. *Reflections on Mormonism: Judaeo-Christian parallels* (pp. 1-12). Provo, UT: Brigham Young University.

Bushman, Richard L. (1984). *Joseph Smith and the beginnings of Mormonism.* Urbana: University of Illinois Press.

Douglas, J.D. (Ed.). (1991). *20th-century encyclopedia of religious knowledge* (2nd ed.). Grand Rapids, MI: Baker Book House.

Farlee, R., Tonsager, Steven R. & Jones, Susan (Eds.). (1985). *Our neighbor's faith.* Minneapolis, MI: Augsburg Publishing House.

Ferm, Vergilius. (1945). *An encyclopedia of religion.* New York: The Philosophical Library.

Florinsky, Michael T. (1955). *Russia: A history and interpretation* (vol. 1). New York: Macmillan.

Friesen, John W. (1983). *Schools with a purpose.* Calgary, AB: Detselig Enterprises Ltd.

Hoekema, Anthony A. (1976). *Seventh Day Adventism.* Grand Rapids, MI: William B. Eerdman's Publishing Co.

Kach, Nick. (1984, November). The acculturation of the Old Believers. *Multicultural Education Journal, 2*(2), 19-26.

Mead, Frank S. (1983). *Handbook on denominations in the United States.* Nashville, TN: Abingdon.

Newman, Albert Henry. (1953). *A manual of church history* (2 vols.). Philadelphia: The American Baptist Publication Society.

Nock, David A. (1993). The organization of religious life in Canada. In W.E. Hewitt (Ed.), *The sociology of religion: A Canadian focus* (pp. 41-64). Toronto: Butterworths.

Persuitte, David. (1985). *Joseph Smith and the origins of the book of Mormon.* Jefferson, NC: McFarland & Co.

19

Off the Religious Map
The Cults

Readers are asked to "bear with us" because of the brevity of this chapter; the fault resides entirely with the author's lack of interest in, or experience with, these movements. Still, though small in terms of numbers of adherents, these groups draw more than their share of attention from the press and therefore at least deserve mention here. In terms of media coverage, who has not heard of the followers of Jimmy Jones mass suicide event in 1979, the David Koresh fire in Waco, Texas in 1992, or the tragedy of deaths connected to the Order of the Solar Temple in Switzerland in 1994. The good news is that while this kind of group adherence peaked in the 1970s, since then their numbers have dwindled. The bad news is that they are probably being replaced by other organizations also committed to mind control. Perhaps these too will fade in time. In any event, though youth are mainly attracted to new forms of religious expression, few of them remain committed to them. Studies show that in the final analysis, nine of ten children who make radical departures from their families to join religiously ideological groups, return within several years to pick up their lives where they left off (Kent, 1993). In the strictest analysis, "while the political aspects of New Age bear watching, the likelihood is that it will eventually prove itself to be sterile and simply whither away in the face of modern technology" (Douglas, 1991).

Cults specialize in emphasizing the virtues of an identified individual or individuals who have allegedly received special revelation from God. This apparently places them in the unique position of singly judging which behaviors are to be adhered to within a given organization. A cult usually promises to "save the world" solely through its means, and demands absolute faithfulness to the espoused doctrines which will allegedly bring about this goal. Religious cults frequently engage their members in menial tasks as a means of controlling them. Sanctions and taboos are myriad in number and there are penalties for even the most insignificant infractions. Cults insist that adherents isolate themselves from all aspects of their former life, including family and friends. They also discourage outside investigations by reporters and academics and they are often quite unfriendly and even belligerent to those who enquire about their operations (Stoner and Parke, 1977).

A variety of schematics are available to assist with identifying cults, and no one likes to think of being affiliated with them. Certainly cult adherents have more complimentary words to describe their affiliation. Viewed entirely from the perspective of known, established and respected religions, cults may be differentiated from mainline religions according to the following criteria:

The Cult	The Established Church
*Uses deceit in recruitment	*Features openness in Recruitment
*Seeks control over recruits	*Offers freedom of choice
*Threatens family unity	*Promotes family unity
*Isolates its members from society	*Encourages societal integration
*Dictates form of personal development	*Encourages open personal growth
*Exploits and manipulates members	*Offers supportive sympathetic understanding
*Encourages lifetime commitment	*Encourages thought before entanglements and commitment
*Intimidates critics with legal threats	*Welcomes criticism (debate)

No attempt is made in this chapter to provide an exhaustive list of cults active in Canada, and even now many of their labels are fading from memory or slipping into the woodwork of the mundane, e.g., Children of God, the Divine Light Mission, the Occult, Satanism, Spiritualism, Transcendental Meditation, the Way International, Wicca, or even the Hare Krishna. Several exemplary groups are summarized to make the point that though the claims of the cults vary according to each "guru," their ways and means tend to reflect a similar style.

New Age

About a decade ago the attention of North Americans was drawn to a new mind-set triggered by a book written by Marilyn Ferguson called *The Aquarian Conspiracy*. Since then the term "New Age philosophy" has virtually become a household word, and attracted international figures like James Beverley, the founder of theosophy, John Nasbitt and Alvin Toffler, both prominent futurists, David Spangler, Edgar Cayce and movie star Shirley MacLaine. For a long time MacLaine's book, *Out On a Limb,* even became a bible of sorts for her followers. Since the movement has such diverse makeup, both in terms of leadership and beliefs, it is difficult to estimate the number of "formal" adherents.

The essence of New Age actually seems to build on the foundation established by Christian Science – that of using one's mind to build inner spiritual strength. It is believed that the spirit world of astrology can be tapped which, combined with one's very best efforts, will help transform the self and make the world a better place to live (Bibby, 1993).

There is a great deal of variation in interpretation among individuals who spout New Age ideas, and thus there are many contradictions among the principles espoused by its promulgators. New Age comprises a reaction against traditional religion, and it even agitates against such revered institutions as medical practice. Some New Age believers are churning out alternative forms of therapy to substitute for a trip to the doctor's office. Even the Aboriginal or First Nations peoples have not escaped the onslaught of New Age, for many New Age belongers are also checking out traditional Indian practices for therapy, i.e., healing circles, sweatlodges, the medicine wheel, vision-seeking and other rituals. Set within the context of Native religion many of these practices have a certain validity; within New Age they tend to be altered almost beyond the point of recognition.

Quite bluntly, no one really knows what New Age is, since it borrows so freely from so many non-traditional sources for its ideas. A systematic delineation is not available, and one must rely on any group of soothsayers for their rendition of it. What I know for sure is that as a reactionary movement, New Age is selling a lot of books, in many different kinds of stores, and making a lot of money for a lot of very different people. As Albert Einstein has been quoted as saying, "The universe is stranger than we imagine" (*Maclean's* 10 Oct 1994, 48). Perhaps even stranger are the belief systems that are originated to explain the workings of the universe.

Scientology

This organization was founded in the USA in the 1950s by a fiction writer, L. Ron Hubbard, on the basis of his book, *Dianetics: The Modern Science of Mental Health*. The headquarters was moved to England in 1954.

Scientology is an eclectic movement combining the elements of science fiction, psychiatry and religion. Essentially non-Christian, the system is basically a humanist organization which offers no basis for belief in God. People can apparently realize their full potential through study and self-effort. Since the death of its founder, the organization has been rocked by internal disagreements and analysis and severe scrutiny and criticism by the media. Scientology has a following of about 700 people in Canada.

Unification Church

This group originated in the efforts of Rev. Sun Myung Moon who was raised in North Korea by Presbyterian parents. In 1936 he claimed that God spoke to him and ordered him to "finish the work of Christ on earth." The organization he subsequently founded was called the "Holy Spirit Association for the Unification of World Christianity." His followers are sometimes nicknamed "Moonies" and there are only about 300 left in Canada today.

Moon's book, *Divine Principle* (1957), spells out the main beliefs of the organization. These begin on the premise that Satan seduced Eve in the biblical account of the Garden of Eden, she polluted Adam and thus brought the human race into sin. Jesus was apparently born to start the "pure" family but since He never married the job was never finished. The Lord of the Second Advent (Moon himself) was then charged with completing the work of Christ. There are reports that Moon at times conducted marriages between hundreds of people in an effort to get the "pure" family expanded. Moon predicted that when the "pure" family has been completed all people will be in harmony with one another and with God.

Criticism against the Unification Church has included complaints against Rev. Moon's lavish lifestyle, the fact that his writings are the sole authority for the organization's beliefs, and Moon's claims that he will usher in the messianic age. Also the procedure by which new converts join the organization has been subject to severe criticism. When young people are contacted by their parents they refuse to leave the group. When they are forcibly "captured" a period of formal deprogramming becomes essential before individuals are able to be function in their family home or in society.

References

Bibby, Reginald W. (1993). *Unknown gods: The ongoing story of religion in Canada.* Toronto: Stoddart.

Boa, Kenneth. (1977). *Cults, world religions, and you.* Whitby, ON: Victor Books.

Douglas, J.D. (1991). *20th-century encyclopedia of religious knowledge* (2nd ed.). Grand Rapids, MI: Baker Bible House.

Kent, Stephen A. (1993). New religious movements. In W.E. Hewitt (Ed.), *The sociology of religion: A Canadian focus.* Toronto: Butterworths Canada.

Stoney, Carroll & Parke, Jo Anne. (1977). *All God's children: The cult experience – salvation or slavery?* Radner, PA: Chilton Book Co.

20

Even Less Religious Atheists & Agnostics

A wag once remarked that in the interests of trying to provide something for everyone, the local telephone company had installed a dial-a-prayer for atheists. It worked this way, "You dial the number and nobody answers!" It is probably for the same reason – something for everyone – that a book of this sort should include a chapter for the "religious none's and sheilas" (Nock, 1993) of our community.

It is very difficult to actually identify an atheist, if indeed there are any. Most so-called atheists, like fundamentalists, are angry at earlier (childhood?) experiences they may have had with their church-going parents or with religious people. As Shakespeare put it in *Macbeth,* "Methinks thou doest protest too much" is also too often true of atheists. According to their tradition atheists are supposed to be people who get along quite nicely without God; in fact, they are not supposed to believe He exists. Even if God *does* exist, this knowledge is not supposed to make any difference to the atheist. What happens in actual fact is that most atheists appear to believe very much in God, but they are very angry at Him and at any organization (like the church) which professes to know something about the workings of God. The protest of the atheist is often so dogmatic and so insistent that what a person encounters is not an atheist but an *anti-theist.*

According to the dictionary, atheists apparently *profess* to know that there is no God; that is they make a claim about it. This suggests that they must have done some research on the topic and the results of their findings prove *beyond a reasonable doubt* that there is no God. By contrast, agnostics have a different problem; they do not claim to know whether or not God exists; they make no claims of any kind on the subject. They are convinced that there are no reasonable grounds to make any metaphysical claims. Agnostics quite frankly doubt the existence of anything, material or spiritual, and doubt that *anything* can be claimed – and certainly not proven.

It is very difficult to engage in a calm or objective conversation about religious matters with an "atheist." If you want to test this theory, simply invite a professed atheist to church, and you will undoubtedly get an earful of protestations. Mention that you have read somewhere that atheists are supposed to be objective, scientific-minded people, always in search of the truth; then suggest that all purported vehicles of unknown or unproven phenomena (like any religious institution), should be investigated by these objectivists, and you will likely get another earful. The atheist will contend that this is not the time for further research. Not unlike the fundamentalist preacher, Jerry Falwell, he or she will insist that this is a time for pronouncements like, "there is no God!"

Pedigree

Atheism is at least as old as humankind, and the New Testament certainly takes cognizance of its claims. The psalmist makes note of this in the Old Testament statement, "The fool says in his heart, 'there is no God' " (Psalm 14:1). By New Testament times there were other "complications" such as the Gnostic movement which specialized in fusing Christianity with Greek ideas. Proponents of this view usually took liberties by borrowing and adapting ideas for their own purposes without regard to the original intent of those ideas (Douglas, 1991).

The atheist/agnostic cause got an extra boost in the 1960s when the "God is dead" movement made headlines (Altizer and Hamilton, 1966). Perhaps in an effort to make old truths stand out as new, three young theologians and a sociologist used the "God is dead" slogan as a central theme in their publications and teaching. In 1963 Thomas J.J. Altizer taught the death of God as an historical event, meaning that God had indeed died as a contemporary happening. Altizer rejected historic expressions of doctrine and belief but insisted that Christian theologians should be loyal to Jesus Christ, not to the organized church. His colleague, William Hamilton, suggested that technology had already become the alternate god of society. Naturally, the God is dead slogan alarmed traditional Christians who feared the authors had gone mad. Non-believers (like atheists) took more than a little joy in the debate. To them it was just another indication that the whole "cult of godism" was fraught with philosophical difficulty.

Altizer and Hamilton were in good company. Decades earlier, philosopher Julian Huxley questioned the claims of theists suggesting that he obtained a sense of spiritual relief by rejecting the idea of God as a supernatural being. His conviction arose from attempting but failing to bridge the gap between the religious and the scientific approach to reality (Huxley, 1964). Bertrand Russell's difficulty with Christianity came from similar reasoning, except he also indicated that people basically accept religion on emotional grounds, not on the basis of philosophical or scientific arguments. Russell also contended that religion is based primarily on fear (Russell, 1957).

On the theological side, in 1963, John A.T. Robinson, Bishop of Woolwich, suggested that traditional notions of God were outdated. After his book *Honest to God* was published, Robinson was accused of going on public record to apparently deny every Christian doctrine of the very church in which he held office (Robinson, 1963). Then, Harvey

Cox of Andover Newton Theological School in Massachusetts suggested that traditional religion was dead because of a new freedom and scope brought to individuals by secularization and urbanization. In his book *The Secular City*, he reminded his readers that the new freedom also required a new maturity and sense of responsibility (Cox, 1966; Callahan, 1967).

Perhaps the most recent seeming onslaught against the Christian church (and religion generally), has been the work of Reginald Bibby, a sociologist at The University of Lethbridge. Having no religious axe to grind other than telling things the way his research shows them to be, Bibby has been awarded a variety of unpleasant titles by religious stalwarts. With more than two decades of religious research under his belt, Bibby has been accused of employing a weak methodology and making erroneous definitions. In studying church growth, for example, Bibby is chided for interviewing church leaders rather than converts (Hexham, 1993). It would be difficult to imagine that converts would have a more objective perspective than church leaders. Still, despite accusations of being too critical, Bibby takes special care in going beyond his role as a sociologist and outlines what the Christian church needs to do if it wants to continue in the Canadian religious mainstream (Bibby, 1993). According to Statistics Canada, 1 386 000 citizens lay claim to belonging to the atheistist "religious" camp, so the potential field of converts for the church is certainly ample.

Principles, Policy and Practices

If we start with the proposition that atheists *claim to know,* we need to know what the underlying proofs of their claims are. Classical atheism was bent on proving the nonexistence of God. Volumes have been written dedicated to the single task of proving in intellectual fashion that *there is no God*. This perspective induced religious leaders to respond in fashion; they felt called upon to *prove* the existence of God – intellectually, of course. Even then, very few of them managed to supercede the genius of the 13th century theologian, Thomas Aquinas, in his *Summa Theologica*. Eventually, arguments on both sides, atheists and theologians, deteriorated to a level of intellectual gymnastics using rhetoric and logic to debate matters of faith (Strunk, 1968).

Contemporary atheism does not spend much time debating the existence of God, nor trying to prove that God does not exist. Rather, the argument proceeds on the assumption that there is no God and goes from there. Another feature of the new atheism is that it tends to be a populist movement, usually attracting first-year college students. It appears popular to be able to state unequivocally that God does not exist even before one has allegedly and officially begun one's "search for truth." Currently the gospel of atheism is being peddled as a trendy, fashionable thing; atheism is being marketed as a non-religious form of morality with a high degree of sensitivity to mankind's finite condition (Strunk, 1968; Douglas, 1991).

It is interesting to note that few of the world's great thinkers and leaders have been avowed atheists. The exceptions include Friedrich Nietzsche, Karl Marx, Friedrich Engels and Sigmund Freud. Although John Dewey is often included in this list it would probably be more accurate to say that Dewey injected a form of agnosticism into his pragmatism, always leaving a little room for doubt in any of his stipulations.

On the affirmative side one can accumulate an impressive repertoire of quotations about God, religion or the Bible by revered political and philosophical leaders, which suggest that not every "great" man has been an atheist. The list includes Abraham Lincoln, George Washington, Napoleon, Thomas Carlyle, Thomas Huxley, Immanuel Kant, Charles Dickens, Goethe and Henry Van Dyke (Halley, 1958).

One reaction to the postulates of contemporary atheism is the phenomenon of "Christian atheism" which arose partially out of the God is dead movement. The believer's mandate advocated by this perspective was to follow the model of Jesus as an answer to human problems, but without carrying along excessive theological baggage. What emerged from the discussion was a form of Christian religiosity without any consciousness of a transcendent God.

A modified form of the theology of Christian atheism is Christian skepticism, whose proponents profess not to have left their brain in the narthex of the church, but have remained in full possession of their intellectual capacities while engaged in worship. From this perspective, Christians are not people who surrender their integrity to the community, but are recognized by the community as qualified spokespersons. They do not "assassinate" their brains just to become members of the faith (Ridenour, 1974). This bulldoggedness sometimes erupts into "family" quarrels, although the whole family allegedly believes in the same things: belief in God the Father, Jesus Christ the Son, the Holy Spirit and the Holy Catholic Church (Shideler, 1968). Christian skeptics can never take a break from analysis, however, and their worship is an admixture of self questioning and answering – another kind of Christian humanism.

Still a little further on the left is the avowed agnostic whose belief it is that absolute or *certain* knowledge has not been attained (i.e., belief in God) either in some particular field or in any and all fields of supposed knowledge. Agnosticism is a form of "fulltime" skepticism; you can never take a break from honest query, except that the agnostic leaves open the possibility of future knowledge while the skeptic never even gets to consider that question. The term "agnostic," by the way, was first employed by Thomas Huxley in 1869 (Ferm, 1945). He apparently based it on a scripture passage in Acts 17:23 citing the apostle Paul when he was in Athens, "For as I walked around and looked carefully at your objects of worship, I even found an altar with this inscription, TO AN UNKNOWN GOD. Now what you worship as something unknown, I am going to proclaim to you."

Peculiarities

A basic assumption of this discussion is that it is virtually impossible to engage in an objective discussion about religious phenomena – even with those who profess no knowledge or who have "healthy" doubts about the subject. This observation has a parallel application to the world of agnostics, atheists, humanists and skeptics. In a strange sort of way, members of these camps may be closer to a worshipful relationship with the Almighty than those whose minds have been made up and then closed forever to *any* form of query. As theologian Martin Buber once noted, "The atheist staring from his attic window is often nearer to God than the believer caught up in his own false image of God."

Even a little questioning is better than none at all, for honest open query can provide enhanced conceptualizations. When one's religious or spiritual quest comes to any sort of a complete end, no room is left for possible enhancement or growth. Suppose one's concept of God, for example, is somehow in error. Suppose God is "bigger, more powerful, and even more sensitive" than imagined. Would a continued quest not benefit from this realization? To this suggestion ardent believers will respond that when you already have the "right" concept of God, why bother with a further search? The proper response to this position is, that up until now you thought only God has the full and correct concept of Divine Self. What's it like to take His place?

References

Altizer, Thomas J. J. & Hamilton, William. (1966). *Radical theology and the death of God*. New York: Bobbs-Merrill Company.

Bibby, Reginald A. (1993). *Unknown gods: the ongoing story of religion in Canada*. Toronto: Stoddart.

Callahan, Daniel (Ed.). (1967). *The secular city debate*. New York: The Macmillan Company.

Cox, Harvey. (1966). *The secular city*. New York: The Macmillan Company.

Douglas, J. D. (Ed.). (1991). *20th-century encyclopedia of religious knowledge*. (2nd ed.).. Grand Rapids, MI: Baker Book House.

Edwards, David L. (Ed.). (1963). *The honest to God debate*. London: SCM Press.

Ferm, Vergilius. (1945). *An encyclopedia of religion*. New York: The Philosophical Library.

Halley, Henry H. (1958). *Bible handbook* (21st ed.). Chicago: Henry H. Halley.

Hexham, Irving. (1993). Canadian Evangelicals: Facing the Critics. In W.E. Hewitt (Ed.), *The sociology of religion: a Canadian focus* (pp. 289-302). Toronto: Butterworths.

Huxley, Julian. (1964). *Religion without revelation.* New York: The New American Library.

Nock, David A. (1993). The Organization of Religious Life in Canada. The Organization of Religious Life in Canada. In W.E. Hewitt (Ed.), *The sociology of religion: a Canadian focus* (pp. 41-64). Toronto: Butterworths.

Ridenour, Fritz. (1974). *How to be a Christian without being religious.* Glendale, CA: Regal Books.

Robinson, John A.T. (1963). *Honest to God.* London: SCM Press.

Russell, Bertrand. (1957). *Why I am not a Christian.* New York: Simon and Schuster.

Shideler, Mary McDermott. (1968). *A creed for a Christian skeptic.* Grand Rapids, MI: William B. Erdmans Publishing Company.

Strunk, Orlo Jr. (1968). *The choice called atheism.* Nashville, TN: Abingdon Press.

PART FOUR
The Challenge

If you have read this far in the book you must surely be either fatigued or somewhat confused. But now it is time to make a decision; which of the outlined creeds do you wish to follow, if any? Perhaps you are tempted to stake out a new religious territory for yourself and elaborate a personally-satisfying creed – maybe even try to attract a following? Perhaps you have recently "experienced a vision," perhaps while reading these pages. That is how most new religious organizations start, with someone's personal vision. In any case, before we end this part of the journey there are a few additional things to keep in mind as you travel on. These suggestions are abbreviated in the remaining section. Good luck in finding your way.

In a lighthearted essay, essayist Paul Iorio (*Details*, Oct. 1994) describes his dilemma in trying to choose the right religion. In the first instance he claims to crave access to all of the traditional benefits of organized religion – "the soup kitchen, salvation and friendship," but the myriad of membership requirements are confusing. Conversion is available, but there is a price to be paid.

One day Mr. Iorio embarks on his quest to find out how to get to heaven since this is apparently the specialty of most world religions. To millions of the faithful, the password to heaven is a simple, "I'm sorry." This apparently qualifies as the act of repentance. Iorio's version of the Catholic interpretation is, "Commit any sin during the week, confess it on Saturday, and you're pardoned if you promise not to do it again – no matter what the offence." Under this arrangement, forgiveness would apparently have been available even to Adolf Hitler. That sounds good, but there is more. According to Iorio, Lutherans believe that the only unforgivable sin is unbelief. Match this up with the theology of the Jehovah's Witnesses, however, and the news is that traditionally only 144 000 guests (apostles) are eligible for admission to heaven. That number has recently been updated to include 12 000 guests for each apostle, but is it enough to include people like Iorio?

Iorio suggests that living up to the intent of the ten commandments is pretty heavy, but discovering that Judaism has an additional 613 commandments is downright depressing. Add to this the strict diet requirements of Islam, the fasts of Baha'i, the pentecostal need to speak in tongues, the availability of a wide variety of Krishna gods from which to choose, and the searcher is thoroughly baffled.

Fortunately for most searchers the initial point of departure is quite uncomplicated. Few people need to begin their exploration from square one since they already have a starting point, the one that has been assigned to them at birth by the society or cultural configuration in which they first wake to personal consciousness. The key to the next step is "consciousness," which implies an awareness of the workings of one's assigned faith and knowledge of any approved alternative behaviors that might be permitted in practicing it. Without the benefit of an informed perspective it will be difficult to proceed intelligently and rationally. Hopefully, spiritual peace will be the logical result of this journey. Alternately, if no investigation in undertaken, an alternative perspective might be simply to react against one's birth religion or perhaps assume the position of being anti-religious, or anti-theistic or prematurely, a half-informed, uninformed or ignorant atheist.

Knowledge is one thing, but reacting to it with reason and wisdom can be an all-consuming life-long pursuit.

21

Now That You Know

We live in a society that lauds informed decision-making. There is no reason why this approach ought not also be taken with regard to the realm of selecting a personal belief system. Since religion deals with that which transcends everyday experience, its validity cannot be assessed exclusively by common sense nor science. It is primarily the domain of faith, and faith cannot be based on scientific evidence. Still, placing one's faith in an established, institutionalized response to metaphysical questions should not be a blind act. Thus any knowledge or assistance one may gain in differentiating between/among alternatives in choosing a route for one's spiritual path should be of value. Hopefully, the preceding chapters have been beneficial in this regard.

The Starting Point

A useful concept to bear in mind as one tries to find one's way through the religious maze of possibilities is to differentiate between religion and spirituality. Spirituality has to do with the need to be fulfilled in terms of ultimate meaning, that is, to find a cosmic purpose for oneself. The primary question is, why are you here in an "ultimate" sense? Is there an afterlife? If so, where are we going after death, and what will it be like when we get there? Out of these concerns arises this question: If there is a God, what does God want of us in this life? Does God have a preference about how we should live?

Organized religions offer a series of a preset response patterns to this question and most religious adherents of any brand would be quite prepared to share their version of what they perceive to be pretty well anyone's purpose on earth.

Most religious denominations and organizations perceive themselves primarily to be concerned with spirituality, but their recipes leave little room for creative personal adjustment to the calling of the universe. The concept of spirituality, on the other hand, implies a wide range of bonafide responses. Some religionists, in fact, might even go as far to suggest that their creeds and routines comprise the sole avenue by which spiritual peace can be attained.

Religious organizations and church denominations are often accused of being engaged in empire-building. Leaders of a few religious bodies might admit to a certain amount of this kind of activity, but they will also argue that it is an essential and unavoidable component of the responsibilities assumed in guiding their followers along the route to gaining spiritual peace. After all, the more converts they convince with their message the better off more people will be. Evangelism is thus regarded as a practice spawned from unselfish motives and it is to be undertaken primarily for the benefit of the recipient. Most religions postulate that people are spiritual beings, that is, we have a need to pursue and solidify a personal peace treaty with the universe. Anti-theists may attempt to explain away this apparent need or "weakness" on the part of human beings, but religion appears to live on despite their disillusionment with it or their complaints about it. Today some world religious organizations are even growing in numbers, a strong testimony to the fact that many people convinced by anti-religious arguments are perhaps diminishing in number. The need for an individual expression of faith is stronger then ever. Therefore, if one is going to join the increasing throngs agitating for religious fulfillment, it behooves one to be well-informed about the alternatives.

Available Options

The plethora of contrived recipes to attaining spiritual satisfaction range from a strong denominational affiliation to individually-contrived formulae. Those who spend an exorbitant amount of time in denigrating existing structural forms, however, will probably be short on positive delivery systems and thereby also cheat themselves of fulfilling their own spiritual need. Many complainants about organized religion can readily demean the various denominational options, but they offer no alternatives to attaining spiritual satisfaction. Don't be fooled by those who have a quiver full of arrows to shoot at the "enemy" without also putting forward some kind of fulfilling resolution to individual spiritual questing. On the other hand it might be wise to avoid what obviously appear to be individually-designed formats, whose advantage may be primarily for the inventor of the approach. This is known as missing the forest by concentrating on the individual tree.

A friend told me recently that the way banktellers are trained to spot counterfeit money is by having them concentrate on good money. When their eyes have been trained to perceive reputable forms of currency, fake forms readily stand out. On a parallel note it should be relatively simple to identify positive forms of religion or faith so that counterfeit forms pale by comparison. The Bible records that Jesus always concentrated on helping, healing, encouraging and uplifting. The only harsh words He ever had for any questioner were directed to religious bigots, self-styled critics and legalists. While He spent his time healing and encouraging, his critics indulged in criticizing his methodology. What an empty life they must have had!

The Search is Personal

An advantage to checking out the religious scene is that there may be some benefit in it for the sincere searcher. After all, if being "complete" is the objective of human existence, it behooves us to research all of the various components of what might make up that existence – social, spiritual, cognitive, emotional, etc., and the alternatives within them. Who knows? A spiritual search might be the most rewarding of all pursuits. Spiritual peace might be achieved via a thorough search of the available religious packages – starting with one's own. In one sense there is nothing alarming about the variety of religious systems or denominations available to be checked out. Most of them have geographic, nationalistic or ethnic origins, and all of them represent human attempts to systematically explain the workings of the universe and mankind's response (and perceived responsibilities) to it.

If it is conceded that religion is a vital part of culture, and often the driving force behind it, or the glue that holds it together and gives it meaning, it logically follows that to understand one's culture, and perhaps oneself, is to investigate one's heritage. So if a cultural/metaphysical root search is undertaken, the religious stem should certainly be included. It just may turn out to be the tap-root of one's inherited moral code. An honest investigation should not be confused with the conclusion that an inherent commitment to that background will result. It's an *honest* search – remember?

A fruitful root search can provide authenticity to being. If one becomes aware of the various subtle forces of one's institutional affiliations – family, religion, media or vocation – one cannot be unduly influenced by them. Nor will one's resultant behavior merely comprise a reaction to those forces. Personal authenticity implies a calm assessment of a given situation resulting in a deliberated conclusion based on an assessment of all relevant information. This can only come about by being informed of the various aspects pertaining to making that particular decision. Since religion comprises such a vital component of most people's personal backgrounds it becomes mandatory to gather information, sift through it, and via careful analysis become aware of its various operations, influences and impacts. To settle for anything else is to opt for a situation of reaction to, or being manipulated by, external influences. All of us deserve better than that.

It makes sense to commence one's personal journey by starting with familiar ground. Start with who you are. Start with where you are. If you happen to be born into a particular culture, religion, nationality, belief system or race, start there. Find out why your institutional compatriots feel it is so important for you to belong – to conform to their expectations. Try to determine why they so greatly fear that your potential apostasy would make such a difference to your salvation, to their composure and happiness, or even to the possible workings of the universe. There has to be a reason for their undue concern. Is it an important reason? If so, to whom? To you? Are valid reasons being offered for you to make a certain decision to stick to a particular value frame? On whose grounds? Yours, or someone else's?

Face it; if there is a caring metaphysical "Ground of Being" (Personality or God?), in charge of the universe, why would your personal quest for inner peace not be a valid component of concern of that Being? It only makes sense. After you have completed your homework, go ahead, pick one!

Culture and Faith

It would be difficult to understand Canadian religious institutions without recognizing the links between religion and ethnicity in Canadian history. Since most religious institutions originate from very specific ethnocultural or national configurations it is logical to assume that some of the trappings of such heritage might be worked into their corollary recipes for spiritual fulfillment. To illustrate this, the Roman Catholic faith community is a good example. Though the doctrines of the Church may be common to all countries in which the faith has been endorsed, the way it is lived out reflects its cultural surroundings. Thus adherents to Catholicism in France will have a slightly different lifestyle than the Italian Catholic Christians or the German Catholic Christians. It is to the credit of the Church that this reality is possible. It underscores both the efficacy and applicability of the Gospel and the flexibility and adaptability of the church.

Separating culture from faith is virtually impossible but sometimes necessary. One can of course become a cultural convert just as easily as a religious convert, but it should be an informed choice. In many cases, when one examines a potential religion the differentiation between cultural trappings and religious essence will not be explicitly elaborated. In fact, it is doubtful that many adherents to religious forms are even aware that this is the case. Thus they continue to espouse cultural forms combined with, or disguised as, the implicit religious message.

This point can be illustrated with reference to my own Mennonite upbringing. While growing up I discovered that despite very convincing evangelistic pulpit preaching, the conversion rate was very low, except for those of us whose parents already belonged to the faith. When outsiders did take an interest in the Mennonite Church, for whatever reason, they often discovered that a certain amount of cultural heritage was carefully interwoven into both church doctrine and practice. Reactions varied; some found the acculturation process too severe and went elsewhere, while others undertook some adaptations to their lifestyle in order to fit in with their new-found "faith." It was embarrassing at times to witness outsiders trying to comprehend references made to culturally parochial happenings or "inside jokes," or even worse, to have to listen to them being told in the German language. It was not always like this, but those instances did happen. I doubt very much that it could be different with other ethnic faith communities or church congregations.

The separation of culture from faith is a personal matter, at least it should be, but it may be a very complex and difficult undertaking to try to differentiate the two factors. Without this knowledge one may very well buy into a religious system and, at the same time, inadvertently adopt a well-disguised cultural configuration. Faith should supercede culture, and even function independently of it and reward the seeker regardless of the cultural configuration in which it is set. Does it *really* work that way? I believe it does, but it will be up to each seeker to check this out for themselves. The important thing is, don't get caught in the web of lifestyle when the object of your search is much deeper than that.

Fruits of the Search

Let me reiterate that there are many reasons why the religious base of society should be investigated, not the least of which is to understand our national origins and institutional operations. The pursuit has implications beyond the personal realm. It is a corporate concern because all of us have a need to believe in something beyond ourselves, a goal, a set of values, a caring Being. Religion gives us a framework within which to deal with experiences beyond our control. We all have to deal with crises at sometime or other, and it is then that religion helps us adjust. Why should a loved one die young? Why must we suffer illness? Why should a person go on living when his or her love is not returned? Such questions demand meaningful answers. Following up on one's faith quest, therefore, is not an irrational activity. The 13th century philosopher, Thomas Aquinas, tried to show that the existence of God could almost be proven by rational means. He has been quoted a lot since, and by a wide variety of religionists, so there must be something to his argument.

Faith seekers and worshippers of the supernatural have no reason to apologize for their endeavors, nor do they have to leave their intellectual capacities in the church narthex when they worship. Seeking for God is a noble activity. On the other hand, a certain amount of analysis *should* also go into the study of faith pursuits, particularly when one considers taking up (or transferring) allegiance to an already established form of religion. When this tack is assumed it will not take long to discover that the framers of that creed will already have built into the schematic a certain amount of rationalized justification for the system. But surely it is not necessary to accept their rationale in blind faith? Why not do a little personal investigating, preferably before joining? This orientation should not be resisted by the authorities; after all, nearly every religion tries to make a case for their encouragement of individuality within its own confines. Many past thinkers have done a little juggling of established creeds, but they did not do too well. Apparently we have come so far since then that questioning tradition is virtually a national past-time. Why not test it and see for yourself?

Finally, we are constantly bombarded with the presupposition that the current generation is enlightened; this is the thinking generation. The upbeat citizen of today expects proof for claims made, and they are not willing to accept things at face value. If this is so, it may be possible that religious claims are being more closely scrutinized today than in the past. Modern seekers want to know the nature of the underlying rationale for what they are being told (and sold). However, one should proceed with sincerity and objectivity and with an open mind and heart. No one can rightfully make any claims about the benefits or detrimental effects of a whole sector of society without examining it. Following this logic, it should be valid to project that an enhanced interest in religion will dominate the headlines of the near future. A truly scientific approach begs for it. Who knows? Perhaps the end result of this kind of personal journey may even have unforseen benefits.

Some Comparisons

The initial plan of this book was to conclude by presenting a comparison chart of religious systems to illustrate to the reader the options available for personally appropriating a belief system. Now that the work has been completed it somehow appears more important to illuminate and underscore the similarities of the various systems. Thus I have come to this conclusion. The end result of an honest and open search for spiritual satisfaction will bring the seeker overwhelmingly to the realization that he or she is engaged in a universal human activity. Only the labels of the various concocted systems may be confusing; the need for the quest is not.

Points of Consensus for World Religions

Traits	Aboriginal	Baha'i	Buddist	Christian	Confucian	Hindu	Islam	Jewish	Sikhs
Originally initiated by personal vision	x	x	x	x	x		x	x	x
Historic hereditary or appointed leadership	x	x	x	x	x		x	x	x
Specified or implicit code of ethics	x	x	x	x	x	x	x	x	x
Belief in grace and forgiveness	x		x	x	x	x		x	x
Sacred writings		x	x	x	x	x	x	x	x
Designated "clergy"	x	x	x	x	x	x	x	x	x
Concept of personal transformation	x	x	x	x	x	x	x	x	x
Full or partial dress code							x	x	x
Portrait of "ideal saint"		x	x	x	x	x	x	x	x
Positive future envisaged state	x	x	x	x	x	x	x	x	x
Claimed equal status of the sexes	x	x	x	x	x	x	x	x	x
Interested in evangelism of outsiders		x		x			x		

Comparative Chart on major Christian Denominations

Traits	Anglican	Baptist	Catholic	Lutheran	Pentecostals	Presbyterian	United
Literal view of Bible	no	some	no	no	yes	no	no
Trained Clergy	yes	some	yes	yes	some	yes	yes
Hierarchical governance	yes	no	yes	limited	no	limited	no
Local governance	no	yes	no	limited	yes	limited	limited
Belief in Sacrements	seven	none	seven	two	none	two	two
Infant Baptism	yes	no	yes	yes	no	yes	yes
Belief in Divine healing	no	no	yes	no	yes	no	no
Belief in Charismatic Glossalia	some	no	some	no	yes	no	no
Eschatologic-ally inclined	no	yes	no	no	yes	no	no
Adhere to common lectionary	yes	no	yes	yes	no	yes	yes